BOLDLY
I OBEY

Do not withhold good from those to whom
it is due, when it is in your power to act.
Proverbs 3:27 (NIV)

BOLDLY
I OBEY

THE *Journey* OF
MAX *and* DIXIE EDWARDS
FROM AN *Indiana Farm* TO
Brazil AND *Beyond*

DANNA JO MATSUKI

OMS · ONE MISSION SOCIETY

One Mission Society is an evangelical, interdenominational faith mission, focusing on multiplying disciples, churches, leaders, and missionaries. We engage the one to reach the many throughout Africa, Asia/Pacific, Europe/Middle East, and Latin America/Caribbean to make a global impact.

One Mission Society
PO Box A
Greenwood, IN 46142
317.888.3333
www.onemissionsociety.org
http://oms.media

Boldly I Obey – Danna Jo Matsuki
Copyright © 2021 by One Mission Society
Paperback ISBN: 978-1-62245-753-3
eBook ISBN: 978-1-62245-754-0
Cover design by Jonathan Lewis.

BIOGRAPHY & AUTOBIOGRAPHY / Religious

10   9   8   7   6   5   4   3   2   1

Contents

Preface

I will sing of the LORD's great love forever;
with my mouth I will make your faithfulness known through all generations.
Psalm 89:1 (NIV)

God is in the business of using ordinary people to do extraordinary things. Don't believe it? Just ask my grandparents.

This is their story—or rather, God's story of His work in and through their lives. And I think it is a rather special story. As I am their grand-daughter, you may say that I am biased, and no doubt, you are right. I think most people have a special place in their hearts for their own family's history. The choices that my grandparents made impacted not only their lives but also my mother's life and, in turn, my life. Their legacy of family and faith is one of the things that most profoundly influenced the home that I grew up in and even the home that I am now creating with my husband. So yes, I'm biased. I think my grand-parents are awesome, and I tell people that when I grow up, I want to be Grandma Dixie.

That said, this book is more than a family story or a family history. It is a story of God's faithfulness. And because it is not just Max and Dixie's story but also God's story, it has touched hundreds of people who have heard it. Over the years, my grandparents have shared their story with dozens of churches, mission teams, friends, and others; it has repeatedly inspired others because it shows what God can do with one or two people who are willing to say yes to His call.

For years, friends told my grandpa that he should write his story down, so that it would live on when he could no longer tell it. And for years, Grandpa Max dismissed the idea; he knew that he was nothing special, so he felt it unnecessary. However, about 10 years ago, these friends began to win him over. Grandpa wanted no glory or attention for himself, but he began to see the value in recording the story of God's work in his life—not to give Max fame or glory, but so God may be glorified for what He has done. Around this time Grandpa was beginning to experience the first signs of Alzheimer's.

At this same time, I was in college at Taylor University in Indiana, just an hour from my grandparents' home. My parents were still working overseas as missionaries, so my grandparents' place became my home base when I was a college student and afterward, until I was married. I had the privilege of living with them when I was on breaks, and seeing their constant faithfulness to and reliance on God lived out in day-to-day life, even in the struggles that come from old age and sickness. I was a history major, and somehow I was recruited to put together their story.

It has been such a privilege and a joy to be the "family historian" for these last several years. I have transcribed old letters, interviewed family members and friends, pored over old prayer letters and pictures, and prayed a lot. I don't feel adequate to write such a book, but Grandma keeps reminding me that it is God's story, and we trust that He is retelling that story through us.

Family stories tend to outline only the highlights—the big events that give inspiration and create interest. And this book is probably not much different. Nevertheless, I am reminded that most of life is not the big events; it's the day-to-day struggles and routines. And how we respond to those struggles determines how we will respond to the big events. I think this is my grandparents' secret to success—their faithfulness to God and those around them in their day-to-day life. Grandma's weekly letters to her parents when they were in Brazil show her giving thanks to God and reciting Romans 8:28,[1] even when the washing machine was broken, no one showed up for Sunday school, and Max was away on a trip. I also saw their faithfulness when I lived with them

---

1   "And we know that in all things God works for the good of those who love him, who have been called according to his purpose" (NIV).

as a young adult. Grandpa got up every morning at 4 to read his Bible; Grandma prayed over every little thing; they recited verses together, sang together, and shared things that God taught them.

Today Grandpa is no longer able to tell his story, but that story lives on. It lives on in the lives and hearts of everyone who was impacted by his ministry. It lives on in the minds of those who have heard and experienced his story. And now, it lives on in this book.

All Grandpa ever wanted was to obey God and to glorify Him. That is all that he desired for this book, and that is all we seek to accomplish. My prayer for you as you read is that you will be reminded of how great, good, powerful, and loving our God is. We may not always understand what He is doing, but we know that our lives are always safest in His hands. May this book encourage you to follow boldly wherever He leads.

—Danna Jo Matsuki

Therefore, since we are surrounded by such a great cloud of witnesses, let us throw off everything that hinders and the sin that so easily entangles. And let us run with perseverance the race marked out for us, fixing our eyes on Jesus, the pioneer and perfecter of faith. For the joy set before him he endured the cross, scorning its shame, and sat down at the right hand of the throne of God. Consider him who endured such opposition from sinners, so that you will not grow weary and lose heart. Hebrews 12:1–3 (NIV)

est. 1956

Audacter Pareo

Introduction

Edwards Family Motto: *Audacter Pareo*

By Joe Edwards

I recall seeing the Edwards family crest on the wall in my grandparents' house throughout my preteen years. The crest was a red lion with a blue tongue on a shield, with black on top and argent (silver or white) on the bottom. When I asked about it, Grandpa Russel said that Grandma Maud had paid someone to research the family, and this is what the research yielded. Through my own research, I learned that the Edwards name (a derivative of "son of Edward") apparently came from both Wales and England; it appeared in colonial America by 1622. A strict male line of succession must be known for family members to be allowed to use emblems from a U.K.-based coat of arms. As a family of "American mutts" grown from the land we've farmed for generations, we certainly don't have official documentation or the British throne's authorization to use the emblem. Nevertheless, the themes of blood and spiritual heritage are important to me, so the emblem is one of the ancestral customs that caught my interest. I learned that the family motto, used along with the emblem, was whatever the bearer felt best represented him and his family unit. Future members of his family could choose to keep the motto or change it as the family tree forked.

I was at a family gathering, thinking about this idea, when two moments in the recent Edwards timeline came into sharp contrast for me. The first was a terrifying moment my Grandpa Russel had as a three-year-old boy—a scar he carried with him to his grave. In this memory, he and his four-year-old brother were held in the iron grip of a groundskeeper at the Randolph County orphanage, kicking, crying, and trying to run after their mother's carriage as it disappeared down a long driveway. Their father, my great-grandpa Austin, had abandoned his wife. The county forced her to place two of her four children, all under the age of four, in an orphanage. She regrettably had to give up the two oldest kids, the three- and four-year-old.

The second moment that came to mind was a family gathering of the Max and Dixie clan. As I observed an entire tribe dedicated to serving God with 100 percent of the couples living in strong marriages while making a positive impact on the world together, I wondered, *How did we get here from there?* How did the Edwards heritage from my great-grandfather who abandoned his family translate to what I saw around me? Well, his heritage clearly didn't. Something radical happened to change the trajectory of this family.

The first generation of change was Russel, who worked hard to overcome a difficult start in life at just three years old. His history of moving beyond abuse and scorn and carving out a life for himself and Maud is a story in and of itself. The second and most remarkable generational change came with Russel's son Max.

You will read his and Dixie's story in this book, but I want to highlight how Max told his own story. He would say, "Well, God wanted people to work in Brazil and serve Brazilians, so more of them could know about Him. He asked the educated men at the top of the barrel—the cream of the missionary crop, men who had college degrees and were good at languages and theology—but they said no. He went down a bit to men who were at least good at one or two of those things. They also said no. So God scraped the bottom of the barrel; He found this hog farmer in Indiana with no skills, but He asked anyway, and the hog farmer said yes."

Dad always figured he was a project for God, since the way he saw it, the raw material was so poor. But he made a decision to always say yes to God. Always. You'll read in this book how that meant leaving a successful farm operation, uprooting a wife and kids, and struggling with grueling work, hardships, broken hearts, and more. But the constant theme you will hear through it all is saying yes to God.

A motto is meant to sum up a family in a few words—a tall task. And a motto can be created to stand for something new or distinct when the trajectory of a family shifts. Max and Dixie's faithfulness and unwavering obedience to say yes changed this particular family line radically.

Audacter Pareo means "Boldly I Obey." When I presented my thoughts and suggested the motto to Dad and Mom, Dad said, "Yes, that's who we are." He was delighted with the idea and proudly wore clothes we had printed for him with the insignia and motto.

As of 2021, the grandson of a man who abandoned his family has a family with 12 Christ-centered marriages across two generations. The son of a man who rarely picked up a Bible has 4 kids, 11 grandkids, and 14 great-grandkids, with all those of age having committed themselves to following God. The man from a line of rural American farmers has a family with members from Brazil, Canada, and Japan. Today the flags of the countries where family members have called home hang on the walls of their Indiana farmhouse: the U.S., Brazil, Mexico, Canada, Panama, Spain, Indonesia, and Kenya. The man who struggled with language has a family that speaks English, Portuguese, Spanish, Indonesian, and Japanese. How did we get here from there? *Audacter Pareo,* bold obedience, from a couple who decided to say yes to God.

Mom and Dad were not saints. They made mistakes like everyone does in their journey. But they said yes to God. Coat-of-arms rules do not force the next generations to take the motto upon themselves. In the same way, God's rules ensure that each person must make the individual choice to live for Him. Each generation has the privilege, weight, and ultimately the choice to live up to that motto and example of faith, or not.

So, *Audacter Pareo* is a fitting description for this couple whose last name happens to be Edwards, and their family after them certainly must choose to live out the meaning of that motto purposefully. But *Audacter Pareo* is also a call to anyone reading these words, a call to see an example, in spite of difficulties and mistakes, of what God can do with a servant who says yes, a servant who boldly obeys. *Audacter Pareo.*

Chapter 1

Thunder in the Night

For it is by grace you have been saved, through faith—
and this is not from yourselves, it is the gift of God.
Ephesians 2:8 (NIV)

Spring 1945

*M*ax Edwards stepped out onto the steps of the family farmhouse. The cool March wind bit his ears and cheeks. He
squinted as the setting sun shone in his eyes. The big Indiana sky was
streaked in shades of pink, purple, and blue. Green grass was starting
to peek out in the yard, framed by the bare trees and the brown fields
beyond. The earth felt so big and fresh in the spring.

Russel Edwards, Max's dad, pulled up in the family's black 1936 Chevy,
and the whole family piled in. Max followed his sisters Keturah and
Nina into the back seat. Little Janice sat on his mother's lap in the front.

"Hey, don't muss my skirt!" one sister complained as Max plunked
himself down. He grunted, not particularly concerned.

"Everyone in?" Russel asked.

"Yes, sir!"

"Okay." Russel drove down the lane and turned left onto Bloomingsport
Road toward church.

Keturah, Nina, and Janice, Max's sisters, were still chatting, but Max
had stopped listening. The girls were always talking and rarely about
anything important, in his opinion. If they were to talk about spring

planting or the cattle or the hogs—now *that* would be interesting. But it usually seemed to be about clothing or friends or other girly stuff.

Max tugged absently on the collar of his shirt as he looked out the window of the car. With services every evening, they were halfway through the two-week revival at church. In some ways, Max didn't mind revival services. He always sat in the back and joked around with his friends anyway. Most importantly, the spring revival meant that planting season was almost here. They always held the revival at this time of year, before the farmers got busy with planting. Max pushed back his dark hair and pressed his forehead against the window. The fields were empty now, but soon they would be abuzz with activity as every farmer hurried to plant his crops as early as he could. And Max would be right there with them. Sure, he had school to go to, but he would help every day when he got home. Planting season meant working as long and as hard as they could every day, until the work was done. It was exhausting but exhilarating at the same time.

Max leaned back and frowned. His breath had fogged up the window. He wiped it with his sleeve. Thinking of spring planting reminded him of what he didn't like about the revival services. They had work to do! Preparations to make! Why were they wasting time going to church?

The car turned off the road into the parking lot of New Liberty Church. Max turned his attention back to his family. The girls were still talking. They climbed out of the car and headed inside.

His dad said very little. Max knew that he wasn't an especially religious man, but his mother insisted that they all attend church together, at least some of the time.

They walked into the church and were greeted by many faces, all familiar. As they entered the building, Max felt the warmth created by the crowd and by the two large stoves on the sides of the sanctuary. The fires crackled, while the air smelled of smoke and old hymnals. Keturah and Nina had already left to find their friends, and his mother and dad were heading to their usual pew with Janice in tow. His mother shot Max a look that said, "Be good." Now that Max was 12, she rarely said it to him directly, but he could hear it all the same.

Max spotted his friends gathered around one of the stoves. He grinned as he joined them.

"Hey, Max!" they greeted. Max looked around at the happy faces; his friends were all there. They were just like him in their jeans and school shirts—their skin too white from the long winter, their eyes tired from hard work every day, and their cheeks ruddy from the nearby fire. Max was glad to see them as he sat on the edge of a nearby pew and leaned toward the fire. This was their habit every evening during the revivals—to sit around the stove and tell each other less-than-holy jokes. It was certainly more entertaining than listening to the preacher.

That night, however, Max could not help hearing some of what the speaker was saying. The message was about heaven and hell, about how good it would be to go to heaven, and how bad it would be to go to hell. The preacher was very descriptive about hell and how awful it was.

"Do you think you know what hell is like?" the preacher called out. He was really getting into it. "All of the worst things you have experienced here on this earth, you will find tenfold in hell! Have you ever fallen from a high place? Do you know the terror, the helplessness of that feeling? In hell you will feel as though you are falling, and the fall will never end. That terror and helplessness will go on and on. Do you know what it feels like to burn? Surely many of you have experienced small burns now and then."

Of course, Max thought carelessly. *I burn myself sometimes while working. It's one of the most uncomfortable kinds of injuries—everyone knows that.*

The preacher went on. "Do you know how the Bible describes hell in Revelation? It is called a lake of fire. In hell you will burn, and burn, and continue to burn throughout eternity."

The preacher was getting loud. "That burning sensation, which you have only felt in small ways here, will be all over your body forever and ever. Is that what you want after you die?"

Max shifted uncomfortably in the pew and focused on his friends, trying to block those words out.

After what seemed like forever, the preacher wrapped up his message. "Jesus could come back anytime!" he exclaimed. "Are you ready?"

The people stood and started to sing the invitation song. Max was shaking a little, but he continued to smile and chat with his friends, hoping they wouldn't notice. As was the custom during revivals, the

3

preacher walked through the congregation, inviting people to respond. He made his way back to the stove on the south side and headed straight for Max.

"Would you like to accept the Lord?"

Max was surprised and embarrassed. The man didn't seem to notice any of the other boys there; he spoke only to Max. Max could feel the eyes of his friends watching as the preacher repeated his invitation. He shook his head. He wasn't about to go forward—not in front of his friends and all these people. The man moved on, but Max was more nervous than ever.

That evening as he was getting ready for bed, Max couldn't shake the preacher's words from his head. If Jesus came back, what would happen to him? Where would he go?

He slipped into his bedroom. Wilbur, the older boy that Max's folks had taken in to raise, was already in his bed on the right-hand side. Max's bed was on the left. As he climbed in, he glanced at the window just in time to see a flash of lighting, followed almost immediately by a loud rumble. A spring storm was brewing. He pulled the covers up and closed his eyes, willing himself to fall asleep.

Another flash and a crash, seeming even faster and closer. Against his will, Max's heart beat harder and his breaths came quicker. The storm continued, sounding louder and louder as Max tossed and turned. Even though it was cold, he felt sweaty. He held his pillow over his face, but he only saw people falling and huge flames. Suddenly, he heard a loud clap at the same time as a flash just outside his window. Peeking out, he saw that a bolt of lightning had struck a tree just a few feet away, splitting it in half. The words of the preacher echoed in his mind: "Jesus could come anytime."

Max couldn't take it any longer. He scrambled out of bed and crawled into the dark space underneath.

"God," he said, "if you'll just wait and come tomorrow night, I'll give my heart to you. I promise."

Max slept underneath his bed that night. The next day he was relieved to find that Jesus seemed to have taken him up on his deal; He hadn't come yet. Max went about his regular activities—morning chores, school, afternoon chores, supper—but he still felt more distracted than ever. He wasn't thinking about planting anymore; he had something even more pressing on his mind. He just had to make it to the evening service. He would do it. Jesus just had to wait a few more hours.

Finally the time came for that evening's revival service. At the service, Max sat with his friends as usual, but he listened to the sermon this time. As far as he was concerned, it was the same message as the night before—about heaven and hell. And once again, during the invitation song, the preacher came straight to Max.

"Would you like to accept the Lord?"

This time Max nodded and stood. The preacher smiled and motioned for him to go to the altar at the front of the church. Max walked up the aisle, looking straight ahead. He saw the cross on the wall behind the pulpit. This night he would become a follower of Jesus. He had to. Max knelt at the altar, folded his hands, and bowed his head. Repeating after the preacher, he said the short prayer, giving his heart to the Lord. Immediately he felt his whole body relax. He was part of God's kingdom now. As he looked up, his eyes widened in surprise. Several of his friends—at least eight of them—had followed him to the altar. Max grinned. They would all have to start paying attention to the sermons now.

The preacher spoke to each person who had come forward that night; he encouraged and exhorted them. When he got to Max, he smiled and clapped him on the back. Holding out his Bible, he showed him a passage in Revelation.

"Your name is now written in the Lamb's Book of Life," the preacher said. "And when you die, you can go to heaven, and they will open that book and find your name and let you in."

Max nodded and said, "Thank you."

"Go in peace." The preacher moved on.

Max did feel peaceful. He went home with his family, carrying out the same evening routines as always. But he knew that he was different inside.

That night there was another storm. Max lay in bed, wide awake but no longer frightened. He clasped his hands behind his head as he listened, relaxed and smiling.

"God, you can come anytime now."

~ * ~

Summer 1947

Dixie Brumfield climbed to the top hay bale and came to a shaky stand. She pushed her curly brown hair out of her face.

"Here I come!" she called, leaping into the air. She squealed in excitement as she landed in the huge pile of hay.

"My turn! My turn! Get out of the way, Dixie!" her sister Judy called from above. Dixie rolled out of the pile and leapt to her feet. The prickly hay clung to her hair and clothes, but nine-year-old Dixie didn't care. Smoothing down her old dress, she looked around. This big barn was one of her favorite parts of their new home in Lynn, Indiana. With the haymow full of straw and loose hay, it was the perfect playground for kids. Low moos and snorts came from the animals below. Up here, the air was dusty and dry. Dixie felt around in her pockets for her hankie. She found it just in time—"Achoo!" she sneezed.

All of a sudden, one of her friends was beside her, poking her arm. "You just gonna stand there all day, Dixie?" she asked.

Dixie smiled, shoving the hankie back into her pocket. Dixie's friend grabbed her hand and led her across the haymow, where friends were building something out of the bales.

"We built a tunnel leading to the jumping pile!" another friend explained. "If you can make it through, you get to go again!" Dixie grinned and got down on her hands and knees to enter the tunnel. She squinted, trying to see the way with the limited light filtering through the straw. Rubbing the dust out of her eyes, she started forward. Another friend followed her.

Dixie smiled to herself. She was lucky to have found so many friends so quickly here in Lynn, especially since she was so shy. It was only a few months ago that they had moved back to Indiana from New Mexico. But soon after they had moved in, some people from nearby New Liberty Church had come and invited Dixie's mother and daddy, Pauline and Joe Brumfield, to their Sunday school parties. Dixie was surprised that they had accepted; her parents weren't church people. Nevertheless, the whole family found that they loved Sunday school parties. Her mother and daddy made friends with the other adults, and there were lots of children to play with Dixie, Judy, and little brother, Jerry. Friendships developed naturally in these situations. In fact, these were the Sunday school kids they were playing with in the haymow.

There was the light! She was almost to the end of the tunnel. Dixie grinned and sped up, ignoring the soreness in her knees and hands. She was small but quick. Coming out, she leapt to her feet.

"I made it!" The big pile of hay bales was right in front of her now. Carefully she climbed up, looked to see that the way was clear, and jumped again. She laughed as she landed in the soft and prickly hay. She would never get tired of this.

"Okay, kids, that's enough for tonight." Joe Brumfield's voice rang through the barn. Dixie popped up and crawled over to the ledge that looked over the barn's main floor. She peeked over the edge. Her father was standing in the doorway, holding an already-sleeping Jerry. *Plop.* A friend landed in the hay behind her. Judy was poised on the stack of hay above.

"But Daddy! It's still light out!" Dixie protested.

Joe smiled. "That's because it's summer," he said. "It's late. Time to do evening chores and go to bed." He looked up at all the children in the haymow. "Your parents are getting ready to leave, so you all had better come on down," he called, with a twinkle in his eye. "Else you might get lost in the hay and never be found again!"

"Yes, sir," the kids responded reluctantly. Dixie said farewells to her friends and headed into the house. Her mother was inside washing dishes. She stood bent over the sink; dishes seemed to fly through her hands. Her dark hair was pulled back, but a few strands escaped, sticking to her face in the humidity of the summer and the warm dishwater. She was strong, weathered, and tanned—signs of years of hard work—but still so very beautiful. She finished and straightened up, wiping her hands on a towel, just as Dixie and Judy walked in.

"Well, aren't you a sight to behold!" she exclaimed as she looked at their dusty appearance and picked some strands of hay out of Dixie's hair. She smiled, but there were dark circles under her eyes.

Why did Mother always look so tired and sad? Dixie wondered.

"Go get ready for your baths now."

"Yes, ma'am." Dixie slipped by and headed to their room. Judy followed behind her. Their mother always seemed to be looking for something. Dixie wondered if she might be hoping to find it in the Sunday school people or maybe even in church. Maybe church could be the answer to what Dixie was looking for too. Though she was still young, Dixie felt distinctly that there was something wrong with her. She knew that Grandma Brumfield—Daddy's mother—was a bit concerned about her family and was always praying for them. But Dixie wasn't sure quite what was wrong, or what she could do about it.

Dixie's family started attending New Liberty Church regularly, and Dixie enjoyed it. She learned a little bit about the Bible and the teachings of the church. She liked seeing her friends and sitting with them in the front pew during services.

The following January, there was another session of revival meetings at the church. Since the Brumfields were now regular attenders, they figured they might as well go to the revival services too.

It was so very cold. Dixie, Judy, and Jerry huddled together in the back seat of the car to try to keep warm. When they got to the church, they jumped out and ran in just as quickly as they could.

Big fires roared in the two stoves on the side of the church, warming the air a little bit, but Dixie was still cold. Her bare legs felt numb under her dress. Rubbing her hands together, she looked around for her friends. They had been in the church for half a year now, and she was getting better at remembering people's names. She passed the group of teenage boys around one of the stoves. One boy's blue eyes twinkled as he chatted with his friends; she thought his name might be Max. Dixie ducked her head and moved on. Though she was starting to get to know people, she was still too shy to talk to anyone besides her own friends.

"Dixie, over here!" someone called. Dixie looked up and smiled to see the familiar face. She dodged her way through the maze of adults and grabbed her friend's hand. They went together to their usual pew in the front.

Dixie did her best to listen to the message, but the preacher used a lot of big grown-up words that she didn't understand. She glanced over at her parents. Her daddy didn't seem to be paying much attention, but her mother was listening intently. There was a strange look on her face—like she was finally understanding something that she never grasped before. Or maybe it was that she was finding that something, the something that she had always been looking for.

When the preacher got to the end of his message and gave the invitation, Pauline Brumfield stood up right away. She marched to the front, excitement and determination on her face. She knelt at the altar on the side, just a few feet away from Dixie. Several members of the church gathered around her to pray with her as she accepted Christ as her Savior. After praying, she smiled and looked upward, tears streaming down her face. Dixie gaped—her mother was transformed, and her face was glowing.

Dixie didn't really understand what had happened to her mother, but she knew it was something wonderful. The people around her were all singing, crying, and praying. After the service, many people came and talked to her. Dixie heard her say, "I looked up, and there wasn't any ceiling there—I looked straight into the heavens."

The family was quiet on the drive home. Dixie's mother was so happy and peaceful, but her daddy seemed a little uncomfortable.

The next morning, while Dixie and Judy were eating their breakfast of eggs and toast, their mother came in and sat down with them at the table. She was holding a big book that Dixie recognized as a Bible.

"You girls know that last night I went to the front of the church, and I prayed to ask Jesus into my life," she said. "Today, I am a Christian, and we are going to read from this book, the Bible, every day and pray."

So Dixie's mother opened the Bible and read. Dixie saw that there were tears rolling down her cheeks again—tears of happiness. She didn't look tired or sad anymore; she seemed like a completely different person. Dixie was so happy for her mother, but she still had that feeling inside—the feeling that she needed something too. Was it the same thing that her mother had needed?

A few nights later at the revival, Dixie again sat in the front pew with her friends during the service. It was January 10, 1948. As she sat there at the end, she suddenly felt that she was the worst sinner in the world. She was starting to understand the teaching that she had been receiving at church. She knew that she hadn't done a lot wrong, but she also knew that she was born a sinner, and that she needed God to save her. She wanted to go up to the altar; she needed to go up. It was just a few steps in front of her, but she was too scared to take those few steps. She wasn't brave enough; she couldn't do it. So she just sat there and started to cry.

Suddenly, her mother was next to her, reaching for her hand. She must have been watching. "Dixie, would you like to go pray?" she asked.

Dixie nodded and allowed her mother to walk her up to the altar. They knelt together, and the preacher came over to pray with her. Dixie, crying because of her sins, confessed her sins and asked Jesus to come into her heart. Immediately, she felt such relief and freedom! After the service, as she was riding home with her family, she looked out the window into the cold night. Bright stars filled the sky. She smiled and thought, *If I wasn't in this car, I bet I could just fly!*

~ * ~

Throughout the rest of the revival, the church members focused their prayers on Dixie's daddy, Joe Brumfield. His family was Christian, but he had walked away from God a long time ago. On the very last night of the revival, one of the church members went up to Joe and invited him to come to the front. And he went! Joe Brumfield accepted the Lord that night, and Judy and Jerry not long after. They were now a Christian family.

The Brumfields became regular members of New Liberty Church and were there whenever there were services. Dixie's mother also continued to have devotions with the children at home. She subscribed to a Christian children's magazine that had stories in it. It came on Mondays. Devotions were moved to bedtime, and it became one of Dixie's favorite parts of the day. The three children shared a room; Dixie and Judy slept in a double bed, and Jerry slept on a rollaway bed. So at bedtime, their mother would first pull out the rollaway and fix Jerry's bed for him. Then he would climb in bed, and Dixie and Judy would get in their bed. Once they were all settled, she sat on the rollaway with Jerry and read them the stories from the magazine. Then she would pray with them. If their daddy wasn't outside working, he would join them too. All three of the children loved devotions. They looked forward to the time to relax, be together, and focus on God at the end of the day. Over the years, Dixie watched her mother mature in her faith, allowing the peace of God to inundate her life. From the day she became a Christian, she was a great example to her children of how to pursue God and live for Him every day.

And so, both the Brumfield and the Edwards families continued to attend New Liberty Church, and Dixie and Max learned and grew from the teaching they received. Both remained committed to their faith from the time that they went to the altar. They had become Christians, and they were learning to live like it.

Chapter 2

The Weekly Proposal

But as for me and my household, we will serve the LORD.
Joshua 24:15 (NIV)

When he was 16, Max bought his first tractor for $500 and rented an 80-acre farm to work for himself. He continued to love everything about farming. He liked working by himself out in the fields or in the barns—just him, God, and nature. He enjoyed the risk that came with competition against the elements. He loved the miracle of planting a seed and watching it grow. It was a manifestation of God's presence and work. Yes, this was what he wanted to do for the rest of his life. When he graduated from high school, he enrolled in a short course in animal husbandry at Purdue University and continued to farm, working with animals as well as with the land.

Dixie was also enjoying school, church, and farm life. Her one big struggle was with timidity; she was painfully shy and was terrified anytime she had to do a presentation in school or anything in front of people at church. Her greatest fear was that someday God would call her to be a preacher or a missionary. She just didn't think she could do it. Nevertheless, over time she learned to recite to herself Philippians 4:13: "I can do all things through Christ which strengtheneth me" (KJV). Dixie leaned on this verse whenever she had to do something she didn't think she could do; she knew she was dependent on God's strength to help her. She was thankful to have so many friends at church and at school.

When Dixie started junior high, she and her friends were able to join the youth group. This was exciting, because the youth did a lot of fun activities. One of her first events with them was a summer get-together at a church member's home. The day was warm and sunny, and they took advantage of the long daylight hours by playing outdoor games on their big lawn. For hours the group enjoyed playing Two Deep, Flying Dutchman, and other games. It was a little intimidating to play with the older kids, but Dixie soon forgot her nervousness in the fun of the games. Dixie loved any games that involved running; she was a good runner, and she knew it.

At one point, they were playing a game in which you tag someone, and then they have to chase you around the circle. When it was Dixie's turn, she walked around the circle, watching the backs of the youth. In the late afternoon sun, the bright circle skirts of the girls and the clean blue jeans and T-shirts of the boys stood out against the green lawn. Coming up behind one of the older boys, she quickly tapped him on the shoulder and took off, brown curls flying behind her. As she ran around the circle, she heard someone call out, "You'll never catch her, Max—she's too fast!" Dixie smiled to herself. You'd better believe she was fast.

When they were exhausted from running around, the youth traipsed into the house for refreshments and devotions. Absently nibbling on a cookie, Dixie sat with her girlfriends and looked around the room, watching the other youth.

The girls sat in little clusters, chatting and laughing together. On the other side of the room, the boys were doing the same, but they were much more rambunctious. As they joked around, one young man, Max Edwards, was acting silly. Dixie couldn't quite catch what they were saying, but as she watched, Max collapsed backwards into a chair, laughing. She couldn't help but smile. He seemed like a good guy—and handsome too! Not that she was interested, of course. After all, he was almost a full-grown man, and she was just a junior high student. Still, it was nice to know that there were good people around.

Max enjoyed attending the youth events at church, even after he graduated from high school and worked toward farming independently. Most of the young people, like Max, continued to participate with the youth until they were married. Of course, Max didn't intend to stay unmarried for long. As soon as he was successful enough to have his own home, he hoped to have a wife to partner with him. He just prayed that God would lead him to the right person at the right time.

One late summer day in 1953, when Max was 20 years old, he went to another get-together of the youth. Again they were taking advantage of the warm weather. Among the many who gathered in the yard, Max observed a group of younger teenage girls. One particular girl caught his eye. She had dark, curly hair that she was trying unsuccessfully to keep down in the breeze. While Max was watching, she spun around, her skirt flaring out like the petals of a flower. Her green eyes and beautiful smile lit up her face. Max noted with surprise that the girl was Dixie Brumfield. It seemed like just a few days ago she had been a little girl. Now 15, she was blossoming into a beautiful young woman. He smiled to himself. *That's who I want,* he thought.

A few weeks later, Max approached Dixie at church. "Hello, Dixie," he said.

"Hello, Max," Dixie responded, trying to hide her surprise at being approached.

"I was just wonderin', would you like to go to a movie with me next Saturday?"

It was almost impossible to hide her surprise now. Had Max Edwards just asked her on a date?

"Um … sure." She forced a smile. "That would be nice."

"Great!" Max grinned. "I'll pick you up at 7?"

Dixie nodded, and Max left to rejoin his family. Dixie sank down into the nearest pew, unsure of what to think or do. Max Edwards was interested in her? He was one of the most handsome, strong, and popular boys in church—larger than life, almost. She should be honored that he asked her out, but she couldn't get past being terrified. He was almost 21—six years older than she was. And as much as he liked to laugh and joke around, she knew from his reputation that he was serious when it came to his relationships and his goals in life. He wouldn't ask her out unless he was thinking that she might be a good possibility for a wife. And she wasn't ready to think about marriage! What was she supposed to do?

Her parents, of course, were very pleased when she told them.

"Max Edwards is a good boy," Joe said.

Her mother nodded in agreement. "You couldn't do better with anyone else."

Dixie knew it was true and nervously prepared for her date. He picked her up at 7 on Saturday as promised. They went to see a movie. What movie, she couldn't remember later; all she could remember was how scared she was. He was very kind and respectful and did his best to make conversation before and after the movie. But Dixie, still painfully shy, couldn't think of anything to say.

In spite of the awkward first date, Max didn't give up on Dixie. They went on several dates that fall and spent some time together on other occasions too. Of course, they saw each other at church and at youth events. Dixie's parents often had the youth over to their house for various activities. One thing Joe Brumfield liked to do was convert their dining room table into a ping-pong table, so they and their visitors could play ping-pong. On one occasion that fall, Max visited their house and was playing ping-pong with Dixie.

Max was good at ping-pong, but Dixie wasn't too bad either; after all, the ping-pong table was in her house. The game became quite animated, until finally Max missed the ball, and it rolled to the floor. He walked over to pick it up, but as he bent down, he heard a distinct ripping sound coming from the seat of his pants. Horrified, Max jumped up and pressed his back against the wall.

"I'm sorry, I just have to go now..." he scooted toward the door and went straight out and home. Dixie found out later what had happened!"

In January 1954, Max was drafted into the military to serve in the Korean War. He joined the military police and was stationed in Georgia.

Dixie was somewhat relieved that he was leaving; he was too old and too serious for her. While he was away, they wrote a few letters back and forth. Her sophomore year of high school ended, and her junior year came and went. She went on a few dates with other boys, but not many. She was still very shy and wasn't involved in many social activities outside of church.

In the fall of 1955, Max was released from military duty. As he traveled home, there were many things on his mind. Getting back to farming, of course, was one thing he was excited about. He had bought a new tractor before he left, and by now, his dad had used it more than he had. He also thought about his family; he was released a little early from the military because his mother was having surgery. He was glad he would be there to support his family during this time.

However, one thing, or rather one person, dominated his thoughts more than anything else—Dixie. She was 17 years old now, a senior in high school. She was practically a grown woman. Perhaps she would be more ready to think about settling down. After his time away, Max was surer than ever that she was the girl for him. She was a firm Christian; she was sweet and kind to everyone; and of course, she was beautiful. Max imagined that she was even more beautiful now than she had been a year and a half ago. What's more, she came from a good family, and he knew she would make an excellent farmer's wife. She was used to working hard, and Max was sure her mother had taught her everything she needed to know about caring for a home and a family.

He couldn't wait to see her again. But, *What if she's found someone else?* he wondered. The other boys would be fools not to try to win her affection. And Max had been far away, and he knew his letters were not very good, probably quite unimpressive to an intelligent girl like Dixie. Max was good at farm work and good with people, but reading and writing—really, any kind of schoolwork—had always been difficult for him.

Max decided then and there that seeing Dixie should be his top priority when he got home. He was arriving on a Saturday, and he knew that Dixie worked at the local dime store on Saturdays. So after dropping his things off at home and greeting his family, he drove straight into Winchester to the dime store.

When he walked in, Dixie was at the cash register, helping a customer. Max smiled. He was right; she was even more beautiful than two years ago when he first asked her out on a date. Her hair was shorter and a little more orderly; her navy pleated skirt and white blouse suited her. Overall, she looked more mature and more … womanly.

The customer left, and Max walked toward the cash register. "Hi, Dixie!" he called as he approached her.

Her eyes widened in shock at seeing him. "Hi, Max!" she responded, her voice quivering a little. So she was still shy, it seemed, but Max didn't mind; in fact, he found it made her even more attractive. He smiled.

"I just got home from the military today," he said, "and I wanted to come see you first thing. May I take you home after work today?"

Dixie swallowed and nodded. "Sure," she responded.

"Great!" Max grinned. He stayed a few more minutes, asking about how she had been, about her family, and about the local news. She gave very short, concise answers to his questions, but it didn't seem like she *disliked* conversing with him, so Max decided that all was well. And she had agreed to let him take her home, so she must not be seeing anyone else. He left quite pleased with the way things were going.

Max decided he wasn't going to miss any more chances with Dixie; she was definitely the one for him. After driving her home from work that evening, he asked her if he could drive her to the youth event the following evening; she agreed. Then he asked her on a date, and she agreed again. Soon they were in a steady relationship, together at every opportunity. They had dates on Saturdays and sometimes Fridays, and he drove her home from church events on Wednesdays and Sundays.

On one occasion not long after they had started dating, Max looked at Dixie, his blue eyes twinkling. "So," he said casually, "will you marry me? I love you."

Dixie felt like her heart would stop. She looked up into his face, trying to decide if he was joking. She really couldn't tell. "I … I'm not sure," she answered. "Not now."

"Okay," Max smiled. "I'll ask again."

And ask again he did—almost every time he saw her for the rest of the fall and into the winter.

"Are you ready to say yes yet?" he would ask.

"No, I'm not ready yet!" she would respond.

It became a normal part of their routine when they were together. Dixie didn't know what to do. Many of her friends were going to college after graduation, and part of her wondered if she might like to go too. On the other hand, her parents had never talked to her about college; she thought they would be more pleased for her to settle down and start a family. They loved Max, and they respected his family. Dixie believed that finding a good man to marry was more important than college.

And Max was certainly a good man. As she came to know him better, some of her fear was slipping away, and he was growing on her. He was kind and respectful; she always felt safe when she was with him. She could see that he had integrity and that he would give his full effort to whatever life brought his way. And he was a Christian. What more could she want?

On her own side, she wondered if she was mature enough to get married. How could she know if she was ready? And yet Max was very capable and mature. He would take good care of her. For Christmas, he gave her a Samsonite train case—a very expensive gift. Inside was a beautiful blue cardigan sweater. It was the prettiest piece of clothing she had ever owned. The gift spoke even more clearly of his intention to marry her; he wanted to take her and that train case away on a special trip.

More and more, Dixie realized that Max was the man that she wanted. She looked forward to seeing him, and she found she was happiest when she was with him. She felt instinctively that she could trust him completely. Dixie knew that Max loved her because he told her all the time; and her love for him was growing in response. She realized that she *did* want to marry him, not just because it was what he wanted or what her parents wanted, but because she loved him and wanted to be with him.

But when would she tell him? He asked her every time he saw her, but she didn't want to say 'yes' over sodas at the diner on some ordinary date night. She wanted it to be special. So, she picked a special day to say yes: Valentine's Day. On that day, they went on a date, and then he brought her home as usual. As they stood in the cold on her front porch, he asked again, "Are you ready to marry me yet? I love you."

Dixie smiled. "Yes!" she responded. "I believe I'm ready." She watched the expression on his face, surprise that was overcome almost immediately by joy. Grinning from ear to ear, he reached into his pocket and pulled out a little jewelry box. He opened it to reveal a diamond solitaire ring. Dixie thought it was the most beautiful ring she had ever seen. He slipped it on her finger, and it fit perfectly. Max leaned in and gave Dixie a kiss.

A few minutes later, he reluctantly went back to his car and headed home. When she could no longer see him, Dixie hurried into her warm house and back to her parents' bedroom. They were in bed but wide awake, doubtless waiting for their daughter to come home.

"Max and I are engaged!" she announced, showing them the ring. Overjoyed, they hugged her tightly.

"We're so happy!" they said.

Dixie was happy too. She knew that she had a good, strong, loving man, and she loved him very much. She felt in her heart that this was what God wanted too. And now she knew that God wouldn't call her to be a preacher or a missionary because she was marrying a farmer!

Max and Dixie were married on June 5, 1956. It was a Tuesday night, which was an odd day for a wedding, but they wanted to be married on her parents' anniversary. Dixie was 17 and had just graduated from high school. Max was 23 and was helping his dad farm his land. When Max was teased about "robbing the cradle," his response was, "As I told her dad, I have enough maturity for both of us!" And he did. They were ready to start their own farming family, just as their parents had before them.

~ * ~

A few months after Max and Dixie were married, an elderly neighbor approached Max to ask for a favor. "My wife and I need to get to our winter home in Tucson, Arizona," the neighbor explained. "But we're getting older, and I'm not sure we should drive the whole way by ourselves. Is there any chance you and your new wife would be willing to drive us? We would pay for your train fare home."

Max smiled. "I think we could do that," he responded. "Let me talk to my wife about it."

He discussed the matter with Dixie, and they decided they would go. Soon after, they headed to Tucson with their neighbors.

As Max drove, he had a lot of time to think. Wow, what were the odds that their neighbors' winter home was in Tucson?

Max had actually been to Tucson before. When he was a boy, his younger sister, Janice, suffered from asthma. The doctors recommended spending the winter someplace warm, so one winter, the whole Edwards family had moved to Tucson, Arizona. They lived in a trailer, and Max and his sisters went to school there.

It had been a while since he had thought about that time. Max, who never had trouble making friends, had soon found several buddies in the neighborhood to spend his time with. There had been a little grocery store near their home, which had candy for sale. Max and two of his friends would go there and experiment. They had discovered that if they came in and two of them paid for candy, the third could hide some in his clothes and just walk out. They did this many times. They were stealing, and deep down, Max knew that it was wrong.

Max shifted uncomfortably and adjusted his grip on the steering wheel. At the end of that winter, the Edwards family had moved back to Indiana, and Max had been able to put it mostly out of his mind... that is, until he dedicated his life to Jesus and began to grow in his faith. His sin had loomed larger and larger in his mind, until finally he had prayed and confessed it to God. When he was 17, he made a promise. "Lord, if I can ever get back to that place in Arizona, I will ask forgiveness of that storekeeper."

His heart was free. He knew he would never return to that place.

And now here he was—driving to Tucson, Arizona! What would he do? He had not told Dixie about his sin or his promise. It was a private matter, between himself and God. As they entered the city, Max could hardly believe it; they were going to the same area where he had lived as a boy. As they got closer, he realized that he had no choice; if he wanted to follow God, he had to keep his promise. The Lord was clearly bringing him here in order to give him that opportunity. They arrived at their neighbors' winter home. As Max helped them unload their things, he took a deep breath, then approached his neighbor.

"Hey, do you mind if I borrow your car for a few minutes?" he asked. "There is something that I need to do." He tried to ignore Dixie's questioning look.

"Sure, no problem," the neighbor responded.

"Thanks!" So Max and Dixie got back into the car, and Max drove straight to the grocery store. They were so close to where he had lived before that he knew exactly where it was. When they arrived, he turned to Dixie. "Can you wait in the car for a few minutes?" he asked. "I'll explain everything later."

Still confused, but not wanting to question her husband, Dixie nodded. "Thanks," he said. Max turned off the car and slowly climbed out, his heart pumping wildly. Would the same grocer be there who had run the store when he was a kid? What would he think of Max's confession? What were the chances that he even remembered him? Wasn't this kind of silly? Maybe he should just go home. After all, it was just a little candy, and it was so many years ago.

But as Max stared at the weathered front of the grocery store, he knew that it *did* matter. It mattered because he owed a debt to this grocer; and it mattered even more because it was a sin that stood in the way of his relationship with God. Slowly Max walked up the steps and entered the building.

It was almost closing time, and the shop had no customers. The vegetables, breads, and other foods sat in tidy rows on the shelves, ready for the following day. The only other person present was the grocer, who was bent over his broom, sweeping the floor. Yes, it was the same man; he was a little older, but for the most part, he was just as Max remembered him.

Gathering his courage, Max strode up to the man and held out his hand.

"Hello," he said. "My name is Max Edwards, and my family lived here for one winter when I was a boy." He briefly told his story, then said, "I want to pay for the candy I stole as a kid." Max pulled out his wallet and found a $20 bill.

"Take this. I'm sure it will more than pay for all the candy I stole." The grocer had not said much. But as Max looked up and handed him the money, he saw that there were tears in the man's eyes.

"You are the only one who has ever returned and confessed," the grocer said, his voice catching a little. "I knew you kids were stealing, but your folks were buying groceries from me, so I let it go." At that moment, Max knew that it was worth it to do the right thing—even when it was scary and even when it was about something small like candy.

They chatted a while, then Max went back to the car. Now he was able to share the story with his new wife. He could see how God had worked;

the storekeeper was left impressed with a Christian life, and Max was free of a heavy burden. God was working in his life and maturing him.

~ * ~

Max and Dixie returned home from Arizona and continued their new life together. For a while, they lived on a farm that belonged to Max's dad, Russel Edwards, while Max farmed with his father. Their first child, Jay Dee, was born there in October 1957. However, there was not enough land for two families, so Max rented a different farm and then another. In 1960, they moved to a 360-acre farm just down the road from New Liberty Church, where they would live for the next eight years. They had two more children: Jan, their daughter, was born in October 1959; and Jeffry Max, another son, was born in June 1963.

Max was a good farmer, and he did well working the land and raising hogs, beef cattle, and sheep. Dixie was a good housewife and enjoyed working at home and raising her children. Both continued to be involved in their church. Max was the church youth leader and treasurer, and Dixie started a children's choir called the Sunbeams. God was growing them, and they were applying what they learned to their ministry at church and to their work at home. This was the life they had always planned on living, and they were content.

Chapter 3

"Drop the Cookie!"

I will instruct you and teach you in the way you should go; I will counsel you with my loving eye on you.
Psalm 32:8 (NIV)

February 15, 1964

The cold wind bit Max's face as he steered his tractor through the field. As usual, he was getting an early start in preparing for planting. Today he was spreading fertilizer on his fields. Max took a deep breath. The earthy smell of the fertilizer mingled in the air with the gasoline smell of the rumbling tractor. To Max, the scents were sweet; he was excited for the new season—seeing God perform the miracle of growth all over again.

How much fertilizer had he spread now? He'd better check the spreader to find out what was left. Max turned the tractor motor down and dismounted.

He walked around the tractor and leaned over to check the fertilizer. Suddenly Max felt a jerk and was dragged backwards. His coat had caught in the power takeoff shaft of the spreader. Max grabbed the fender of the tractor and pulled, trying to wrench himself free. Though he was strong, he was no match for the machine. As he strained and pulled, the spinning shaft pulled back, grabbing his coat, then his sheepskin vest, then his hooded sweatshirt. His neck would be next. Covered in sweat, he felt his arm being torn out of its socket as he held on to the fender. He yelled in pain, the sound echoing across the quiet fields. Max began to panic. This machine was going to kill him!

Just then the motor stopped running, and the shaft stopped spinning. Max could hardly believe it. Pain shot through his left arm as he let go of the fender and sank to the ground. He was hurt, but he was alive.

"Thank you, Jesus."

Nearly fainting, Max used his right hand to grab on to the spreader and drag himself to his feet. With some trouble, he freed himself from all the clothing wrapped around the power takeoff shaft and disconnected the spreader from the tractor. Then, wearing only an undershirt, he got on the tractor to drive back to the house.

A quarter mile had never felt so long. With his left arm still hanging limp, he maneuvered the tractor with only his right hand, gritting his teeth against the cold and the pain. Finally, he reached the lane.

"Dixie!" he yelled. "Bobby! Kids!"

Bobby, the hired hand, ran to him. Max stopped the tractor and Bobby helped him down, pulling Max's arm over his shoulders.

"Mrs. Edwards!" Bobby called as he helped Max to the house. "Mrs. Edwards!"

Dixie and Jay appeared at the back door. "Oh, my!" Dixie exclaimed. "Max, what happened?"

Max faltered and sank to his knees. Bobby picked him up and carried him to the back door. Max hurriedly told them the story as he stumbled through the door and sat down on the back porch. Dixie grabbed an extra jacket and wrapped it around his bare shoulders.

"Jay, go back into the house where it's warm," Dixie said.

"Yes, ma'am."

"We need to take you to the doctor," Dixie said to Max. "I'll call your mother and see if we can drop the children off at her house." She looked at Max. "Can you make it to the car?"

"I'll help him," Bobby said. "Then after you leave, I'll take care of the tractor and the spreader."

Max smiled weakly. "See if you can get it to give my coat back."

Dixie called her mother-in-law while Max gave Bobby some additional instructions. Then Dixie piled the family into the car and, after dropping off the children, drove Max to the doctor's office. The doctor took them to the emergency room to give Max a muscle relaxant and put his arm back into the socket. He then told him to keep his arm in a sling for six months, and sent him home.

As Dixie drove, Max leaned back in the passenger seat and closed his eyes. All of that, and all he had was a sling for six months? God had miraculously spared his life. Max was one very thankful man. He felt sure that the Lord must have a purpose for this. Could it be that there was more in store for him than farming?

In the following days, Max sought the Lord more than ever before. He wanted to know God and to be obedient to whatever He had for him. He started by making his daily devotions a top priority. Every day, he would spend time reading his Bible and praying—no matter how much he had to do around the farm. He became engrossed in the Bible like never before. Through these devotions, Max began to see things in a different light. He learned a great deal for his personal life, and he also learned how to better relate to his wife and his children. God was working in his life.

Later that year, a missionary came to speak at New Liberty Church. His name was Dale McClain, and he was serving in Hong Kong. Max and Dixie, impressed by his message, decided to support him financially. He visited them several times in 1964 and 1965, and the Edwards family came to know him well.

Soon after, the Edwards family began to support another missionary—this one working in South America. Austin Boggan, a missionary to Brazil, had a passion for ministry and a dynamic personality. He was a fiery, articulate, and charismatic communicator. He also visited often, sharing his passion with Max and Dixie.

A friend gave Max some books about fasting, and he made this spiritual discipline a part of his life as well. He fasted for days at a time, drinking only water, even when he was working hard outside. On one occasion, he happened to be fasting over Thanksgiving. The family went to his parents' home for the holiday, and he sat at the table with one of the children on his lap, hoping to make the situation less awkward. Still, it was clear to all who were present that he was not eating, and his mother was concerned about him. Was he becoming some kind of fanatic?

Dixie was also concerned and somewhat frightened. She did not know what was happening to her husband. Why all of the changes? Though she appreciated that he was growing in his faith and learning to be a better husband and father, some of his actions seemed a little extreme. Dixie didn't want anything to change; she liked things just the way they were.

~ * ~

Max closed his Bible and sighed, looking out the living room window. His devotional reading that day had been particularly convicting. The sun was coming up, and the sky was tinted in purples, pinks, and oranges. He had a lot to do, and yet, his work was no longer foremost in his mind. Not like it used to be anyway. What was this stirring in his heart?

He had seen the changes in his life since the accident. It wasn't just about being more interested in his devotions or in missions—it was about a shift in his focus and his priorities. It was confusing but also intriguing.

Others around him had noticed the changes too, but they seemed more concerned than intrigued. *I guess I can't blame them,* Max thought, *considering the way I've been acting.* And yet, all he sought was to know God better, to listen to the Holy Spirit, and to be obedient to Him. After all, wasn't that what life was all about for a Christian?

He looked down at his Bible again. No matter what anybody said or thought, there was no going back for him. The passages that he read convicted him; they urged him to be increasingly dedicated to the Lord.

Max whispered a prayer under his breath. "God, I will do anything you ask me to do, no matter how unusual it might be."

~ * ~

Go to the church right now.

Max suddenly awoke. Dixie was sleeping soundly beside him. He rolled over and checked his clock—2 a.m.

Go into the church, kneel at the altar, turn on the cross light, stand behind the pulpit, and read a message from the Bible.

Go to the church? At 2 a.m.? Really? The voice wasn't audible, and yet it could not be mistaken. He knew it was the voice of the Holy Spirit. He could get into the building; as youth leader and treasurer, he had a key. It was only half a mile away. But Max was terrified. What if someone saw him?

Max realized he didn't have a choice. If he wanted to obey God, he had to go to the church right then. Reluctantly, he got out of bed and got dressed. He crept out of the house and into the cold night. It was February again, a year after his near-fatal accident, and the air was crisp and fresh. He got into his car and turned it on. Was it always this loud? He carefully drove down the road and turned into the church parking lot.

He got out of the car and walked up to the church. Max was scared to death. He could think of so many reasons why he shouldn't be there. He knew that the sheriff spot-checked the churches for burglars. If he came to check New Liberty, what would he think of Max? How would Max explain himself?

His hands shook a little as he got his keys out and opened the door. He walked inside and closed it softly behind him. The church was dark and quiet, but Max knew his way around. His eyes adjusted to the darkness as he walked up the aisle in the sanctuary. So much had happened in this little church. In the darkness he could almost see his group of friends, sitting around the furnace telling jokes. Now they were all grown up, most still attending this church with children of their own. Max reached the front of the church and approached the altar—the same altar where he had knelt all those years ago and given his life to Jesus. He knelt and bowed his head, praying a short prayer. Standing up, he walked over to the wall and flipped a switch. The cross behind the pulpit flickered, then lit up, casting a soft light on the platform.

Max took a deep breath, squared his shoulders, and walked confidently up to the pulpit like a preacher on a Sunday morning. He laid his Bible on the pulpit and opened it to the book of Acts. Somehow, he knew that this was what he was supposed to read. By the light of the cross behind him, he began:

"The former treatise have I made, O Theophilus, of all that Jesus began both to do and teach, Until the day in which he was taken up, after that he through the Holy Ghost had given commandments unto the apostles whom he had chosen" (Acts 1:1–2 KJV).

Max continued to read, his voice echoing through the empty sanctuary. He read the first chapter of Acts, then the second, then the third. He read all the way to the end of the seventh chapter, which was about Stephen, the first Christian martyr. "And they stoned Stephen, calling upon God, and saying, Lord Jesus, receive my spirit. And he kneeled down, and cried with a loud voice, Lord, lay not this sin to their charge. And when he had said this, he fell asleep" (Acts 7:59–60 KJV).

Max took a deep breath. In his heart, he heard the Holy Spirit speaking to him again. *If you're as dead to everything you ever wanted to do as Stephen was, then you can go home.*

Heart thumping, Max closed his Bible, turned off the light, and headed home. Much to his relief, he made it safely without being seen or questioned. He went inside and got back into bed. Dixie was still asleep.

Max was learning to hear and obey God's voice.

~ * ~

Dixie took another egg out of the basket, cracked it, and poured it into the pot with the others. She hummed to herself; Jay and Jan were doing so well with their new song, "I Wouldn't Take Nothing for My Journey Now." The two were talented; they had been singing duets together since they were five and three. Nothing could make Dixie happier. She loved music and loved developing the musical abilities of her children.

Actually, New Liberty had many talented singers. Dixie's children's choir included many of them. Working with children was the perfect ministry for her. It was right within her gifting, and it was not frightening in any way. She really felt like she had arrived in the search for a place to serve God.

Dixie frowned at the bubbling eggs. From her perspective, Max had found his place too. He was working hard, farming 700 acres, and being involved in church as the treasurer, youth leader, and a Sunday school teacher. And yet it seemed like he wanted something more. What exactly he wanted, she didn't know; maybe he didn't know either. But it seemed like he thought something was missing—like there was something else that God wanted him to do or be. Just the other day he had told her about his little late-night adventure, which had apparently happened several months ago. What was that all about? Going to the church in the middle of the night to read from the pulpit? Did Max think that God wanted him to be a preacher? He was a farmer! Dixie loved her husband, but she was so confused about what all of this meant.

Max came out of the bedroom, ready for work. He looked so handsome and strong in his overalls and plaid shirt.

"Mornin', Dixie!"

"Good morning, honey!" she replied, smiling as he kissed her on the cheek. "Ready for breakfast?"

"You bet!" Max sat down at the table while Dixie put some of the poached eggs and toast on a plate for him.

"Thank you, honey."

"You're welcome." Dixie grabbed a glass from the cupboard and went to the refrigerator to get him some milk. While she poured, she stole a glance at Max. He was chewing thoughtfully, staring at nothing in particular. "You're awfully quiet this morning," she commented, as she set the milk in front of him.

Max looked at her, then back at his food. "I had a strange dream last night," he said, "and I can't seem to get it out of my mind."

"Oh? What kind of dream?"

"Well ..." Max took a deep breath. "I was drivin' down the road on my tractor, and then all of a sudden, there wasn't any tractor."

Dixie raised her eyebrows. "What do you mean, 'there wasn't any tractor'?"

Max threw up his hands. "It was just ... gone. Then I woke up." He looked up at Dixie. "Do you suppose it means something?"

Dixie was at a loss for words. "I don't know, Max," she said. "I don't know what to tell you. I don't know about things like that."

Max looked back down at his eggs. "Yeah, me neither."

He finished his breakfast, thanked his wife, and headed outside. The sun was shining, and the sky was clear and blue. It was a beautiful day. *Thank you, Lord, for the sunshine and the good weather,* he prayed silently, taking a deep breath. He walked into the barn and looked at his hogs. With everything going on in his heart, he was a little worried that he would lose his edge in caring for his livestock. Everything on the farm was still going well, and Max had not neglected anything, but what if he started to? The farm was not his main passion as it had been for so long.

And what about this dream? Did it mean that there would come a time when he would no longer farm? In the following months, Max asked everyone that he could for advice. At one point, a preacher visited their home, so Max asked if he had any insight. Unfortunately, he had no more answers than Max did himself.

When his missionary friends visited, he told them about the dream, as well as about the other things he had been experiencing.

Dale McClain thought that he shouldn't read into it too much. "Missionaries need people like you to stay on the farm," he said, "and give money." He told him that God was calling him to grow in his walk with the Lord and to continue to be a faithful layman.

Austin Boggan, on the other hand, wanted everyone to be a missionary. He suggested that Max do some extra Bible study "just to be prepared" for whatever God had planned. Max didn't really expect to ever leave Randolph County, but he consented. He figured that it would make him a better Sunday school teacher and would give him more to offer to the youth as their leader.

Austin gave him the name of a correspondence school based in Kansas, and Max agreed to contact them. Before he knew it, he was taking classes by correspondence, studying the Bible systematically, and writing sermons.

He also continued giving money to missions. In addition to their regular support for the McClains and Boggans, he decided to dedicate three hogs to the Brazil field. While speaking at New Liberty, Austin mentioned that the missionaries in Brazil needed money to buy a VW bus for their transportation. The three hogs yielded a good profit, and Max sent it all to Brazil for the purchase of that vehicle. After this, Austin talked to him more about taking a trip to Brazil.

"You need to get down there and ride in your hogs!" he joked. Max laughed and nodded, hiding the idea in his heart. Perhaps, someday, he would get to visit the mission field.

Max continued to learn about listening to the Holy Spirit and obeying. At one time he felt that God was telling him to go to the nearby city of Richmond, Indiana, and hand out tracts in taverns. He wasn't sure whether the idea was really from God or not, so he discussed it with a friend. The friend encouraged him, saying, "Even if this direction isn't from the Lord, it couldn't hurt anything."

So Max did. He went to Richmond one Saturday night, shared about Jesus with people in taverns, and handed out tracts. He never knew whether his actions that night impacted anyone, but he proved once again that he was willing to do anything that God might ask him to do.

On another occasion, Max came in from work to find that Dixie had made his favorite cookies—chocolate chip. He sat down at the table, poured himself a glass of milk, and chatted with his wife. He ate several cookies, then picked up another.

Drop it.

Max was so startled that he immediately dropped the cookie. It was that voice again—internal, but very real. He drew back his hand and stared at the plate.

Dixie looked at him in surprise. "No more?" she asked.

Max shook his head. "I've had enough."

Another time, as Max was working in the barn, he suddenly felt that God had another task for him. He was to go up to the haymow, set up seven bales of hay, and preach to them. Max looked out the open door of the barn. It was raining hard, and the hired hand wasn't around today. Still … preach to the hay? Sometimes seed salesmen came by, even on rainy days. Or neighbors. Everyone was already starting to think he was a little crazy.

Again, Max realized that if he wanted to obey God, he had no choice. The voice in his heart was unmistakable. He decided he was more afraid to disobey God than he was of embarrassment. Taking frequent glances at the door, he climbed up the wooden ladder into the haymow. He wiped the dust and sweat off his face with his sleeve. Seven bales of hay. He began to pull the large, rectangular bales off the piles at the end of the haymow. As he set them up, he imagined that each one was a person who needed to be saved. He talked to them—quietly at first, then louder and stronger as he gained momentum. His voice echoed through the barn, rivaling the sound of the rain pounding on the roof. As he preached, his thoughts were all about Acts 1 to 7. Nothing was more important than this—reaching the lost and advancing God's kingdom. The bales of hay were cold and indifferent, but they allowed him to preach his entire sermon! No one came looking for him, and he was obedient once again.

It was now the spring of 1966. In his correspondence course, he was studying the deliverance of the Hebrew slaves by Moses and the Red Sea story. He wrote a sermon on how God caused the wheels to come off the chariots as the Egyptians were pursuing the Hebrews through the sea. He wrote about the way that God gave the victory as Pharaoh's army was destroyed. His sermon was good enough to merit an "A" from the teacher who graded his paper. Max, the farmer, was writing sermons.

Chapter 4

"I don't want another man!"

Whether you turn to the right or to the left, your ears will hear a voice behind you, saying, "This is the way; walk in it." Isaiah 30:21 (NIV)

October 1966

*D*ixie sat down at the kitchen table and took a deep breath. She finally had a moment to do her devotions, while three-year-old Jeff was taking his nap. Jay and Jan, now ages nine and seven, were at school. She opened her Bible and turned to 1 Samuel 10, where she had left off last time. It was the story of Saul, the first king of Israel. He was a young man, a mostly ordinary Israelite, but through a series of events, God called and appointed him to be the king. Dixie knew the story well. Suddenly, verse 6 jumped out at her: "And the Spirit of the Lord will come upon thee, and thou shalt prophesy with them, and shalt be turned into another man" (KJV).

Immediately, Dixie thought, *Max!* He was becoming another man. Startled, she chided herself, *That's ridiculous. This is talking about Saul.* She finished her reading, prayed, then hurried to get some housework done before Jeff woke up. She pushed any thoughts about Max and Saul from her mind.

That is, until the next day. Continuing with her devotions, she should have begun with 1 Samuel 11. And yet, as she opened her Bible and began to read, her eyes fell on chapter 10 verse 6 again: "...and shalt be turned into another man." Again the thought thundered in her head, *Max!* A wave of fear rolled over her. She began to pray aloud. "Lord, I don't want another man. I like him just like he is!"

~ * ~

The next Sunday

"Okay, I think that about does it for today," Max said. "I'll see you all upstairs." The room filled with the sounds of scraping chairs and closing Bibles as the youth stood. They chatted and laughed as they left the Sunday school classroom. Max smiled. He enjoyed working with the youth; they had so much energy and potential.

He stepped out of the classroom into the common area in the New Liberty basement. All around, people were coming out of their Sunday school classes, Bibles tucked under their arms. Children darted through the crowd of adults, holding freshly completed crafts. Max chatted with the other men about this year's harvest as he made his way to the sanctuary upstairs. It was the same as every Sunday morning; all the people and routines were familiar. Upon reaching the sanctuary, he went to his family's usual pew, where he was soon joined by Dixie and the children.

The organist finished the prelude, and someone stood up to give announcements. Then, in Max's heart, the announcer's voice was overpowered by the voice of the Holy Spirit.

Go to Peaceful Valley Church.

Peaceful Valley was a small Friends (Quaker) church about eight miles away. It was another country church but different from New Liberty in that most of the members were factory workers, not farmers. Max only knew one or two people there. Why would God want him to go there? He shifted uncomfortably in his seat and looked around at his family and friends. There was no way to leave without being noticed. But he could not shake it.

Go to Peaceful Valley Church now.

Max leaned over to whisper in Dixie's ear.

"I have to go," he said. Her eyebrows rose. He swallowed and continued. "I need to go to Peaceful Valley Church."

Dixie frowned. "Peaceful Valley?" she whispered. "Why would you need to go there? Max, the service has already started!" They were getting looks for their whispering.

"It's just something I need to do. Your parents can take you home after church." And with that, he stood up and left.

Max walked out of the sanctuary as quietly and inconspicuously as he could, though he knew that everyone saw him. He felt bad about leaving Dixie; she was clearly confused and embarrassed. But what was Max supposed to do? He had to obey God. He prayed that she would understand.

As he drove the quiet country roads, Max wondered why the Lord would want him to go to Peaceful Valley. The church had been having some trouble; their pastor had left abruptly just a week or two before. But there wasn't anything Max could do about that situation. Surely God didn't expect …? Max began to sweat a little as he pulled into the church parking lot.

When he arrived, the Sunday service was just about to begin. Max crept in and slipped into the back pew, keeping his head down. The leader of the service was in the middle of the difficult task of explaining to the church that they had no pastor. When Max settled into his seat and looked up, he saw that the man speaking was Lowell Pearson, an old friend of his. They had attended New Liberty together as boys. Their eyes met, and Max gave him a small smile.

Lowell's face suddenly broke into a grin. "But friends," he continued, "many of us have been praying all week that God would send us a messenger for this morning." He looked straight at Max, eyes twinkling. "I think that odd one who just slid down in the seat in the back needs to come up here and mind God. Max, would you like to share?"

Max gulped. So this *was* what God expected. He had thought that maybe he would be asked to share his testimony, but now it was clear that he was supposed to preach. Slowly, he rose and walked to the front, as scared as he had ever been.

He walked up behind the pulpit, set his Bible down, and looked out at the people. "Um, good morning," he said, smiling tentatively.

"Good morning!" the people responded.

"I'm Max Edwards, and I'll be sharing from …" he looked down at his

Bible. He didn't have his sermon with him, but he had only written one. "Exodus 14," he said. Using his Bible and his memory, he preached the sermon he had written for his correspondence course. He preached about how God had caused the wheels to come off the chariots of Pharaoh's army and had delivered His people. And that day, God delivered Max from his fears and insecurities as he preached his first real sermon.

After the service, many of the church members approached Max to introduce themselves and thank him for sharing. Max was surprised and thrilled. He couldn't believe that he had really preached a whole sermon, not to an empty church or to hay bales, but to people! As he drove home, he thanked God for what He had done and prayed for wisdom and guidance going forward.

As soon as he got home, Max went to the kitchen to find Dixie. She was waiting for him. "Dixie! You'll never believe what happened this morning!"

"What happened, Max?" She looked up from the stove, nervous and confused. "Why did you go to that other church?"

Max beamed at her. "I gave the message there this morning!"

"You *what?*"

"I went there, and they didn't have anybody to bring a message. Lowell Pearson called me up, and I preached!"

Dixie looked at him in disbelief. She didn't know what to think or what to say. Suddenly, she remembered again the passage from 1 Samuel 10:6: "And the Spirit of the LORD will come upon thee, and thou shalt prophesy with them, and shalt be turned into another man" (KJV).

Was this the "another man" that Max was becoming?

Max realized that Dixie couldn't understand his excitement at what the Lord had done in and through him. In her mind, Max wasn't a preacher; he was a farmer. Max knew that, and he agreed. Farming was his profession and his passion. But it seemed like, at least for now, God wanted him to preach too.

Max felt certain that God wanted him to speak again at Peaceful Valley, and after the warm reception he had received, he expected someone to call or visit and invite him back. In anticipation of this, he prepared another sermon, spending much of his spare time in study. The days rolled by—Monday, Tuesday, Wednesday, Thursday—no call or visit. Sunday morning came, and he still hadn't heard anything from Peaceful Valley. So, he took his family to New Liberty as usual.

As he sat in the pew with his children, Max's heart was eight miles away in that little Quaker church. He heard the voice speak to him again.

The only invitation you need is my command. Get out of this church and get over there!

Max looked around. Dixie was at the piano this week, sitting with her back to Max and the children. He leaned over and whispered to Jay, Jan, and Jeff, "I have to go. You kids are gonna sit with Grandpa and Grandma today." As quietly as he could, he shuffled the children over to where Dixie's parents were sitting; then he headed out.

When Max walked into the sanctuary at Peaceful Valley, he had the strangest sense that they were expecting him, and even wondering why he hadn't arrived earlier. He was motioned to the pulpit, and the leader sat down. So he preached the message that he had prepared that week. Obedience felt so good!

After the service, he learned that they *had* been expecting him. A committee of three had met the previous Sunday and decided to invite him back. However, God had allowed a confusion among them. Each one thought another had invited him, when in reality, no one did. Max could see clearly that this was God's doing. The Lord had allowed this confusion in order to teach Max to obey Him rather than any human authority.

When the confusion was understood, it was quite humorous to all involved. After a good laugh and an apology, Max was invited to return for a third Sunday.

~ * ~

So Max preached at Peaceful Valley the third Sunday and, once again, was invited back. On the fourth Sunday, Dixie and the children were already home when Max returned. He strode into the house and put his arms around Dixie. He looked into her face and smiled, his blue eyes lighting up.

"Honey, the people have asked me to pastor the church. I know in my heart it's what God wants me to do. So I said yes."

Dixie looked up at him, dumbfounded. She had been watching Max slowly change over the past couple of years, but she had always told herself, *He's just going to be a better husband, daddy, and Sunday school teacher. After all, he is a farmer!* She had repeated this to herself, even as she felt God telling her that He was changing Max and doing something new. She had pushed away any thoughts that he would actually make significant changes. But now … now he was really going to be a pastor! As this truth slowly penetrated her understanding, she found her tongue.

"Max, if God had wanted you to preach, He would have called you before you were 34!" She felt tears begin to prick her eyes. "I can't leave my church. I don't want to take the kids there. I can't leave the Sunbeams." She was really crying now, but she didn't care. How could Max do this to her? How could God do this? Didn't they know how hard it was for her to do new things? Didn't they know that she was just a simple country girl and that she didn't have the courage or the skills to be a pastor's wife? Her insecurities loomed around her as her world came crashing down. She had never agreed to this.

Max did not try to preach to her or quote Bible verses at her. "I understand," he said. "God called me. And when God calls you, then you will go." He kissed her forehead and smiled.

How could he be so relaxed when he was taking on such a big job—one that he had never done before? Peace was written all over his face. There was no anxiety or worry there. He knew that he was doing what God wanted him to do. Dixie, on the other hand, could feel nothing but anxiety and fear. A pastor's wife had to be involved in everything. She had to know everybody, and she had to set an example for the whole church. Dixie didn't even know the people at Peaceful Valley. She just couldn't do it!

So the following Sunday Max went to "his" new church, Peaceful Valley, and Dixie took the children to "her" church, New Liberty. Max told his congregation, "If you want a pastor's wife, you'll have to pray her here!" They did pray for Dixie, and she knew it.

Dixie felt burdened, depressed, and embarrassed. She knew that everyone was talking about her farmer-turned-preacher husband. In her spare time, she struggled, prayed, thought, and cried. She didn't sleep well. She didn't want her life changed, but God had changed it. She was angry with Him. One never wins an argument with God, so she knew she would have to change. But how could she? She felt certain that she could not be a pastor's wife. She wasn't good enough, strong enough, or smart enough.

At the end of November, New Liberty held a series of revival services. They brought in song evangelists for the occasion, and Dixie was asked to accompany them on the organ. On Sunday morning, they started with the song "He Touched Me."[2] One of the evangelists was at the piano, and Dixie was playing the organ on the platform.

> They began to sing:
> Shackled by a heavy burden
> 'Neath a load of guilt and shame
> Then the hand of Jesus touched me,
> And now I am no longer the same.

The words sank into Dixie's heavy, heavy heart. The burden she had been carrying for the past six weeks was more than she could bear; her heart was crying out for Jesus' touch. Dixie glanced sideways at the altar, just a few feet away. She wanted to go and pray, but she didn't want to cause a disturbance—imagine the organist leaving her seat during the opening song! Her heart was beating faster and faster. She struggled to breathe as she felt the weight of her resistance to God pressing on her chest. *I just might die right here on the organ bench if I don't obey God,* she thought. The Holy Spirit was calling her to complete surrender.

So the organ music came to an abrupt stop as the organist left the bench, scooted around the side, went down the steps, and knelt at the altar. Everyone could see her; perhaps many were already praying for her. Her mother was soon by her side, praying with her. There she was, at the same altar where she was saved as a girl of nine, where she was married, and where Jay, Jan, and Jeff were all dedicated to God as babies. Now she was here again—needing to surrender her life to God. In reality, she needed to give her husband to God for His own purposes. She

---

2   Bill Gaither, 1963.

had tried to hold him prisoner in her heart, telling herself *he's a farmer, not a preacher.* Max was free. She was the one who was a prisoner.

She had a clear picture of what she needed to do. She prayed a prayer of surrender. First she surrendered Max to God's own purposes. Then she prayed and gave each of her children to God once again. Finally she prayed, *Lord, I give you my life. Lord, I give you the Sunbeams. And please make me a good pastor's wife. I can't do this on my own.*

As the evangelists continued to sing, the words of the chorus reached Dixie's consciousness:

> He touched me, O He touched me,
>> And O the joy that floods my soul;
> Something happened and now I know,
>> He touched me and made me whole.

Dixie finished praying and shakily rose to her feet. At that moment, she felt peace wash over her from the top of her head through her body and down to her feet. Finally she relaxed. She had surrendered to God, and that heavy burden was gone. Yes, He had touched her!

That Sunday night, Dixie went with Max to Peaceful Valley and became a pastor's wife. The whole family began to attend there and made Peaceful Valley their church. It was an adjustment for them all. Dixie sang with the Peaceful Valley children, though they were never a choir like the Sunbeams. Jay and Jan did not like the move at first, but after a while, they felt at home and enjoyed playing with the other kids. They also enjoyed hearing their daddy's messages. He used lots of word studies and illustrations. And Dixie learned to be a pastor's wife, even as she continued to be a farmer's wife. Yes—obedience felt good.

Chapter 5

Unconverted Hogs

Then he said to his disciples, "The harvest is plentiful but
the workers are few. Ask the Lord of the harvest, therefore, to send out workers into his harvest field."
Matthew 9:37–38 (NIV)

1966

*M*ax closed the door as Austin Boggan drove away. Austin's
words echoed in his head.

*Go to Brazil! You will be used by God to change lives there. You should
go on a Men for Missions crusade to see the field and be a witness.*

Go on a mission trip? Max had never thought of it until recently, but
as Austin continued to urge him, the invitation was sounding increasingly appealing.

This was Austin's second visit in recent months. The other missionary Max and Dixie supported, Dale McClain, had visited several times
recently as well. Dale, however, continued to encourage Max to stay on
the farm and support missions financially. Max respected both men
deeply—and yet, they expressed opposite views.

Both Austin and Dale were missionaries with OMS.[3] That summer,
in June 1966, Max and Dixie had attended the annual OMS convention
at Winona Lake in northern Indiana. It was a beneficial experience, but

---

3   This organization was founded in 1901 in Japan as The Oriental Missionary Society. The
    name was changed to OMS International in 1973, and then to One Mission Society in 2010.

both Max and Dixie felt out of place there. Dixie especially felt intimidated around so many spiritual people. The two of them had attended for one day and were glad to get back home where they belonged.

At the convention, Max had briefly met Harry Burr, the international director of Men for Missions, or MFM. Max had heard about MFM. It was a ministry of OMS that organized short-term mission trips and fundraising efforts.

After Austin left, Max changed into his overalls and headed towards the hog barn. He was beginning to think that he should pray seriously about going on one of those MFM trips. He grabbed his bucket and walked toward the feed bin. *I think I'll ask God for a sign,* he thought. He set the bucket down and took a deep breath.

Lord, he prayed, *if the next time Austin comes here he has his wife and three sons with him, I'll accept that as a confirmation that I should join an MFM team and visit Brazil.*

In his recent visits, Austin had always come alone; he hadn't brought his family along in a while. Now Max waited to see how God would answer his prayer.

~ * ~

The rain pattered gently on the windows as Dixie cleaned the kitchen. Max sat at the kitchen table, working on next Sunday's sermon. The children were in bed, and all was quiet and peaceful, until Max and Dixie heard knocks on their door.

Max looked up from his studies, and Dixie put down her dishrag.

"Who would come calling at such a time?" Dixie wondered aloud.

"I guess we'd better find out," answered Max, heading to the back door.

The sound of the rain was louder on the back porch. Max opened the door, and there stood the tall figure of Austin Boggan.

"Hello, Max," he said.

Max's heart leaped inside his chest, remembering his prayer. "Austin! Welcome! What a surprise!" he exclaimed. Then, unable to contain himself, he blurted, "Is your family with you?"

"Yes," Austin answered, still standing outside, his blonde hair soaked by the rain. "May we come in?"

"Oh yes, of course!" Max recovered his senses and sprang into action. He stuck his head back into the kitchen to tell Dixie who was there, then went out to help the Boggan family bring their things inside. He was embarrassed at his rudeness, wanting his answer before inviting his friend in from the rain. Still, his heart filled with excitement as he realized what this meant.

The whole family stayed overnight and spent the next day at the Edwards' home. Everyone had a wonderful time. Austin's sons were close in age to Jay, Jan, and Jeff, so the kids had fun playing together. The adults enjoyed conversing so much that it was almost noon before Max completed his morning chores. And best of all, Max had his answer.

The next question, of course, was how he was going to pay for this trip. Farming was going well, but they hardly had money for trips to other continents.

Max had a 10-acre field of corn, which he had dedicated to missions when he had planted that spring. Last planting year in 1965, Max had promised God that he would give to missions the profits of anything over 100 bushels of corn. In previous years, Max had been unable to raise 100 bushels of corn from that field. But that year it yielded 130 bushels. Therefore, this year Max had taken the same field and promised to donate all of its profits. At harvesttime, he found that this field yielded amazingly well. As he prepared to give the money to missions as planned, he felt God tugging at his heart.

That's your trip to Brazil.

He looked at the amount of money that he was going to send—$920. It was the exact amount needed for the trip. His way was paid, and he was officially going to Brazil next March.

~ * ~

Dixie did not mind if Max went on the trip. She could see that God had stirred his heart, and she was thrilled to see how He had provided for Max's fare. But of course, she had no intention of going herself. She didn't want to.

It was January 1967, and the deadline to register for the mission trip was approaching. One day while Dixie was out, she ran into her dear friend Evelyn. After they greeted one another, Evelyn asked Dixie if she was going on the trip with Max.

"No, I'm not going." Dixie replied. "I'm staying home with the kids and keeping my fingers on the church." She had been at Peaceful Valley two months, and being a pastor's wife was enough of a challenge for Dixie.

"But Dixie," her friend asked, "have you prayed about it?"

"No, I don't pray about things I don't want to do!" Dixie answered.

That was the end of the conversation with her friend, but the question planted a little seed in Dixie's heart that she could not shake. She had no personal desire to go to Brazil. However, her recent struggle with God over the move to Peaceful Valley was still vivid in her mind and in her heart. She did *not* want to repeat that kind of spiritual battle. So, reluctantly, she prayed about the trip. And sure enough, when she was honest and humble before God, she felt that still, small voice telling her that He did want her to accompany Max. She yielded to the Lord and registered.

But how would her fare be paid? It was now the end of January, and they had no extra money. Max shared her financial need with both of their church families, New Liberty and Peaceful Valley. Various members of the churches donated funds, and within a week, Dixie's fare was paid.

Once again their Lord had provided, and once again Max and Dixie embarked on a new adventure of faith.

~ * ~

March 1967

Max and Dixie followed their group out of the airport into the lively, bustling city of São Paulo. Unfamiliar sounds filled their ears as they walked through the crowd of Portuguese-speaking Brazilians. Their driver was waiting for them with the *Kombi*—the VW bus that had been purchased with Max's "hog money." The driver offered a smile. "Welcome to Brazil!" he greeted them.

The Americans stared out the windows of the vehicle as the driver skillfully directed it to the place where they would be staying. São Paulo was huge. The buildings were tall, the streets were large, and there were people everywhere. And the traffic! Dixie missed home already.

They spent the first week of their trip in São Paulo and the second in a rural area around the city of Londrina. During these times, they visited different churches and shared their testimonies through a translator.

All the people they met were friendly and outgoing. Of course, one-on-one communication was always difficult, as the Americans did not speak Portuguese, and not many of the Brazilians they encountered could speak English. However, Max and Dixie learned a few words and communicated as much as they could through gestures and facial expressions. Max enjoyed this very much, and he loved all of the people he met. It was a bit more difficult for Dixie. She appreciated the people; everyone she met was so kind, open, and loving. However, she was always afraid that she would say or do something wrong.

Everything was so different! All the food smelled of garlic, which Max and Dixie had never tried before. They ate a lot of rice and beans and fresh fruit. Many of the fruits were ones they didn't have available or only found in cans in Indiana. They liked some of these more than others. Dixie decided that she did not like papaya at all. Fresh Brazilian bread, on the other hand, was delicious. It was the best she had ever eaten.

The group had the privilege of meeting many of the OMS missionaries in Brazil. Max and Dixie admired the missionaries; they were working hard, and they were doing so much good. It was amazing to the Edwardses how these men and women had learned the language and adapted to Brazilian culture. The missionaries also treated their American visitors incredibly well. In her heart, Dixie prayed, *Thank you, Lord, for not calling us to be missionaries. I could never attain what I see in these dedicated servants of yours. I'm simply not smart enough.*

For Dixie, this trip was a confirmation that she was very content with her life as a farmer's wife. She missed her children all the time and was counting the days until she could be back with them again.

Max, on the other hand, loved everything about Brazil; he was touched by the work that he saw God doing through the missionaries' ministry. When they went out into the country, he felt a personal connection to the Brazilians who were farmers like himself. The people were so poor, but the Christians they encountered gave their very best to host the American group. On one occasion, Max and Dixie stayed in a pastor's rural home. The place where they stayed didn't seem like much—just a little shack with a straw mattress—but later they learned that it was the pastor's own living quarters. He had stayed in the barn in order to make space for them.

It wasn't only the country churches that touched Max. One of the most impactful moments for him was a service they did one evening in São Paulo. They held the service right on the street—a street called *Rua Direita,* "Straight Street." The MFM team leader approached Max and Dixie as they were setting up.

"We'll have you two give your testimonies tonight," he said. Max and Dixie looked at each other.

"Just us?" Dixie asked.

The leader nodded. "I think that will be enough for tonight."

Soon the Brazilian pastor was calling people to come hear the service. Then it was time for Max and Dixie to speak. With a missionary translating, they shared about how God had worked in their lives. Then the Brazilian preacher stood up again with his guitar. He led the group in singing and gave a message with an invitation.

Max watched the crowd throughout the service. Though he couldn't understand the words being spoken, he could see on their faces that the Holy Spirit was moving and touching hearts. This big city—and this country—held all kinds of people: rich and poor, educated and uneducated, farmers and businessmen, salespeople and beggars. One thing they all had in common was that they needed Jesus. Everyone in the world needed Jesus, but as Max stood here on the streets of Brazil, his heart stirred with a special love for these people. They were listening; they were eager; they just needed someone to tell them and teach them. Jesus' words seemed truer than ever: "The harvest truly is plenteous, but the labourers are few" (Matthew 9:37 KJV).

The preacher wrapped up his message with an invitation, and people came forward. One … two … three … In the end, eight people accepted Jesus that night. The joy on their faces was unforgettable. Max couldn't believe that his testimony had played a part in the Lord's working in these precious souls.

"Pray ye therefore the Lord of the harvest, that he will send forth labourers into his harvest" (Matthew 9:38 KJV).

At the end of the trip, the team had one last group meeting to share their reflections about the trip. Max closed his eyes as his team members spoke. His heart had been stirred in a way that he had never felt before. How could he explain this feeling? What could he do with it?

When his turn came to share, he spoke with deep conviction. "I don't understand my thoughts and feelings." Max paused, then continued. "I know I'm not equipped or trained to be a missionary, but somehow, some way, I believe that God wants me back here. Will you all pray with me that I will understand and follow God's direction?"

Dixie's heart sank. She could understand why Max was so moved, but she longed to be back in her familiar Indiana country home. She couldn't handle any more changes. A fervent prayer rose in her heart. *Oh, Lord, I'm just now recovering from the transition from "my" church to the one we're pastoring. But surely, Lord, when we get home and Max gets back with the church and the hogs, he'll forget about Brazil. Surely ...*

She didn't have to wait long for her answer. On their second day home, Max spent all morning in the hog barn, trying to catch up on his work. When he came back into the house, he had a strange expression on his face.

"Max, are you okay?" Dixie questioned.

He replied seriously, but with a familiar twinkle in his eye. "Well, honey, I've worked with these hogs all morning and haven't converted a one of them!"

Dixie knew their lives would never be the same. She prayed for the strength to accompany her husband wherever their Lord led.

~ * ~

Max's involvement in missions continued to increase. On one occasion, Max heard that the OMS vocational school in Colombia needed an ensilage cutter to chop corn and sorghum for the school's dairy livestock. He went around to local implement dealers to look for one. Unfortunately, the kind that was needed had not been used in their area for years, and none of the dealers had one. When word got around of his search, however, a neighbor told Max that he had one in his barn that he would be happy to donate. With the help of some others, Max saw to it that the machine was sent to Colombia. His persistent work for missions was noted, and an article with a picture of Max and the ensilage cutter on the front appeared in MFM's *ACTION* magazine. He was portrayed as an exceptional example of how much an ordinary farmer, a layman, could do to support God's work in other countries. Max also encouraged other farmers like himself to become involved in giving to missions.

And still, all of this was not enough. Max knew in his heart what that voice was telling him, what the Holy Spirit had been saying ever since that trip to Brazil.

Max finally found a time to sit down with Dixie and talk to her about his feelings.

"You know how I feel, Max," she said. "I am committed to whatever the Lord has for us, but ..."

"Yes?" Max asked gently.

She closed her eyes, took a deep breath, and looked up at her husband. "This life—farm life—it's all either of us has ever known."

"I know."

"I'm scared, Max."

Max nodded. "Me too." They looked at each other for a moment. Max leaned forward. "The center of God's will is always the safest place to be," he said. Dixie nodded, so Max continued. "Let's agree to pray together about what God wants for our future."

Dixie agreed, and for several months they dedicated much prayer and conversation to the subject.

Lord, Max prayed, *please don't let me make a mistake. Too much is at stake.*

They finally reached a point where they agreed on one thing: God did want them to leave the farm. He was calling them into full-time ministry.

"I think that you should get the training to become a qualified minister," Dixie said. "Work as a full-time pastor, here in the States."

"I see," said Max slowly. "Well, I still feel my heart pulled toward Brazil," he said. "I believe God is calling us to be missionaries."

Oh, Lord, Dixie prayed silently, *anything but that!*

Therefore, they still disagreed; but praying together, they told God that they only wanted His plan—whatever it may be.

The Edwardses attended the OMS convention again that July, in 1967, at Winona Lake. While there, Max was encouraged to take the necessary forms and apply to be an OMS missionary to Brazil. He took the forms home with him.

He also decided to contact Dr. Eugene Erny, the president of OMS. Dr. Erny responded by asking if he could visit Max and Dixie and speak in their church. They willingly obliged and learned much from him while he was in their church and in their home.

Word got around that Max Edwards, the man whose dreams had always revolved around farming, was thinking of becoming a missionary. Max's friends and family warned him to be careful; they didn't want him to make any hasty, foolish decisions. Of course, it was good that he wanted to do so much to support missions, but to go himself would be too much.

On one occasion, Max's mother brought up the matter as she was ready to get in the car after visiting their home. "Dixie," she said, "we're concerned that this might not be a good thing for your family. You're the only one who can talk Max out of this. I know that puts you in a hard place, but …" Dixie carefully considered her response, understanding her mother-in-law's anguish. She answered quietly, "Mom, I can't do that." With love and understanding, Maud nodded and got into her car, with a heavy heart.

Dixie's heart was heavy as well. This was not easy.

Max understood how hard this was for his family. He wasn't taking this decision lightly; he knew all of the arguments against becoming a missionary, and he heard them often. What about schools for their kids? What if they grew up not knowing their relatives? What if it didn't work out and he had lost his livelihood as a farmer? However, his training in the school of the Holy Spirit had taught him that the Lord required obedience, even when He gave no explanation for His instructions. Yes, Max wanted the farm, and the security, and to be there for his family. However, more than that, Max wanted to be the man who always said yes to God, no matter what. So, after much prayer, he filled out his application to OMS and had it ready to go by August.

Dixie tried to do the same, but the longer she looked at that application, the sicker she felt. She trusted Max's judgment, but how could she apply for something that she did not want to do?

After praying, crying, thinking, and reading Scripture, Dixie finally narrowed down her objections to being a missionary in Brazil to three things. She sat down and wrote them out:

1. The language: Their trip to Brazil was the first time Dixie had been in a situation where she didn't understand what was spoken around her, and it had been overwhelming. She was shy enough without the extra complication of not knowing how to speak the local language! Dixie was just sure that she wasn't smart enough to learn Portuguese.

2. Having maids in the home: Really, her objection wasn't just about the maids; it was about adapting to a different culture and way of living. Dixie was used to doing all of her own work at home and helping around the farm; that was her job as a farmer's wife. The missionaries in Brazil, on the other hand, gave most of their time to ministry and hired help to do some of their housework. Dixie just didn't feel like she could make that kind of change.

3. Her children's schooling: Many missionaries had to send their children away from home so they could attend a good school. How could she ever do that? Her heart could not take it. Jay, Jan, and Jeff were now ages nine, seven, and four, respectively. They still had most of their school years ahead of them.

Dixie prayed over these three things every day. One day while she was praying, she simply understood that if God was really leading them to Brazil, He would help her to learn a new language and adjust to a strange culture. She could trust Him with those things. But the third difficulty she continued to pray over for several more days. Dixie felt certain that she could not send her kids away. Finally she realized that such thinking was her problem. She was imagining a potential situation and praying about how hard it was—"praying a problem"—rather than focusing on reality and what God could do. She read 2 Corinthians 12:9: "And he said unto me, My grace is sufficient for thee: for my strength is made perfect in weakness. Most gladly therefore will I rather glory in my infirmities, that the power of Christ may rest upon me" (KJV).

If God called her to send her children away, He would give her the grace to do so at that time. She had to entrust the future unknowns to Him and know that grace would be provided for whatever she was called to do.

Dixie finally completed her application and sent it in. Then all they had to do was pray and wait. Max prayed that they would be accepted, and Dixie prayed that they would be rejected! At the same time, they both told God that they only wanted His will for their lives, whether it was the answer they hoped for or not.

Dr. Erny invited Max and Dixie to visit the OMS World Headquarters in Greenwood, Indiana, and meet with the OMS board of directors. They went on November 22, 1967, the day before Thanksgiving. The board meeting was intimidating for both Max and Dixie. Max felt like a lion in a den of Daniels! The men present were Eugene A. Erny, Wesley Duewel, Dale McClain, Richard F. Capin, Lester S. Ike, and William A. Gillam. All were spiritual giants to Max. They asked questions and discussed Max's situation and call to serve as a missionary. They weren't sure where there was a place for Max—a man with a desire to serve but little ministry experience and no college education. Max didn't have an answer; he only knew that his Lord was again calling him to be obedient. The board told them that they would pray that God would give them the answers they needed.

Just a few days later, the phone rang at the Edwards house. Max answered it. "Edwards residence … Hello, Dr. Erny!" Dixie hurried over to listen to Max's end of the conversation. This was it! the phone call that could change their lives forever! Dixie could hardly breathe.

"Really? … Uh-huh … Uh-huh … Yes, sir! Will do! Thank you!" Max hung up and looked at Dixie. A smile spread over his face.

"We're accepted!"

"Really?"

"Yes! They just have a few conditions that we need to meet first." He counted them off on his fingers. "We need to go to Bible college for some training; we need to complete an OMS Missionary Internship here in the States; and we need to raise the necessary funds." He grinned. "Then we're good to go!"

"Oh, my. We're really going to Brazil? I can't believe it!"

"Me neither!"

Max and Dixie looked at each other for a minute. They didn't know whether to cry out for joy or shock. Max took Dixie's hands in his. "Let's thank God for His answer."

Dixie nodded, and they bowed their heads together. "Almighty God," Max prayed, "thank you for answering our prayers and directing the OMS board. We are trusting that this decision is from You. We know our next step."

The Everlasting Arms

By Dixie Edwards

What have I to dread, what have I to fear,
  Leaning on the everlasting arms?
I have blessed peace with my Lord so near,
  Leaning on the everlasting arms.[4]

I had that picture in my mind again when I sang the song. It never fails. I was 28. It was January 1967. We were farmers.

God had begun to work in Max's life, and I was running in my spirit, trying to keep up with my husband who had yielded his life fully to God—trying to keep up with him first spiritually in his dedication to God and then emotionally, and now even geographically.

I was in Peaceful Valley Friends Church, and Max (age 34) had just begun to pastor there three months earlier. I had joined him after the struggle of my life to yield to God—more specifically, to yield my husband to God.

Max was going to Brazil in March. We had planned this trip—for him. A short trip with MFM. I was going to stay home with our three children, but he wanted me to go.

The picture: I was seated at the piano in the church, playing and singing "Leaning on the Everlasting Arms." I got through the first two verses and then, "What have I to dread, what have I to fear?" It was the message I needed to hear. It was God's word to me that morning. He spoke. I listened. And the peace came. I embraced this truth.

God met the need of my heart at that moment. I knew; I *knew* I could trust Him.

I went to Brazil that March with Max and a group for only two weeks. The rest is history.

I was young then. Now I've lived my life—leaning on the everlasting arms. Surrender is safe. The *arms* are there, but we won't experience

---

4   Elisha A. Hoffman, "Leaning on the Everlasting Arms," 1887.

them unless we fall into them, let down our weight, and make Him the absolute first in our lives.

> The eternal God is your refuge, and underneath are the everlasting arms.
> Deuteronomy 33:27 (NKJV)

Chapter 6

Getting A's With God

The Lord had said to Abram, "Go from your country,
your people and your father's household to the land I will
show you."
Genesis 12:1 (NIV)

January 1968
Sunday afternoon

*D*ixie stared idly out the passenger window. Max was talking to the children, who sat in the back seat of the station wagon along with their two boxer dogs. The family's possessions were piled up in the back. Four-year-old Jeff was asking, yet again, about their new life.

"Where will we live?"

"A nice couple in Fort Wayne named Ross and Ethel Sills are letting us stay in their house for free, 'cause they just moved into a smaller house."

"Why are they letting us stay for free?"

"Because they care about missionaries."

Jeff's face scrunched up as he tried to process the information. "Missionaries ... like Mr. Boggan?"

"Like us, silly!" Eight-year-old Jan answered. "Don't you remember? We're missionaries now."

Max smiled. "Well, not yet, but we will be soon!" He looked straight ahead, determination on his face. "We will be soon."

"And then we'll go to Brazil to tell people about Jesus," said Jan. "Right, Daddy?"

"That's right, Jannie."

"Is Brazil in Fort Wayne?" asked Jeff.

"No, Brazil is in South America," said Jan.

"What's South America?"

Jan thought for a minute. "I don't know!" she said finally. "But it's really far away. Too far to drive in our car. Fort Wayne is closer because we can drive there in one afternoon!"

Max spoke up again. "Jeffie, before we go to Brazil, your daddy and mother have to learn how to be good missionaries. So first we're going to Fort Wayne so we can take Bible classes."

"Oh," said Jeff thoughtfully.

Jay had not said anything. Dixie glanced back at him. He was just staring at the fields rolling by. He looked like Dixie felt. If anyone had wanted to stay on the farm more than Dixie, it was Jay. Yesterday was their farm sale. They had sold the cattle, the hogs, the farm machinery, and even some of their household items. At 10 years old, Jay was already a farmer at heart. He knew better than to question his parents' decision, but he was certainly hurting inside.

"What's gonna happen to our church?" Jeff continued with his questions.

"We'll come home on weekends so I can keep pastoring for now."

"Will we stay at our house?"

Dixie saw Max struggling to hold in a sigh. They had explained all of this to Jeff many times, but it was hard for his young mind to comprehend.

"No, son, we'll stay with Grandpa and Grandma. My parents and Mother's parents will take turns having us." He forced a smile. "Won't that be fun?"

"Yeah!" Jeff said. He thought for a minute. "I'd rather stay at our house though."

"Jeff!" Jan said, exasperated. "We don't have a house anymore! We moved everything out yesterday and today. Remember?"

Dixie chimed in. "That's right, and after everything was out, you helped me sweep the kitchen floor."

"Oh," said Jeff again. "So do we have a new house?"

And they were back where they started.

Fortunately, it only took an hour and a half to drive to Fort Wayne, and the excitement of the new place distracted Jeff from his questions.

The family spent the rest of the afternoon unpacking and getting comfortable in their new home. The house was furnished, which was a great help. Yet even after they unpacked, it felt like someone else's home, not their own.

Before bed, Dixie sat at the table with a map of Fort Wayne. She ran over their schedule again. In the morning, Jay and Jan would take the bus to their new school; then she had to take Jeff to day care for part of the day. Where was it again? She traced the route with her finger on the map. After this, she would go to her classes at Fort Wayne Bible College, then pick up Jeff before coming home to meet the kids and make dinner. Max was studying full-time, so he would be in classes all day.

Dixie leaned back and closed her eyes. *What have we gotten ourselves into?*

~ * ~

Max shifted uncomfortably in his seat. He hadn't been in a classroom in more than a decade. The young people around him looked like they were fresh out of high school.

The professor was laying out the course requirements.

"By the end of the semester," he said, "I expect you to be able to write these 110 verses—word-perfect—including spelling and punctuation."

Max looked at the list of verses. He felt he would be lucky if he could read the verses perfectly by the end of the semester, let alone write them. His dyslexia had caused him to avoid endeavors that involved reading and writing as much as possible; he preferred working with his hands.

When class was dismissed, he introduced himself to the professor. "You know, the only thing I've studied in the past 17 years is the *Farm Journal* magazine," he joked. "All of this study and memorization is gonna be a little challenging for me."

The professor looked at him seriously. "Brother Edwards," he said, "this is the Word of God. Nothing is more important to study and write on our hearts."

"Of course," Max agreed wholeheartedly. He chatted a couple more minutes and then headed out to his next class.

Of course, he repeated to himself. *He's right; nothing is more important than knowing the Word of God. And if knowing these verses is what I need to complete this requirement and become a missionary, then God will help me do it.*

He straightened himself as he headed into another class full of young, intelligent faces. *With the Lord's help, I can overcome all the odds.*

~ * ~

For Dixie the classes were the easy part; studies had always come naturally to her. However, everything else was hard. The house was dirty and musty, and with her new schedule, she had no time to clean it or make it suitable for their needs. Jan developed allergies of some kind, and Jay had nightmares about the farm. Neither of them made friends at their new school. Jeff seemed content enough, but Dixie didn't like leaving him at day care every day. They had so many different schedules and only one car; it felt like they were always driving, driving, driving.

All of the familiarity and normalcy were gone. The expectations had changed, and Dixie didn't know how to meet the new standards. All of that driving meant a lot of time for thinking, and the thoughts that came were not at all helpful. *I can't do this. I will fail. This was a mistake. I can't do this ... I can't do this.*

As these thoughts pounded in her head and in her heart, Dixie felt depression fall on her, hard and heavy. She hardly knew what had hit her; she only knew that this new life was more than she could handle.

One evening as she finished cleaning up after supper, she felt like she couldn't keep moving forward. Overwhelmed and discouraged, she told Max, "I cannot do devotions with the kids tonight. I just need to go to bed."

Max looked at her, concerned. "Tired?" he asked.

"Yes. I need rest."

Max nodded. "Okay, I'll go do devotions and pray with the kids tonight."

"Thank you." Dixie went to the bedroom, got ready for sleep, and lay down in bed. She stared at the ceiling, the thoughts continuing to run through her mind. *I cannot manage this new life. I will fail. I cannot do this.*

After a little while, she heard Max come back down the stairs. He peeked into the room to check on her. Thinking she was asleep, he left to work on his homework.

In terror Dixie realized that she could not move. She tried to call out to Max, but no sound came out. She tried to lift her arms—nothing happened. She tried to move her legs, still willing her voice to call out to Max. Again, nothing happened, and panic rose inside her chest. Finally, in one forceful effort, she kicked her legs out and screamed.

Max came running. "Honey, what happened?"

Dixie sat up and put her hands on her face. "Oh, Max." He came and put his arms around her. As he held her close, she cried and poured out her heart to him. She told him everything she had been struggling with. When she finished, he prayed with her and then suggested that she quote all of the Scripture she knew.

"Fight the devil with the sword of the Word of God," he suggested. She followed his advice, and after a while she was able to sleep.

However, her struggle was not over. As she went about her daily activities, she continued to feel hopelessly inadequate. Those thoughts of defeat would not leave her alone.

A few days later, she was driving from class to Jeff's day care. As she drove, she felt like her world was crumbling around her. *I cannot manage this new life. I am a misfit. I will not succeed. Max would be better off without me to hinder him.*

She reached a complicated intersection, which she had maneuvered many times. She needed to turn right. If she continued straight, she would drive into oncoming traffic. *I can't do this ... Max would be better off without me to hinder ... Don't turn. Go straight into the traffic. This is your best way.*

What? That message was not her thoughts. It was the enemy! She gripped the steering wheel with sweaty hands and answered aloud, "Get thee behind me, Satan. Help me, Jesus!" Trembling, she turned right.

Dixie was still shaking when she picked Jeff up. Something clicked in her mind that day. These thoughts, which had been tormenting her day after day, weren't truth. They were lies of the devil, meant to drag her down. It was a lie that Max would be better off without her. On the contrary, she was key. Max could not do this alone. He needed her to support him and care for the family. God had called him to be a missionary, but if the devil could bring her down, the plan would fall apart. She was called too. That's why the enemy had targeted her in this way.

It was also a lie that she was destined to fail, that she could not succeed in this new life. Max was trusting God to help him overcome the odds as he studied and prepared to be a missionary; and just as God was enabling him, He would enable her to stand by her husband's side. They did have an enemy—one who wanted very much for them to fail. But God wanted them to go to Brazil, and He would give them the power to be obedient to His call.

~ * ~

The seventh week of classes

Max strode down the hall with his bag of books and notebooks slung over his shoulder. The dean of students had called Max into his office. His stomach churned nervously. What could it be about? He reached the office and knocked on the door.

"Brother Edwards! Please come in. You may close the door behind you." The man smiled, but it was not a happy smile; it was the smile of someone who wants to appear friendly. Max closed the door and lowered himself into the chair; he set his bag of books down next to him.

The dean opened a folder and looked up at Max. He cleared his throat nervously. "Brother Edwards," he began, "it's my duty to inform you that you are failing in most of your classes."

Max felt like he had been hit across the face. Hadn't God sent him here? How could he be failing?

The dean's voice was gentle and kind. "Could it be that maybe, perhaps it is God's will for you to go back to the farm?"

Max looked down at his lap. His rough overalls had been replaced with a pressed shirt and pants, his tractor with a book bag. He hardly recognized himself. Could he really have mistaken God's direction?

The dean continued to speak. "Don't misunderstand me," he was saying. "You are welcome to stay if God so guides you."

"Sir …" Max's voice trembled, but he forced himself to look up. "I've burned my plow. There is no going back for me."

The dean nodded. "Very well then."

Max thanked the man, picked up his bag, and left. His head was spinning. He didn't feel nearly as confident as he sounded, but what he had said was true. He had no farm to return to; everything had been sold. If he had missed God's call, he was in a desperate situation indeed.

When he arrived home, he went through all the motions of their regular evening routine. He couldn't say anything to Dixie; he didn't know what to say or how to say it. That night after everyone else had gone to bed, the farmer-turned-student knelt at the couch in prayer before his God. He determined to stay there.

"Lord, did I miss Your direction? Surely I cannot fail in what you called me to do. Please show me, Father. I won't leave this place until I hear from you."

He waited and prayed. His knees hurt and the dust from the couch tickled his nose, but he didn't care. He was desperate; he could not leave until he heard from his God.

Around 2 a.m., Max felt a warm touch on his shoulder. Thinking that Dixie had come to bring him to bed, he turned around, but there was no one there. Then he heard the voice of the Lord in his heart. *You are mine. You are right where I want you. You are getting A's with me.*

Suddenly, Max felt the heavy burden lift from his heart. He was in God's plan for his life. He got up and went to bed, feeling as free as a bird.

After that, Max saw his learning experience improve. One professor, Dr. Wes Gerig, was a special teacher to him. He used illustrations that were biblical, basic, and practical—some of which Max remembered for the rest of his life. He also learned the value of Scripture memorization from his professor who required the 110 verses. Max worked hard on the verses; he wrote them all out on 3-by-5 cards and preached them to his family to try to seal them in his memory. His hard work paid off. When the time came, Max made only two errors, and he completed the course with a *B*.

By the time both spring and summer sessions were completed, Max had A's and B's in all of his classes! God had taught him to learn.

~ * ~

"Amen!" the last child finished his prayer. It was bedtime, and as always, Dixie was doing devotions with the children.

"All right, time for bed," Dixie said.

"Good night, Mother." Jan gave Dixie a kiss and then scurried off to her room.

"Good night," said Jay. He lay down in his bed and pulled up the covers. Four-year-old Jeff climbed into Dixie's lap.

"Please don't go, Mother," he said, burying his head in her shoulder. "I'm scared."

Dixie sighed and looked around. The attic room where the boys stayed was a little scary, and it felt isolated from the rest of the house. She could understand why Jeff was fearful, but what could she do? She forced a smile.

"You don't need to be scared, Jeffie. Jay is here with you, and more importantly, Jesus is here too. He is always watching over you."

"I know," Jeff said, his voice muffled by Dixie's shirt. "But sometimes, it's hard to remember."

After more comforting and praying, Dixie finally went downstairs. She picked up her Bible. *Lord, please help me to find some comfort for Jeff,* she prayed.

As she flipped through the Psalms, her eyes fell on chapter 4, verse 8: "I will both lay me down in peace, and sleep: for thou, LORD, only makest me dwell in safety" (KJV).

Perfect! She found a piece of construction paper and wrote it down. The next night, she brought it with her to devotions. "All right, kids," she said. She got out some tape and taped the piece of paper to the wall above Jeff's bed. "We are going to memorize this new verse and say it every night after prayer." She looked at Jeff. "It's a verse to help us remember that God is always with us and protecting us."

The Edwards children soon learned the verse, and saying it with devotions became a family tradition. Later, they would teach it to their children, who would in turn teach it to their children. Through all of the changes and moves, it was a continual reminder that God was the One who was watching over them, and that He was all they needed for peace and safety.

~ * ~

July 1968

"Here's this morning's offering." Lowell Pearson handed Max a pile of money and other miscellaneous items. Max smiled. This week there were two Mars bars for him. Some time ago, one of the children at Peaceful Valley had learned it was his favorite candy bar, so this young person had put one in the offering plate for Max. It was the beginning of a tradition at the church to put candy bars and other interesting items for the pastor in the offering plate.

Dishes clinked, and Max looked up from the Pearsons' dining table. Lowell's wife, Jenny, was clearing the table. Lowell had disappeared, but Max knew where he was. The Pearsons worked at a meat market, and they had made a habit of collecting groceries throughout the week for the Edwards family. They loaded their car with meat, bread, eggs, and other items on Sunday afternoon before they drove back to Fort Wayne. Max was struck again with thankfulness. Throughout the spring and summer terms, the weekly freewill offering at Peaceful Valley had been their only source of income. Though the congregation members were not wealthy, they were generous, and the Edwards family had not lacked anything they truly needed ... or Mars candy bars!

Max thanked the Pearsons, gathered his family, and got in the car. This was one of the last times they would make this drive. After they completed their summer classes, they would be cleared by OMS to move to the next phase of preparation—missionary internship. No one in the Edwards family would be sorry to move on from Fort Wayne. At the same time, it was nerve racking to be making another transition so soon. Would they have the same struggles all over again?

Lord, if it's Your will, please let the next phase be easier for our family, Max prayed. He thought again about the ways God had provided for them during their time in Bible college. Yes, even though it had been difficult, the Lord was always faithful. Max needed to continue to trust Him.

~ * ~

September 1968
Missionary Internship

"This is the street," Dixie said, squinting at the map. "Everyone start looking. It's called Central Free Will Baptist Church."

The children obediently leaned toward the car windows and pressed their faces up against the glass, rumpling their good Sunday clothes. Already they had been staring; the suburb of Royal Oak in the Detroit area was the most metropolitan area they had ever visited. The buildings, the shops, the many different kinds of people—they had never seen anything like it. And they were going to live here for almost a year.

"There it is," said Max, pointing at a huge building.

The kids' jaws dropped. That was a church? It was so big even Dixie's eyes widened a little. Max turned into the parking lot where there were rows and rows of cars. He parked, and the family got out, still staring at the large, colorful brick building. Dixie took Jeff's hand as they walked into the church together. All of a sudden, she felt small and out of place. Max had said that the average weekly attendance at this church was 600. What place was there for a family of rural Indiana farmers?

They entered the church foyer, and many smiling faces greeted them. As the morning progressed, the family relaxed. This church was big, but the people were genuinely warm and welcoming. The service was good; the children enjoyed their program as well. Dixie could see why so many people attended here.

The church leadership had already determined where the Edwards family would serve during their missionary internship there. "You will each teach a Sunday school class," the pastor told them. "Max, you will have the 13-year-old boys, and Dixie will have the 13-year-old girls." Max and Dixie nodded as the man continued. "In addition, Max, you will participate in the church's bus ministry." The pastor handed Max a piece of paper that looked like a map. "Every Sunday morning, you will be given a bus and a driver to cover this route," he said. Then he looked up at Max, smiled, and winked. "Work it!"

"Will do!" Max replied, grinning.

The bus ministry was an excellent fit for Max's outgoing personality, and with great enthusiasm he tackled the challenge of filling "his" bus. Using the map, he covered the route on his own during the week; he met people, especially young people, and talked to them about coming to church. Then on Sunday he went with the bus and the driver, picked them up, and brought them in. Soon Max's bus was regularly filled with kids, always excited to be coming to church. The church leadership was impressed at the effort he put into this task. One Sunday the bus arrived with 82 people on board; this was a bit *too* full!

Dixie was able to find a ministry that suited her gifting and personality as well. The Edwardses were surprised to discover that, though the church was large, there was no children's choir. Max approached the pastor to ask if Dixie could start one.

"This has been tried a number of times and has never worked," the pastor responded. "She may try if she wants, but be prepared to be disappointed."

She decided to give it a try. One Sunday evening before the service, she gathered about 10 kids around the piano, including Jay and Jan, and started singing. They liked it. She soon organized a choir of children ages 8 to 12 and called it The Singables. She attracted the children with fun songs and treats and brought in many of the kids from Max's bus ministry. She discovered there was quite a bit of talent among them. By Easter they had a choir of 110 children, singing praises in two-part harmony.

The whole family adapted well to life in Detroit. They all enjoyed the church. Besides their regular assigned ministries, Max and Dixie helped in other ways, and the kids pitched in wherever they could. The church loved them and supported them, and it wasn't long before the

Edwards family felt the same love for them. Furthermore, Jay and Jan did well at their new school. They made friends and were able to participate in extracurricular activities. They were content and thankful for this refreshing season.

~ * ~

For their missionary internship, the Edwardses were on a four-week rotation: three weeks at the church, then one week at a nearby retreat center, receiving training along with other missionary interns. These weeks at the retreat center were enriching, sometimes grueling, and always challenging. Max and Dixie absorbed the books they were assigned to read. One book called *Have We No Rights?*[5] opened their eyes to what being a missionary meant. It challenged them with the idea that they were called to give up every "right" for the sake of Christ. Dixie cried her way through the book. Both of them wondered if they could really do it. They were also introduced to Oswald Chambers' *My Utmost for His Highest,* which continued to inspire them for the rest of their lives. They knew that their teachers were dedicated to God and to them, and they felt privileged to have this training, even though it was not always easy.

During their time at the retreat center, their instructors assigned the interns with various tasks to help them prepare for missionary life. On one occasion, Max and another intern were assigned to wash all the dishes, while the others went on to an activity. The other intern was not pleased with this arrangement.

"A man of my education and experience should not be wasting my time doing dishes," he complained. "I should be at the activity. I should be leading the activity."

Max gave no response. About halfway through the job, the other man left and joined the activity. Max finished the dishes on his own.

One of the lessons they were given in their sessions was the story of Abraham who "went out, not knowing" where God would take him (Hebrews 11:8 KJV). Max was really impacted by this. He could identify

---

5   Mabel Williamson, China Inland Mission, Overseas Missionary Fellowship, *Have We No Rights?* (Moody Press, 1957).

with Abraham; they were going to Brazil and did not know what they were going to do there. It was an unusual situation, to say the least. Max was thankful to be reminded that the God who led Abraham to the Promised Land was the same God who was leading him to Brazil. God was always faithful.

~ * ~

Shortly before their internship ended, Max was invited into the pastor's office at the church. The pastor greeted Max, leaned forward, and looked him straight in the eye. "Brother Edwards," he said, "we have been praying for a long time that God would send us a youth pastor. Could it be that God has taken you off the farm and brought you to us?"

Max was surprised. Was he really being offered a position in the church? The pastor continued, "I don't want to tempt you. If God wants you in Brazil, then we do too. Talk to Dixie about it; think and pray. You are invited to stay if God thus guides you." The accompanying salary was to be more than Max had ever made farming.

Max went home and told Dixie about his conversation with the pastor. Dixie's heart leapt. Oh, how she wanted to stay. She felt like here, in this church, she had finally found her place. But she knew her heart and emotions were easily swayed. She told Max, "I don't trust my feelings, so I cannot help you make the decision. I trust my life to God through you." Max understood. He also knew what she wanted.

Dixie went to her Bible and found a verse that had popped into her head—Psalm 37:4: "Delight thyself also in the LORD: and he shall give thee the desires of thine heart" (KJV). That really said it for her. She knew what the desire of her heart was. So she knelt and prayed that verse.

"Lord," she said, "Please let us stay here, if it is Your plan." As she was silent before Him, she felt a gentle reply.

My child, you are not delighting in me. You are delighting in the work.

She knew it was true. She surrendered again.

Max prayed in earnest for direction. He knew that he had felt called to Brazil before, but he also saw that God was using him and his family for ministry in Detroit. What was God's direction now? The Lord answered him in a unique way.

There was a man in the church named Roscoe Bird who was a bar-ber. When the Edwards family first came to Detroit, he volunteered to cut Max and his sons' hair every three weeks. Now, Max, Jay, and Jeff were going to him for, presumably, the last time. When Max sat down in the barber's chair, Roscoe walked in front of him and pointed his scissors in his face.

"Max Edwards," he said, "God has called you and your family to Brazil. Don't even think about anything else." Roscoe looked at him intently, his eyes piercing through his glasses. Max looked back, stunned. It seemed the Lord had spoken through his friend.

A smile played around Roscoe's mouth. "Really, you're too old and too ugly and not smart enough to make a good missionary." He gave a warm, friendly laugh, tapping his scissors on his hand thoughtfully. Then he pointed them in Max's face again. "But I'm going to support you because I've been watching how you and Dixie are raising your children." He nodded toward the two seated in the waiting chairs by the wall. "I consider you a good investment because I believe you will go to Brazil and raise missionaries."

In fact, Roscoe was right. Jay, Jan, and Jeff would all become mis-sionaries when they were grown. Max didn't know that in 1969, but he did know that God had called his whole family—including his children. Once again, the Lord had given him an answer.

On their last Sunday night in the church, the closing song was "I'll Go Where You Want Me to Go."[6] Max picked up a sleeping Jeff to carry him out, and Jay and Jan followed. Dixie brought up the rear, carry-ing their things. She saw in her mind's eye their family walking out of that church and right down to Brazil. And she praised the God who was going before them.

~ * ~

In reality, the Edwards family had one more step to complete before they could go to Brazil: fundraising. In June 1969, they moved back to Winchester to complete this phase. Max had retained a small piece of land, 80 acres, which his dad was now farming for him. This land

6   Mary Brown, 1899.

contained a house, which became home base for the Edwards family while they raised funds.

It was a blessing to be back in their home community for this last step, but at times it felt like they weren't really there. They traveled every weekend to a different church to share their story, and Max traveled on his own throughout the week.

Everyone they encountered was impressed by Max's testimony and by the whole family. Whenever the family went together, the children would sing while Dixie played the piano. They called their little trio "The 3Js," and they were a big hit. Everyone loved to hear them sing, and people were especially impressed with Jeff.

"Such a little boy, but with such a strong voice," they would say. Jeff carried the melody while Jay and Jan filled in with harmony.

And so, Max would speak; Dixie would play the piano; the children would sing, and the Edwards family found supporters everywhere they went.

On one occasion, a friend encouraged Max to join his children in singing to make it a whole family performance. He obliged; however, singing wasn't one of Max's best talents. After the service, nine-year-old Jan approached her daddy.

She climbed up onto a chair in front of him, stood, and put her arms around his neck. "Daddy, God called you to preach. Leave the singing to us!" she exclaimed. From then on he took that advice.

Veteran missionaries had told Max that it would take him at least a year to raise funds, and probably longer. He had a large family and therefore needed more funding. He also had very little education and training. They told him it would be more difficult to raise funds. It didn't help, either, that he still didn't know what he was going to do when he got to Brazil.

However, the Edwards family visited mostly small, rural churches, and the people were very generous toward them. Church members identified with them and were impressed that a successful farmer would give up everything and choose to become a missionary, even though he wasn't "qualified." They were amazed at Max's faith and thrilled with his testimony of how God had called them. Many were glad to support them financially.

By September, they had the minimum that OMS required them to raise. By December, they were overfunded and had completed their deputation. It was record time for OMS. They obtained their tickets to leave for Brazil in January.

Fundraising is never easy, and it was not easy for the Edwards family. However, they focused on "forgetting those things which are behind" and moving forward (Philippians 3:13 KJV). They knew where they were called, and they pressed on toward the goal their Lord had given them.

The Ford 4000

Thou shalt have no other gods before me.
Exodus 20:3 (KJV)

By Jay Edwards

As I got off of the school bus, my mind was on one thing only—getting to the field and helping my dad plow. I was 9 years old, going on 18. The year was 1966, and Daddy was pulling a 6-bottom, pull-type plow with a 120-hp Ford 6000 diesel. My tractor was a Ford 4000, select-o-speed, which struggled with a 3-bottom, 3-point hitch plow. I entered the house and greeted Mother, and she made my sister and me some fried eggs and toast. While we ate, she fixed something for Daddy and put it in a brown bag. Mother then gave the instructions: "Daddy is plowing in the back 60 by the woods. You are supposed to fill the tractor with fuel and drive down the lane to meet him there. He hopes to get the field done tonight, so he wanted you to help him until your bedtime."

Bedtime? Bedtime? I thought. *If he is trying to finish the field, why do I have a bedtime?* I changed clothes and bundled up; the night would be cold. The fall sky was still well lit, but evening was quickly approaching as I ran down the path from the back door to the fuel barrel and the awaiting tractor. Jumping up on the lower cross-brace of the fuel tank and holding on with my right hand, I struggled to loosen the fuel hose with the other. Eventually, it came unhooked, and I jumped down onto the oil-stained gravel.

Now came the challenge of climbing onto the tractor while holding the fuel hose. Unable to manage this task quickly, I draped the hose over the tractor hood and climbed up onto the front wheel; then I straddled the hood and scooted back to the fuel cap and quickly took it off. Placing the nozzle into the hole, I squeezed the lever and allowed the fuel to flow freely. Oops! Why hadn't I remembered to get a little rock to hold it open? Now I would have to keep switching hands every time one of them got too tired. No problem. My father needed me, and I would rise to the occasion and get to the field quickly.

The tractor started easily, as if it had just been waiting on me. It wanted to run. What a wonderful sound of power and partnership. The tractor and I were going to plow. I raised the implement, put it in gear, and started rolling. The front end skimmed along the ground just barely touching. Oh yes, now that the loader was off, I needed to remember to steer just a little with the brakes, a skill that I had recently learned. I opened the gate to the barnyard and drove through, got off, and closed it. It was the same with the next gate leading to the access lane. In 15 minutes or so, I was back at the field, but my dad was at the other end; it would be 20 minutes before he would be back to my end. I had hurried and hurried, and now I'd have to sit and wait.

I studied the turnaround patterns for a long time until I determined that two lands had been started and plowed out to about the same size, and now he was plowing out the middle. *I could start,* I thought, because the plow was probably still set from yesterday. However, I knew I should wait for Daddy to start me. So I sat there and let the engine idle, since that's what farmers do. I guessed it was because they like to hear the sound of a diesel or that they were afraid it might not start the next time, so they didn't want to shut it off.

After what seemed like an eternity, Daddy arrived at my end, pulled out of the furrow, and roared up beside me. Throttling down, he climbed off the tractor and came over to me.

"Did you already eat supper?" he asked.

"Yes, sir," I said as I handed him his brown supper bag from Mother.

"Do you have any homework before Monday?"

"No, sir."

"Did you fill your tractor with fuel?"

"Yes, sir."

Daddy was tired and dirty but happy and glad to see me. He knew how much I loved what we were doing. It was my life, my very blood. I was a third-generation Edwards farmer.

"Conditions are tougher today, Jay, so I'm going to lower the furrow wheel one notch like I did on the 6-bottom, so they'll cover equally. I went over the plow earlier so you shouldn't have any problems, but things can always happen. Remember, sit sideways in the seat and look backwards at that plow just as much as you look forward. In the bottom ground, she'll have a tendency to pull out of the furrow; ride the right brake just a little, and she'll come back. Don't ride the brake too long, or it will get hot. If you're on the brake a lot, lift the plow just a little bit and the front end will set back down; as soon as you're through the bottom ground, lower it again. I'll go first, because the 6000 is faster. It will take a couple of hours, but when I catch you from behind, stop at the end and let me around. When it comes time to finish a land, I'll get you started on the next one and then go back and plow out the headland. When I go back, you stay on the new land where I started you. And if you get sleepy, STOP! I don't want you falling off the tractor. When I turn my lights on, you turn yours on. You got all that?"

"Yes, sir." I already knew all of that, but it was good to hear it again; it kind of made me feel important. These were instructions for a boy who was doing a man's job. It made me proud and just a little scared.

Daddy got back on his tractor, swung it out toward the fence, then back in and lined up with the furrow. I followed. He dropped the front moldboard, then the back of the plow, and then opened up the throttle. Black smoke poured out of the exhaust pipe. With the fuel pump turned up, his tractor sure had the power. I pulled into the furrow he had just left, lowered my plow, and opened up the throttle. A little smoke came out of my stack, but nothing like Daddy's. I wished my pump were turned up too. I looked back; the plow was slowly sliding through the ground, corn stalks under, dirt on top. Conditions were good. There was just enough frost in the stalks to make them stick and turn under without balling up. I knew the days like this would be very few, and as much as possible, we had to farm around the clock. That's what my dad was doing, and I was helping.

Hour after hour I followed my father around the field. This was our calling. The work had to be done. We were up to it. I made up games in my mind about the cornstalks fighting the plow. The stalks always lost. They were weak; the plow was strong. The plow looked ahead to next year when there would be soybeans planted in this field. If we didn't keep the plowing going, the stalks would fight with the beans.

The soybeans' only hope was the plow. We had to make it happen. I was the captain, and I commandeered the mighty plow.

It was 10 p.m. when I pulled out at the end and saw Daddy's tractor back about in the middle of the field; he flashed his lights at me. I flashed mine to show that I'd seen the signal. Slowing the engine to an idle, I stopped, knowing that the flash meant for me to wait here for him to talk to me. We'd already filled up once, and I still had half a tank of fuel. I was pretty sure there wasn't anything wrong with my plow, or was there? I dismounted and cleaned off the stalks and shook the cover boards. None were loose. Try as I may, I couldn't see anything else wrong with the plow. Nevertheless, I kept looking at it until Daddy came alongside. He got off the 6000, and I met him there. He stretched and patted me on the shoulder and said, "Son, it's past your bedtime; you need to get on up to the house." I looked at him in disbelief.

"Daaaddy," I whined, "I can't quit until you do!"

"Aren't you sleepy?"

"No."

"Not even a little bit?"

"No, sir, not even a little bit!"

"Your mother won't like you staying out longer than this."

"Well, I don't have school in the morning."

"I'm afraid you'll get sleepy and fall off of the tractor."

"If I get sleepy, I'll stop. I don't want to leave until you do. We need to get this field done."

My father was weighing things in his mind. His son wanted to keep plowing and was apparently not sleepy. His wife wouldn't like it for the boy to be out so late if he stayed much longer. Even though the boy's tractor was small, it helped quite a bit to have nine bottoms going around the field instead of six; it was 50 percent more productivity. Conditions were optimum; if ever there was a time to stretch the rules, it was tonight. No school in the morning.

"Okay, Jay, we'll keep rolling." I was so elated inside I could hardly contain myself. Outwardly, I smiled and hugged my father to reassure him that he had made the right decision. Back to work we went. At midnight, it was time to fill up and check everything again. Daddy stopped for fuel and tightened things on the plow. Arriving at the end,

I also drove over to the fuel wagon as it was starting to snow just a little. Daddy came over, I supposed, to fill my tractor; but no—

"Jay, you go on up to the house now, we'll fill your tractor out of the main tank tomorrow."

"Daddy, I'm not sleepy!"

"You have to be sleepy; your bedtime is 8:30."

"Well, I'm not. Really, I'm not sleepy. Are you going to quit?"

"No, I'm going to finish the field."

"I don't want to quit until you do."

Somewhat reluctantly, my father once again weighed the factors. Fifty percent more productivity meant his son's intense desire once again prevailed. He filled my tractor and checked my plow, and we were off. Oh, glorious day. I had never been up this late in my entire life. I felt sorry for every boy I knew who didn't have a father who farmed. After another hour into the night, I was getting sleepy. In all fairness to my father, I knew I had to quit, but … just one more round. On the last round, things blurred a little and somehow, in some strange way, the front wheel, then the back one, came out of the furrow and the little blue tractor plowed a funny curved path some 50 feet into the stalks.

Oh, no! In shock, I did everything all at once. Throttle down, plow up, clutch in, hit the right brake. The tractor spun just a little to the right and stopped with the plow in the air. Oh what a terrible mistake. What an ugly streak was left behind. *What will Daddy say? How will he plant beans over this mess I've made? Now he'll think I was trying to plow when I was too sleepy.* And I was. *Oh, dear! For Pete's sake! Son of a gun! Shucks!* I thought through my most dramatic vocabulary. I guessed the snow in the headlights had put me to sleep for just a few seconds, and now this. Why hadn't I quit one round sooner?

Okay. Now I was wide awake, so I might as well put the tractor back into the furrow and keep going. At this point in the night, Daddy was catching up with me from behind; he would see this mess in about 15 minutes. When I arrived at the other end, I decided it would be best to wait for Daddy and tell him how terribly sorry I was. There was nothing to do but that. I could not undo what had been done. I'd plowed like a learner and not like the seasoned professional I'd considered myself to be just a few minutes earlier.

I plowed to the end and sat waiting, not a bit sleepy anymore. Daddy pulled out and roared up beside my now-quite-humbled, little blue tractor. Embarrassed, I met him between the two tractors to talk. Before I could even say I was sorry, Daddy reached out and rubbed my head, messing up my hat.

"I think you are getting sleepy."

"Well, I was, but now I'm not. I'm really sorry for the mess I made on the last round."

"That's all right; I already fixed it."

Already fixed it? I thought. *Wow! What a father! How did he do that?*

"Thank you, Daddy. I'm really sorry."

"It's about 1 a.m., Jay; you need to go up to the house and go to bed. I'll have this done before sunup."

He patted me on the shoulder, and I turned to go. It was snowing harder now, but everything seemed fine again. Somehow, he'd already fixed my terrible mistake. I drove up the lane, opened and closed both gates, and parked the tractor by the fuel tank. As I walked in the back door, my mother quickly greeted me and helped me get off my sweatshirts and coats. I was so cold and stiff, it was hard to move around. I had been a big man with my father up to now, but after 1 a.m., it really seemed nice to have a mother also. She told me I had no business being out this late. I knew she had to say it; it was her duty as a mother. I also knew she'd tell Daddy that same thing later, but they'd be okay after they got over it. She tucked me in, and I was out like a light, free now to keep plowing in my dreams.

God was working in my father's life. Everyone knew it. The preacher talked about it when he was at our house; missionaries came and invited him to the mission field, whatever that was, and we talked about it as a family. He was already preaching at a little country church not too far from us. At first I didn't like that, but soon it was okay because after church we played "king of the mountain" on a big dirt mound, "horse and rider," and several other rough games. Most of the kids were teenagers or adolescents, and they let me play but also watched out for me just a little. It was a blast.

This topic of the mission field, which was really not a field at all, kept coming up. I knew it was somewhere called Brazil, but it could have been Mars, and it wouldn't have been any different to me. If we did a mission field, we'd have to leave the farm. I was against that with all of my being. Come to think of it, the farm was my being.

It was my identity, and I thought it was my father's too. Maybe we'd take the tractors to Brazil—or was it Mars?

One day the following year, Daddy and Mother sat us three kids down and told us about their decision. Our family would sell everything, go to Bible school in the far-off town of Fort Wayne, and then go to Brazil. In Brazil we had no idea what we'd be doing, but we'd learn a new language and do something that was not farming. I was devastated. I wanted to be supportive, and I loved my parents dearly, but this was a terrible mistake, and I knew it. My father was not the type to be good at missionary stuff, whatever that was. He was the type to be good at farming. That's what he was good at; that's what I was good at. He wanted to serve God so badly that he'd gone crazy. Although my parents were gentle and understanding, there was really no way of getting around the facts as I saw them.

The newspaper announced, "LOCAL AREA FARMER PREPARES FOR MISSION FIELD." The word was out. At school my friends who were from farms were nice but felt so sorry for me. By their comments, I could tell that their parents had been talking about how Max Edwards had gone off the deep end. What in the world was he thinking? I had a series of emotions that ranged from being mad to feeling sorry for my parents, to deep grief knowing that we were leaving the farm forever, to sharing their excitement about going to the mission field. Some of my classmates assured me that Brazil was in Africa and made fun of it, telling me to say hi to Tarzan and Jane.

The farm sale was set for January. Shortly after that, we'd move to Fort Wayne. In preparation for the sale, neighbors and others I didn't know came and helped Daddy line up the equipment in the small pasture just north of the house. It bothered me to see them messing with our equipment, but I knew that it had to be done. There was no going back. The next day all of my farming school friends were there. The snow was just right for snowballs, and we were having a blast forming teams and throwing snowballs as we dodged in and out of equipment. This was a purposeful activity on my part because every time I heard the auctioneer holler, "SOLD!" it was very painful. At 10 years of age, a good snowball fight is an amazing emotional pain reliever.

All of the smaller items had sold, and the crowd had moved to the last row. This freed up more space for the snowball strategies, but even so, snowball fights were getting kind of dull. We were tired, and one of the boys had already gone home. It was no big deal, but I knew I might never see him again. I knew they were getting close to the little blue tractor. It was surreal. Couldn't something happen to stop this? I ran off to throw a snowball at someone. Auctioneers like to build up their larger items and take more time on them. I have no idea how long it took to sell the Ford 4000, but the timing was impeccable. I had chased and been chased and was stopped and looking right at the tractor when the auctioneer yelled, "SOLD!"

A knife pierced my soul. The crowd was now moving to the big tractor, oblivious to the tragedy they had just witnessed. My stomach was in my throat; it was hard to breathe; tears blurred my vision. I ran for cover under a hay wagon at the end by the apple tree. I sobbed and sobbed. I didn't think any of my friends had followed me. If they did, when they saw I was crying, they left me to mourn in peace. I didn't see the big tractor sell, nor did I see most of my friends go home. After a while, I came out and walked around, helping with this and that and staying out of the way when needed. Daddy found me and gave me a big hug. He'd told the man who bought the tractor that they always referred to the 4000 as "Jay's tractor," and he had said I could drive it down to the neighbor's ramp where it would be loaded onto a truck. I knew my dad had arranged this, and I really appreciated it. It was like going through the goodbye process, which he realized I desperately needed. I talked to the tractor as I drove it in the blistering cold wind. I would not complain about the weather; it was the last time I could do it. Amid tears and more emotions than I'd ever felt before, the little blue tractor was gone.

We moved to Fort Wayne. No one in my new class was vaguely aware of what a farmer, or even a tractor, was. Daddy was in Bible classes with lots of students 15 to 20 years younger than him. He was not doing well at all. When your dad gets excited with Cs and Ds, it is not a good sign. I had known it all along. This was a terrible mistake, but now we had to support each other and try to help Daddy get through this one way or another.

Mother was not happy either. She cried a lot. She didn't complain about anything, but she was really having a hard time, and we kids knew it. Our world had turned upside down, and it was Daddy's fault, but I would never utter those words to him. It would hurt him too much. What I wanted now was for him to pass his classes and for Mother to be happy. I would have given my right arm for this to come true.

At no point in this story had I ever been rebellious. In my 10-year-old intellectual way, I really did want to do God's will. For me, I knew that was to obey my parents, and I did that—most of the time. I believed that God's way was the best way, and that is what I wanted for all of us. It was just all so terribly wrong and hard.

Later I would learn that my parents were going through the worst times of their entire lives. I don't think my mother ever dwelled on suicidal thoughts, but once while driving, the steering wheel was physically pulled into the oncoming traffic, and it took all of her strength to pull it back and keep the car in her lane. She was psychologically fragile and emotionally spent. She told my father about this, and he was devastated. Had he made a mistake?

The house we had rented was very small, and I slept in the attic with Jeffry, my younger brother. Jeffry was probably the only one who was happy at times, as he was four or five and only vaguely aware of the terrible plight of the family.

In the middle of the night, I was sound asleep when I had a wonderful dream that ended as a nightmare. I awoke crying and yelling, "Daddy, Daddy, Daddy!" I would learn later that he had not slept because he had been studying; then he lay in bed questioning life, his calling, and God. Crying, I sobbed out my dream, unaware as to how it might affect him. Between sobs I said, "We were plowing in the field like on that night when you let me plow until 1 a.m. I was smelling the dirt and the diesel, and the plow was turning under the cornstalks so perfectly. I was on my tractor, and the throttle was wide-open. You were on your tractor way on down in front of me in the field, and we were plowing together. It was cold, and every now and then, I had to ride the brake.

It was so real. It was so real, Daddy. Then I woke up, and I was here!" I sobbed and sobbed. Daddy cried too, as any decent father would have.

He spoke with me about giving everything to the Lord. He gently talked to me about how I needed to tell God that I was willing to serve Him in any way He wanted. He talked of how we store up treasures in heaven, and that's what life is all about. He was strong and wise and prayed with me, and I went back into a peaceful sleep.

That "dream turned nightmare" cut him to the very core. He loved me. He loved the whole family. Oh, such pain; maybe he had made a terrible mistake. He was cut as deeply as he could fathom. I think he hurt more at this point than I did when my tractor sold. He would have gone back to the farm if he could have, but he could not. The land had been rented, and the equipment had been sold. My father, mother, and yes, even I, were caught between the sea and the mountain with the enemy approaching quickly.

Only my father could relate the anguish of that night from his perspective. I think he would say that on that night, he absolutely came to the end of himself. There was nowhere to turn. There were no secret plans if things didn't work out in Bible college. There was no way to right the wrongs if he had missed God's will. It was the bottom of the pit for my father. I did not want to hurt my father, but God had used me to do just that. I would not understand until I had a son, what devastation of spirit was caused that night by my dream and my deep pain.

I don't know how to describe it, and maybe I didn't even realize it at the time, but this was a turning point. As he studied in total submission and even abandonment to God, my father's grades began to improve, and I began to think positively about going to the mission field. Mother was happier from that point on, so I guess my two younger siblings were also. It was at this point in my life that I really thought about giving God everything. I heard my parents talk about it; I saw it in their daily lives. It was the beginning of the most important lesson I would ever learn. Not even a little blue Ford tractor could take his place; God must be in first place in my life, like it says in the first commandment: "Thou shalt have no other gods before me" (Exodus 20:3 KJV).

According to Mother, this tractor dream was to repeat itself other times in the months and years following, and I would go crying to her and Daddy. It probably made them rethink their decision and check their hearts, and it probably helped me to stay firmly on the path of commitment to God in my boyish way.

Thank you, Daddy, for the little blue tractor that was mine for a short season, but mostly, thank you for the lesson you and Mother taught us kids about committing everything to God. Now, more than 40 years later, we are farming in Brazil, South America. We have had more opportunity here than we ever would have had in Indiana. Life as missionary farmers has indeed been rich, as God continues to be in first place.

Chapter 7

Mouthwash and Other Essentials

For God hath not given us the spirit of fear; but of power, and of love, and of a sound mind.
2 Timothy 1:7 (KJV)

Miami
January 1970

*J*an jumped and covered her ears at the low bellow of the ship's horn. They were pulling out. She stood with her family on the top deck of the *Leonardo da Vinci* cruise ship. The winds whipped around them and rustled her skirt. They wore special outfits for this occasion—the boys in suits and Dixie and Jan in matching mint-green dresses that Dixie had made. On the shore a crowd of people waved goodbye. All through the city, lights blinked on and off, accompanied by shouting and whistling. Someone even blew a trumpet. One of the other passengers told the Edwards family that they always did those things to say goodbye when a big ship left the port. Jan thought it was exciting. They were really going to Brazil.

Jeff shivered in the cold, so Max took his suit jacket off and wrapped it around him; he held him as they watched the shoreline disappear into the distance. It certainly was exciting. Max was pleased and relieved that they had managed to get themselves and all of their possessions onto the ship on time. Friends had driven them down to Florida from

Indiana—quite a trip with seven people and their boxer dog in one car. Their things were transported separately.

The Rudds, a family who had been in missionary internship with them, had intended to travel to Brazil at the same time. However, their trip had been postponed, so they sent their barrels along with the Edwardses. Between the two families, they had 37 barrels! The Edwards family also had some trunks and a crate, which were all safely on the ship.

The luxury liner was a foreign world of its own for the Edwards family. For the next 12 days, they explored, watched movies, played Rook, visited their dog in the kennel, and swam. They also spent a significant amount of time in their cabins feeling seasick. By the time the ship neared Brazil, they were ready to plant their feet on dry land and get busy.

The Edwards family ate their last dinner on the ship with no regrets; the food was so much fancier than their usual, and by then they had had quite enough.

"I'll be glad to eat your cooking again, Mother," Jay said as they walked back to their cabins. "Are you sure you haven't forgotten how?"

Dixie laughed. "I sure hope not."

Just then the loudspeaker in the hallway crackled. "Hello, everyone," a voice boomed. "This is your captain speaking. Tomorrow at dawn, we will be arriving in the world-famous port of Rio de Janeiro."

The children clapped and grinned.

"It is a sight you won't want to miss," the captain continued. "The water will be a gorgeous clear blue; dolphins will be playing, and you will get a spectacular view of the city and the famous Sugarloaf Mountain, which is solid rock. Don't oversleep! Be there!"

The loudspeaker buzzed and clicked off.

"Hear that, kids?" Max said. "We need to pack up and get to bed early, so we will be ready to see Brazil at dawn."

These instructions were followed dutifully, and before long they wrapped up family devotions. By this time, the whole family knew Psalm 4:8 by heart: "I will both lay me down in peace, and sleep: for thou, Lord, only makest me dwell in safety" (KJV).

Max and the children went to bed filled with enthusiasm, but Dixie felt only anxiety. *Tomorrow is "it,"* she thought. *We are moving to Brazil as missionaries.* Dixie was there in obedience; she recognized that God was guiding their family to Brazil through her husband. And yet, she had not felt a "call" personally, and she still felt so inadequate for the tasks set before her. She thought about their two-week trip to Brazil and how out of place and incompetent she had felt. She wanted to be obedient, but how could she do this?

Even as they had walked onto the ship, Dixie had prayed, *Lord, you can yet stop us if this is not Your plan.* But He had not stopped them, and now … now they were there. *Lord,* she prayed, *please help me.*

Dixie slept fitfully that night and woke several times. Each time, she had similar thoughts: *Sugarloaf … the rock mountain … Christ, my Rock!* "*The stone which the builders rejected, the same is become the head of the corner*" (Matthew 21:42 KJV). "*For other foundation can no man lay than that is laid, which is Jesus Christ*" (1 Corinthians 3:11 KJV). "*The LORD is my rock, and my fortress, … and my high tower*" (Psalm 18:2 KJV). *Christ, my Rock!*

The whole family was up early and on the top deck. The experience was everything the captain had said, and the kids were so excited.

"Look, Daddy!" Jeff said. "Dolphins!"

As the family pressed up to the railing with the other passengers to see the dolphins, Dixie's gaze drifted ahead to the approaching land. There was Sugarloaf Mountain. Suddenly, she knew there was a Bible passage she needed to read. Hurrying down to the cabin, she found her Bible and leafed through the pages until she found 1 Peter 2:6–7: "Behold, I lay in Sion a chief corner stone, elect, precious: and he that believeth on him shall not be confounded. Unto you therefore which believe he is precious" (KJV).

There it was! Jesus was her Rock. The promise that she would not "be confounded" meant she could do it—whatever "it" was. She looked out the porthole and again saw Sugarloaf Mountain. It was solid rock—immoveable, as was her Lord! He was the essence of all that was stable, strong, true, dependable, and secure. All He required of her was her love and obedience. It was God's special promise to her before she stepped on Brazilian soil.

~ * ~

A wave of heat struck the Edwards family as they walked down the gangplank. The dock, beach, and city beyond all buzzed with people. This was the time of *Carnaval,* which was one of Brazil's biggest holidays, especially in this particular city. Max scanned the crowd, looking for familiar faces. He soon found them—Charles and Martha Elkjer, the OMS Brazil directors. They had their son Chris with them. Max and Dixie had met them on their short-term trip. The Elkjers smiled and waved as the Edwardses made their way to them.

"Welcome to Brazil!" they called.

"Woof!" The Edwards' dog, Tramp, greeted in return. He strained at his leash and sniffed at the new people.

"Oh!" Martha exclaimed, surprised but not upset. "You brought a dog!"

"Tramp, down!" Max commanded. The dog obediently backed up and sat. Max then turned and shook Charles' hand enthusiastically.

"It's good to be back!" he said.

After many greetings, hugs, and introductions for the children and dog, they headed off the dock and picked up their hand baggage from customs.

"Your barrels, trunks, and crate won't be processed until after *Carnaval,*" Charles explained. "We will have to come back for them."

The sun beat down on their faces and necks as they loaded their hand baggage into the back of the *Kombi* (Volkswagen bus) the Elkjers had brought.

"Well," said Charles, his face red with heat, "let's go find a place to get a cold drink of water."

They all piled into the *Kombi,* trying to give each other space because of the heat.

"Tramp, get away from me," Jan complained. "You're too hot." She pushed the dog off her lap.

Up in the front passenger seat, Max eagerly took in the city as Charles guided the large vehicle through traffic. They were finally there—and not just for a two-week trip this time. They were there to stay. Max couldn't wait to see what God had in store for them.

After a few minutes, Charles pulled into the parking lot of a small store that sold refreshments. Everyone climbed out of the car and headed inside.

Max boldly strode up to the counter. With an amused smile, Charles followed but stayed off to the side. He would let Max have this experience.

"Water," Max said, waving his arms around. The man behind the counter smiled and answered in Portuguese. Max had no idea what he was saying, and the man clearly didn't understand him either. He acted like he was drinking a glass of water … still no result.

Max looked around, determined to do this on his own. Finally, he walked around the counter, still talking to the man in English and the man still answering in Portuguese. Max found himself a glass and some ice. Pouring it into the glass, he held it up and said in English, "Ice."

The man grinned and responded, "*Gelo.*"

"*Gelo,*" Max repeated. He smiled. He had learned his first Portuguese word!

~ * ~

We live on a row of Missionaries.
—Jan, in a letter to her grandma

The Edwards family spent their first night in Brazil in a little hotel outside the city of Rio de Janeiro. The next day they made the 300-mile trip to the city of Campinas, where they would be living. Max, Charles, and Tramp drove the *Kombi* with their cabin baggage while the rest took the bus. As they rode through the hilly Brazilian countryside, Dixie saw bananas, multicolored flowers, sugar cane, and even cornfields like those in Indiana. Everything was so different here, and yet there were wisps of familiarity. The landscape was beautiful. The fields were dotted with large anthills that looked like rocks—some perhaps three feet high. At one point, Dixie noticed a farmer milking an old cow under a small lean-to.

"I'm afraid to close my eyes," Jan said. "I might miss something." Dixie could understand what she meant. This may be an ordinary day in the life of that farmer, but it was an extraordinary one for these Indiana farmers.

By that evening, the family was settling into their new home. Campinas was a nice, quiet city not far from the much larger city of São Paulo.

They would live there for a year while Max and Dixie attended language school. After that, only God knew where they would go.

Their house was located on a street full of families, mostly missionaries, who would be attending language school with them. Located a few blocks from the school, the road had been nicknamed "Presbyterian Row" because many of the residents were Presbyterians. Within days, the Edwardses were making new friends, and Jay, Jan, and Jeff were learning to jump over the low walls between the backyards to go play with the other kids.

Though they found themselves surrounded by others who were like them, the Edwards family also had to adjust to many new sights, sounds, smells, and experiences. Food salesmen would come down the street in horse carts, advertising their products through loudspeakers. Instead of the large, clean supermarkets, the most common stores were little shops along the street. People were expressive and used lots of hand motions. And most noticeably, they all spoke Portuguese.

Occasionally, the whole family visited the city of São Paulo, where the heavy traffic made Dixie pray harder than ever before. "You have to see it to believe it," she wrote in a letter home.

After a month of settling in, waiting for their barrels to be processed and delivered, making friends, and (finally) unpacking, Max and Dixie were ready to begin language school at the beginning of March. They attended their orientation full of nervous anticipation.

"Learning a new language is a difficult task," the school director said to the group of new students. "It is not uncommon for students to become frustrated and break down in class." The director looked around the room thoughtfully and then continued. "If you become frustrated, we encourage you to release the tension. Cry if you need to. You will all have points when you feel overwhelmed; it is perfectly normal."

Max and Dixie discussed it later over bowls of homemade ice cream.

"I think it will be difficult for both of us," Dixie said, "but I guess all of us students are in the same boat."

Max nodded thoughtfully. "This morning as I was doing my devotions," he said, "I received a promise from God that if we stay in His Word and in prayer, He will give us the language."

"Amen!" Dixie said as she lifted another cold bite to her mouth. "May it be so. I know I can't do it without His help."

"Me either," said Max.

Max and Dixie were right to believe that language school would be hard. Within the first few days, they were already frustrated as they began with sounds. Their mouths just wouldn't move the right way.

"We drill and drill and drill," Dixie wrote in a letter home. "All d's and t's are soft ... tongue goes hard behind the front teeth. The i's are all e's, and the e's are three different 'a' sounds ..."

And so it began. The language program was designed for missionary couples like Max and Dixie, with the men studying in the morning for three hours, everyone together at midday for one hour, and the women studying for three hours in the afternoon. The men made a habit of playing volleyball in the afternoon while the women were in class. This was one way to let off steam. Max soon found another way to release tension—making goodies. Soon the Edwards family was enjoying chocolate chip cookies and fudge made by Daddy.

Dixie felt that learning a language was like dying, then very slowly and painfully being reborn. One has to die to one's own language, to bury it and become as a little child learning new sounds and meanings, word by word.

Though language learning was frustrating, all of the Edwardses were highly motivated to learn it as they ventured out beyond Presbyterian Row. Their inability to speak Portuguese turned ordinary tasks into big challenges. This gave them some interesting experiences—especially Max, who was bold and forward whether he knew the words to say or not.

On one occasion, Max needed to buy mouthwash. When he entered the little drugstore, he discovered that he would need to ask for it from the woman standing behind the counter.

I haven't the foggiest idea what the Portuguese word for "mouthwash" is, he thought to himself. Max scanned the wall behind the counter to see if he could point to it, but he didn't see anything that looked like mouthwash, and of course, he couldn't read the labels. The lady behind the counter was smiling nervously. What to do?

Max started waving his arms around as usual. "Mouthwash," he said, pretending to pour some into a cup and into his mouth. The woman looked bewildered. Max pointed at his mouth. "Stinky!" he said. He didn't know that word in Portuguese either. The woman put a few different products on the counter, but none of them looked right. Finally Max had an idea. Leaning forward, he grabbed the woman's shoulders and blew in her face. Then he tilted his head back and pretended to gargle.

The woman laughed, and her face suddenly lit up. She returned to the shelves and promptly fetched a bottle of the desired product.

Max grinned and picked it up.

"*Obrigado,*" he said in thanks. As he paid for the mouthwash, he also handed the woman a tract in Portuguese. He had no intention of waiting until he could speak the language to start sharing the Good News of Jesus Christ. He just prayed that God would work even through his feeble efforts.

~ * ~

It's going to be very difficult. Please pray every day. I've struggled inwardly about this communication. Without the Lord, I'd either lose my mind or come home. I tend to withdraw, and that's the very worst thing to do. Max plunges ahead making all kinds of errors; laughs and the Brazilian laughs with him. Did you ever have the feeling of wanting to crawl in a hole and pull it in after you? That's me—off & on!! (not all the time) I sometimes consider it a great challenge and am anxious to get into it.
—Dixie, in a letter home

Max and Dixie sat together at the dining table, books and notebooks spread out before them. The children were asleep, but the grown-ups still struggled with their homework. A half-eaten bowl of popcorn sat between them.

Dixie wrote carefully, striving to commit the difficult verb tenses to memory. As she finished her assignment, she sighed. Sitting here at home with only Max sitting next to her, it didn't seem so hard. It was a lot of work and a lot of memorization, to be sure, but she had always enjoyed studying. The problem for her was actually getting out and talking to people. When she sat in class, she felt like she had learned a great deal. But when she tried to talk to someone in real life, she found that she was missing three-fourths of the words she needed to communicate. She felt paralyzed and didn't even want to open her mouth for fear of making a mistake.

Max did not mind making mistakes, but this homework was really something else. Every lesson was a struggle. He watched Dixie close her books and get out a notepad to start a letter to her mother. How did she finish so quickly?

Both Max and Dixie went to bed that night discouraged. They felt like they spent all of their time studying, and progress was so slow. When would they get to do the ministry that they came for?

Lord, Max prayed as he got into bed, *I have remained faithful to You, and I am relying on Your promise. Please do not forget us, Lord. We need the language to do Your work here in Brazil.*

The next day they got up and tried again, discouragement still weighing heavily upon them. Later, after classes and volleyball, Max meandered home, still thinking and praying. As he walked, he absently watched the neighborhood boys playing soccer in the street, as was their habit. Some of them smiled, waved, and called out greetings. Smiling and waving back, Max suddenly had an idea. He walked up to the curb and sat down.

"*Bom dia,*" he called in greeting, his American accent heavy.

The boys were intrigued. A few of them picked up their ball and came over to Max. They chattered in Portuguese, laughing and pushing at each other. Max understood very little, but their enthusiasm warmed his spirit. He sorted through the muddle of words and phrases in his head, searching for ones he could use with these boys.

"*Futebol,*" he said, as he pointed at their soccer ball. The boys burst out laughing and continued to chatter. Max smiled and did what he could to converse with them; he repeated words that they said, and used what he had learned in class. The boys apparently thought he was hilarious. Max was certain he appeared quite ignorant—a grown man speaking like a toddler. Nevertheless, the conversation was a refreshing contrast to his classes. As he said goodbye and resumed his walk home, he thought, *I must become like a little child to learn this new language.*

From then on, Max made sitting on the curb a regular practice, and the boys always came to talk to him and laugh both with and at him.

In their spare time, Max and Dixie did their best to familiarize themselves with Brazil and OMS' work. On one occasion, Max visited one of the local OMS partner churches to share his testimony. After the service, Max stood with the talkative congregation, understanding very little of what they said. The people seemed eager to meet him, and he was happy to interact with them, but understanding their questions and coming up with the words to answer was a challenge. Eventually, the pastor motioned to him that it was time to leave. Max thought about his parting words. He planned to return to this church in a few months, and he wanted to tell them that his Portuguese would be better then.

"*Quando volto,*" he said. Then he searched his memory for the word for "better." "*Eu vou ser mulher português,*" he said.

The people looked confused for a minute, then laughed and answered him in Portuguese. Max wasn't sure what was going on, but he smiled and shook hands and hugged everyone; then he left with the pastor.

When they got into the car, the pastor chuckled. "Do you know what you said?" he asked.

"No," Max answered. "What did I say?"

"You said, 'When I return, I will be a Portuguese woman!'"

Now it was Max's turn to laugh. He had mixed the word for "better," *melhor,* with the word for "woman," *mulher.* He was happy to be among these people who would laugh with him, teach him, and love him, whether he was an American man or a Portuguese woman!

~ * ~

The Edwards home soon became a popular gathering spot; the other missionaries enjoyed their homemade ice cream, Dixie's piano and organ, and the warm and friendly environment. Max and Dixie did their best to invite Brazilians to their home as well, when they met them. They had so many guests, in fact, that Dixie occasionally mandated "family-only" days, so her children would get some rest.

Though the Edwards family loved their American friends, they also saw their need to get out of their American bubble, so they did what they could to involve themselves in Brazilian culture. Only a couple of months after they arrived in Campinas, they stopped attending the American church and began attending a Brazilian church. This was difficult for the whole family, especially at the beginning when they understood so little. However, in time they got used to it and even enjoyed it.

The family became involved in ministry wherever they could, both inside and outside the American expatriate community. Dixie led a Bible club with American children on Saturday mornings. The 3Js continued their singing ministry; they sang in both American and Brazilian settings. They performed in chapels at the language school, at special events they attended, and in churches all over Campinas. Everyone was amazed at their beautiful harmony and especially little Jeff's strong, clear voice. Dixie had some of their songs translated into Portuguese, so they could sing in both languages. Max continued to befriend everyone he met; he handed out tracts and watched for every opportunity to share the Gospel.

At first Jay and Jan attended the local American school. However, when the school year ended in June, the family decided that it would be best for them to go to a Brazilian school in order to learn Portuguese. Jeff, now in first grade, studied with a missionary in Campinas who taught several children in an informal setting. The Edwardses hired a tutor to help all three children with Portuguese in the afternoon. Jay and Jan eventually learned Portuguese, but attending Brazilian school when they had not yet learned the language was very difficult for them. Deciding what to do for the children's education would be a struggle for the family throughout their time in Brazil. However, they trusted in their Lord's plan and knew that He would provide for their family everywhere that He led them.

And where was He leading them? All Max knew was "Brazil!" Now they were in Brazil, and slowly but surely, the language was coming. So, where would they go next?

Chapter 8

Snakes and Rats and Toads

Trust in the LORD with all your heartand lean not on
your own understanding; in all your ways submit to
him, and he will make your paths straight.
Proverbs 3:5–6 (NIV)

It was unusual for missionaries to go overseas without knowing what
they were going to do there. Max went trusting that God had a plan,
even though he didn't know what it was. In Brazil, the OMS field committee of missionaries wasn't quite sure what to do with the Edwards
family. Without a college degree, Max was not qualified for the kinds of
jobs that most of the missionaries did, such as teaching in the seminary.
However, new missionaries always went to the seminary compound in
the city of Londrina after language school to be with the other missionaries while they got used to Brazil. So the board planned to assign
Max to be the caretaker at the compound after his family's year in
Campinas was complete.

However, about halfway through his year of language school, Max
heard that OMS had recently acquired a campground in the interior
of the state of São Paulo. It was intended for use as a retreat center and
church camp. His interest was piqued, so during their semester break
in July, Max, Jay, and fellow missionary Bill Rudd made the 10-hour
trip inland to see the camp.

As they approached the little town of Panorama, Max and Jay saw a
different side of Brazil than the modern city of Campinas. The town was

on the Paraná River, which marked the border between the states of São Paulo and Mato Grosso. The river was about a mile wide at that point, with the other side bordered by thick jungle. The only way to cross the river was by boat. A ferry crossed from town, which was surrounded by wide-open spaces and farms. As he rode along the dirt streets, Jay was enchanted by the "Wild West" feeling of the area. Many of the local people didn't even have cars; they used horse carts instead. The visitors learned that Panorama had about 5,000 people and only one telephone. The nearest city, Dracena, was a 45-minute drive away, and as far as they knew, there were no other Americans for miles around. Max and Jay, still farmers at heart, immediately fell in love with rural Brazil. The space and nature were refreshing compared to the close quarters of the city.

Panorama Camp (*Acampamento Panorama*) was located about five miles outside the town. They planned to spend several days there and attend a camp meeting. As they approached the camp and turned onto the long lane, the camp caretaker and his wife came out to meet them. Max, Jay, and Bill stopped and introduced themselves to Sr. Antonio and Dona Maria de Souza.[7] Grinning broadly, the couple chatted in Portuguese and showed them around the camp. Max, Bill, and Jay focused intently on their words and tried to understand their Portuguese. As far as Max could tell, they were relaying information about the camp and its history. They followed the caretakers through the dusty paths; they surveyed the dining hall, dorm rooms, and bathrooms. In addition to the caretaker's residence, there was a residence for the camp directors, where the Edwardses would live if they were to go there. Max went through the house and looked out the back door. He was delighted to glimpse the river just a three-minute walk from the house. He closed his eyes and took a deep breath of the fresh country air.

This place has so much potential, he thought. *We could build new dorm rooms, a new chapel, a recreation hall, and lots of spaces for sports and games. It's the perfect retreat center.*

As they walked through the grounds, Max noted that Jay lit up in a way that he hadn't since they left the farm. Jay thought the camp was great. *It's just like the Wild West!* he thought. Images filled his

---

7   *Sr.* and *Dona* are Brazilian terms of respect for married men and women, respectively.

mind—Cowboy Jay riding horses, going hunting, and exploring the jungle with a pet monkey perched on his shoulder. Even the run-down buildings contributed to the rustic atmosphere of the place. This was definitely where he wanted to live.

Jay had the opportunity to experience life as "Cowboy Jay" when Max and Bill took a trip across the river to see the city of Três Lagoas and left Jay at the camp. He stayed alone in one of the dorm rooms near the house and ate his meals with the caretaker's family. Before he left, Max gave Jay a talk about how God would take care of him.

"Jay," he said, "it's when men are alone that they find out who they really are."

Twelve-year-old Jay thought a lot about that. He felt like he was a man alone, finding out who he really was. He slept with his hunting knife by his bed—a little scared, but thrilled by the wildness of this place.

Max was delighted with the camp too. Later, as they traveled back to Campinas, he thought of all the outreach they could do through the camp if he were to develop it. *We would minister to the youth between Panorama and the city of São Paulo—a stretch of 500 miles. Young people from the cities and towns could come to the camp to get away, to have fun, and, most importantly, to hear about Jesus. How many lives could be touched through a facility like this?*

The more Max considered the possibilities, the more excited he became. He was sure now; this was where God wanted him.

~ * ~

Max and Jay returned home full of stories of how wonderful Panorama was. The rest of the family soon became excited too. Dixie wasn't sure about moving to the interior, but from Max's description, the place sounded lovely. Besides, their family felt more comfortable in rural situations than in the city.

Max applied to the field committee for permission to move to Panorama after he completed language school. The committee promptly denied his request, saying that the assignment was too challenging for a new missionary fresh out of language school. Furthermore, how would his children receive a good education out there in the middle of nowhere?

The older missionaries believed that it was a terrible place to raise a family. Max and Dixie had discussed this and decided that if they were to move there, Dixie would teach the children herself at home. They were requesting their assignment early (by August), so they would have time to order books from the U.S. for this at-home study. Even at that, the schooling situation was not ideal. In fact, many things were not ideal.

What am I going to do? thought Max. *I know that I am a new missionary, and that the language is not coming easily to me. And yet, I'm also sure that God wants us in Panorama.*

He came to a decision. "I'm going to fast for a while," he told Dixie. "I think I need to fast and pray over two things: our assignment after language school and learning Portuguese."

Dixie nodded. "Okay," she said. "I understand." Sometimes she worried about Max when he fasted, but she knew that these things were weighing heavily on his heart. She joined him in praying for God's direction for their future.

Max fasted and prayed for three weeks in all, and then he reapplied for permission to go to Panorama and was denied again. Max talked to one of the committee members and shared his heart.

"I ask you to fast awhile," he said, "and see if this is not where God wants us."

The committee member agreed to fast and pray. Everyone knew that Max had been fasting; he was getting very thin. Max applied to the committee a third time, and the family scheduled a weekend to visit the camp all together toward the end of August. During this trip, they would also visit Londrina, where they would hear the final decision of the field committee.

~ * ~

The campsite consists of a small main house, two dormitories, a kitchen and dining hall building, and a chapel (which is about to collapse). Sounds great—and it could be with lots of improvement, repair and a manager. We are appointed to be that <u>manager</u>.
—Dixie, in a letter home

The big weekend came. Dixie, Jan, and Jeff eagerly anticipated seeing the place that God had assigned to them. As they neared Panorama, the roads turned from pavement to rutty dirt. Finally, they turned and bumped up the camp's long lane. Dixie's mind was full of pictures that she had created when Max had described the place to her—beautiful palm trees, the river, the house, dormitories, and the dining hall.

Max stopped the car, and they got out. Dixie looked around. *Where is it?* she wondered. She didn't see any of what she had pictured from Max's description. Instead, she saw run-down buildings, peeling paint, broken windows with torn screens, tall grass, and insects.

She walked into the house—the house that would soon be her home. As she entered the living room, all Dixie could see and feel was dark. The furniture was dark, the paint was dark, and the curtains were closed. Everything looked black. Her spirit sank.

She went through the house and into the kitchen where Dona Maria, the caretaker's wife, was cooking; she was expecting them. As Dixie walked in, Dona Maria began chatting to her in Portuguese. Dixie listened carefully, but she couldn't understand a word.

"*Como?*" she asked, indicating that she hadn't caught what the woman had said. Dona Maria repeated her words, but Dixie still didn't understand. Dixie was appalled. She was more than halfway through language school, and she couldn't understand this woman, someone she would be working with in just a few months! More darkness.

The family spent time walking around outside and looking at the buildings. The children enjoyed the visit. They thought that Panorama was great fun. Jan and Jeff enjoyed the wildness of it, as Jay had. After the closeness of the city, the open spaces felt wonderful to them. They had fun playing outside and climbing trees.

When Dixie was outside, she couldn't help keeping a constant eye out for snakes. All the buildings were in a state of disrepair, and the grounds were not in much better shape. Dixie couldn't believe that this was going to be her home in just a few short months.

They stayed overnight at the camp, and Dixie lay awake in bed, thinking about everything she had seen. She heard strange noises overhead.

"Max, do you know what that noise is?" she asked.

Hesitantly, Max asked, "Do you really want to know?"

"Of course!"

"They're rats, honey."

Dixie shuddered.

As they drove back down the lane the next day, Dixie blinked back tears. Max looked at her. "It's not quite like I described, is it?"

"No," Dixie replied. But she remembered what God had taught her so far—that she was resting firmly on her Rock, Jesus. She mustered up all her courage and said, "But if this is where God wants us, it will all be fine."

During that same weekend, they went to Londrina, and Max met again with the field committee. After considering all the options for him and considering his age, maturity, and insistence, the committee finally agreed. He could go to Panorama after language school. He would be in charge of raising the funds to finish paying off the camp as well as the funds for any remodeling he decided to do. But he was permitted to go.

The Edwards family was excited. It wouldn't be easy, but they knew that if this was God's assignment for them, they could do it with His guidance and support.

~ * ~

The Edwards family returned to Campinas with a renewed desire to learn the language and prepare for their upcoming ministry. Max and Dixie continued to struggle with the language, but they also knew that they had improved considerably since the beginning of the year. Max was as bold as ever, blundering along and learning as he talked to people. In a letter home, Dixie wrote, "Max still isn't speaking as well as others, but he communicates better than most."

Their year of language school was to finish in January. In November, the children's books arrived for homeschooling, so Jay and Jan quit Brazilian school and studied at home. It was quite a challenge for Dixie to teach them at home while she was still studying herself. But now they would be ready for their transition to the interior. Also in November, Max made another trip to Panorama to draw up plans for remodeling and make estimates of how much it would cost.

Dixie continued to struggle in prayer over the move to Panorama. It was hard to see how it would all work out with the camp in the condition that it was and her needing to teach the children at home, all while working, cleaning, and organizing. What's more, they were planning to add another member to the family; already in December Dixie was experiencing the blessed symptoms of pregnancy. She and the family were very excited about this, but the situation at Panorama did not seem ideal for her family. And yet, she trusted that God would not put them in the wrong place. She knew that He knew best, and after thinking it over, she also felt excited about the possibilities.

~ * ~

The days will physically be difficult, but know-
ing that all things come from our Father's loving
hand makes it much easier to praise Him who goes
before us and makes "the crooked places straight"[8]
—Dixie, in a letter home

January couldn't come soon enough for Max. He was tired of studying and was ready to get into the ministry. He could hardly wait to work with his hands again. On Sunday, January 10, 1971, they filled the *Kombi* with as many of the family's possessions as they could. Max, Jay, and Tramp drove out to Panorama, where they worked for five days in preparation for a volunteer work team that was coming from the U.S. to help. As they drove, Max thought through their plans again. Just before they left, he had been informed that only a small amount of the money needed was allotted to them at this time for repairs. This limited what they could do; however, Max knew that somehow God would provide everything they needed. He had been thinking and praying about priorities. For now, they would focus their remodeling on their family home. Once they were settled, they would more easily be able to focus on their ministry and on remodeling the rest of the camp.

On Friday, Max and Jay returned to Campinas, and on Sunday, January 17, the Edwards family awoke early to move to the camp. After a long day of driving, they finally bumped down that long lane

8   Isaiah 45:2 KJV

again with their moving truck following behind. Dixie looked around anxiously, hoping that it was not quite as bad as she remembered from her last trip. Her stomach clenched as they approached the house. If anything, it was worse.

Max parked the car, and the moving truck stopped behind them. Though her legs ached from the long drive, Dixie hesitated.

When I step out of this car, she thought, *I am moving to this place. There is no turning back. Lord, help me!* She took a deep breath and opened the door.

The children were already out and running around.

"Be careful, kids!" Dixie called after them. She peered into the tall grass next to the car. The last thing she wanted was to step on a snake. Max walked around the car and offered her his hand. Looking up at him, she forced a smile and took it.

"Welcome home," he said cheerfully. Dixie looked at the house again.

I only hope that someday this can feel like home, she thought.

The air was heavy with heat, and Dixie could hear the mosquitoes and other bugs buzzing around. The noise barely changed when she walked into the house; it seemed to be just as full of insects and other critters as the rest of the place. Oh, there was so much to do and not enough money to do it. Would they even have a clean home for the baby by July?

The next few moments were spent unloading and trying to tell the movers where to put their things. The house was barely useable, certainly not livable. There were three dorm rooms adjacent to the house, which were available to live in. These would have to accommodate their family, the work crew, and any other visitors they had during this time. Luggage would have to be piled everywhere, and their furniture put in the house living room and on the porch.

As soon as he finished giving the movers instructions, Max headed out again—this time to the train station to pick up the work crew. The group of six men had traveled to Panorama by train that very day, accompanied by another missionary. Dixie looked around helplessly as Max drove off. How was she to receive visitors in this place?

Fortunately for her, this group had come to serve, and they did not expect any special treatment. On the contrary, when they arrived and saw the condition of the place, their hearts went out to her. The group came from Indiana through MFM, the same OMS ministry that had brought the Edwardses on their first visit to Brazil. Their names were Jack Hueni, Ken Woodcox, Loren Lobsiger, Wally Yoder, Buss Rassi, and Dick Zeltwanger. They all had wives and families back home, and when they saw the situation, they dedicated themselves to doing whatever they could to make life easier for the Edwards family.

A few days later, Jan walked into the bathroom and wrinkled her nose. A big, fat toad sat in the middle of the room. He stared at her complacently, as if defying her to remove him. Sighing, Jan reached for the broom. At least it wasn't a rat—something she also frequently saw in the bathroom. If it were a rat, she would call for one of the men, but she had learned to handle toads herself.

"Go on, get out of here," she said, pushing the reluctant toad with her broom. With all the bugs around there, the toads were all so fat they could barely move. Still, Jan knew better than to try to kill one; she wanted them to keep eating as many bugs as they could.

Actually, when they weren't invading the bathrooms, the toads were fun. Jay, Jan, and Jeff made a game of feeding them bugs and daring them to eat the extra big ones. There were lots of fun things to do at the camp when they had the time. It was a great place to ride their bikes and run around. One of Jan's favorite things was swimming in the river. It was so hot that they went swimming every day, and she loved it. Everyone loved it.

At the same time, there was so much work to do. Jan helped Dixie with washing, cooking, dishes, and cleaning. Even though Dona Maria was preparing the main meals for the group, there was plenty of work for the rest of them. Jay was helping too, working on the remodeling with the men. Even Jeff pitched in when he could. They were enjoying taking a break from school; there was no room or time for studying.

Jan headed into the house kitchen. Jeff was there, asking Dixie for his daily "ration" of candy. In his letter to the work crew, Max had casually mentioned that they liked Milky Way candy bars. In response, the crew had brought 76! They also brought M&Ms for the children. Dixie said that everyone was allowed one candy bar and one package of M&Ms a day, to make them last as long as possible. Jan liked to save hers, but

Jeff asked for his every day right after breakfast. Moving stiffly, Dixie was retrieving Jeff's portion from the freezer when Jan entered. The mosquitoes and other bugs were biting them all, but Dixie had it the worst. She was covered in large, swollen bites. Jan wondered if she was allergic or something.

The men were working on remodeling the bathroom in the house. Because there wasn't much money, Dixie and Max had to choose what to do first, and they chose the bathroom. They were redoing the whole room, with the tile and fixtures in white and green colors that Dixie had picked. Most of the house was still a mess, but Jan thought the new bathroom was looking very pretty.

The work crew dedicated their time to doing whatever Dixie needed, including redoing the bathroom, doing basic home improvements, and completing various other tasks. This included the challenging task of killing rats. Jay kept track of the number of rats they killed—70 while the group was there. Though resources and time were limited, the men did as much as they could for the family. Every little thing was an improvement.

The men in the work crew never complained about any of the conditions. They worked hard and cheerfully the entire time. When they didn't have something they needed, they improvised with something else. A great team, they added much more than bricks, mortar, and plumbing to the home. They built confidence into the lives of the whole Edwards family.

Max was kept so busy going back and forth to town for supplies that he and Dixie hardly saw each other during that week. Dixie was plenty busy too, as she set priorities and kept everything organized. Max contributed to the food by making ice cream every day! Dixie watched the work on the house with anticipation. She was so grateful for all the work that was being done, and she knew that Max was doing his best to make them all comfortable.

Though the men were only there for a short time, the Edwards family became very attached to this work crew, feeling like they were part of the family. There were tears all around upon their departure.

Over the next five years, the Edwardses would see some 300 men and women come to work at Panorama Camp through MFM. It was through the efforts of these volunteers that Max's dreams of a beautiful facility for ministry would take shape. Many of those who came were farmers who were accustomed to physical labor and knew how to do the kinds of tasks that needed to be done in order to remodel the camp. When the Edwards family had raised their funds in 1969, they had gravitated toward churches in farming areas, as those were the people who could relate to their background. When they were assigned to Panorama, they encouraged those country churches to pray about sending people on these short-term trips to help with the work. Max and Dixie knew that the work was beyond their ability and beyond the skills of most local Brazilians. And so, God used their background to bring to Brazil the kind of people who were needed to remodel Panorama Camp.

During the week that the first work crew was there, the family also had several other visitors. Among the visitors were OMS leaders who gave the Edwardses approval to finish the remodeling of their home even though the money for it had not yet come in. They would borrow from an emergency fund and pay it back later. This was a relief to Dixie and the family; they could continue with the work and have a real home within the next few months.

After the work crew left, the Edwards family traveled back to Campinas for language school graduation on January 29. This marked the end of their year of language study and their official transition to Panorama Camp, their new home. There was a long road ahead, but they were committed and excited to see what God would do.

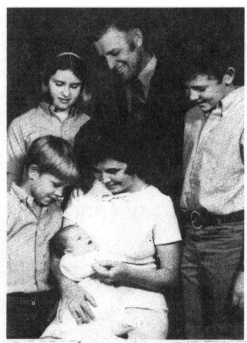

Leaving a successful farming operation in Indiana, Max Edwards with wife, Dixie, and their four J's—Jan, Jay, Jeff, and Brazil-born Joe—find frontier missionary life a rewarding challenge.

Why I Am A Missionary

Max Edwards/Brazil

BY all logic I should still be a farmer. I can think of many reasons why I should not be a missionary, and only one reason why I should be.

First, every born-again Christian is a missionary in the true sense of the word. So let it be understood that I am referring to the role of a professional missionary—one who has left a secular job and works full time at propagating the gospel message.

In 1964 I made a mental decision to walk through every door the Lord opened to me. If there was no door open, I would open one of my choice, believing the Holy Spirit to guide my mind in the decision. If two doors opened, I would consider it a God-given option and act accordingly.

In six years time and after many decisions on my part as well as those of others, I'm a missionary in a foreign country spreading the gospel to the best of my ability.

Why am I a missionary? Because I'm want to be. Because I made a decision and stuck with it. Because God permitted it. Because someone better qualified refused. Because it is God's best for me.

Actually, only one answer really fits. Man was made to worship God. Being a missionary is my way of worshiping Him.

Like childbirth for a woman, there have been many difficult times in the last six years. But also like childbirth, the struggles are quickly forgotten when new life appears, when someone is reborn and love replaces hatred, ambition absorbs laziness, and organization conquers turmoil.

Recently a man who made most of his income on Sunday was converted. He quit working on that day and testifies that God is taking better care of him and his family than he ever did; they want for nothing. Mine was the privilege to assist in baptizing this man, his wife, and some of the older children.

Why am I a missionary? Because I'm well rewarded? Because I'm happy? Because I love to be a part of this kind of story?

Yes, all of these. But mainly it is because I was created to worship God, and this is my place of worship. □

Chapter 9

Camps, Critters, and the Fourth J

"Forget the former things; do not dwell on the past. See, I am doing a new thing! Now it springs up; do you not perceive it? I am making a way in the wilderness and streams in the wasteland."
Isaiah 43:18–19 (NIV)

*A*s soon as they returned to Panorama from language-school graduation, the Edwardses plunged into local ministry. They started a morning Sunday school at the camp. The first Sunday, the only attendees were the caretaker's family and a few others. However, since the caretaker had nine children, Dixie had a class! Later, as word of the Americans' Sunday school spread, more local children and youth began to attend. Dixie taught the children, and Max taught the teenagers and adults. Max and Dixie both struggled as they felt they still did not have the language skills to make their message clear. Sometimes they wondered if the people understood anything they said. Nevertheless, they saw God's blessing on their ministry. Attendance was usually in the 30s for the first part of the year and in the 60s and 70s later, when they moved their location to a small schoolhouse near a brick factory, where many local families worked.

There was also a little church in Panorama that was part of OMS' church denomination in Brazil, *Igreja Missionária* (Missionary Church). The Edwards family soon became involved in ministry there. The church had services almost every night of the week, and Max was often asked to preach. Despite his many language errors, people loved to hear him. He used object lessons to help make his points. Max also served as a mentor for the young pastor of the church, and Dixie started a church choir. Since they had a Jeep-like car and a trailer, they brought people from the countryside with them to church. People gathered on the road near the camp to be picked up. Some weeks Max would make two trips with the car and trailer, carrying 20 or more people in each load.

And of course, their main focus was the camp and its facilities. First, they had to finish remodeling their house, so Max hired local workers to continue the work after the American MFM work crew left. He had difficulties with some of these workers, but eventually he was able to find good help and get the essential tasks completed. One man, Abimael, was a member of their church and skilled in construction work. He helped them with many future projects at Panorama and elsewhere.

After a significant amount of remodeling, repainting, and cleaning, the family finally moved into the house at the beginning of April. They were so thankful to have a home.

It took them some time to adjust to their new life at the camp. After a few weeks of swimming in the river, all three of the children developed bad earaches, which bothered them for weeks. They still had rats, toads, lizards, snakes, and so many insects. There was very little relief from the critters, but over time, they learned to get used to them. When they were still living in the dormitories, every morning Dixie would brush scores of bugs out of their bed. Max said, "I'm getting so I don't mind sleeping with them if they're dead."

Dixie and the children also began a regular school schedule. The children missed almost a month of school with all the activity in January, so Dixie was anxious to get them started again. Jeff was in second grade and able to go through his work quickly. However, with Jay and Jan in seventh and fifth grade, respectively, it was harder to progress without a classroom or formal instructor. Trying to answer their questions kept Dixie hopping, and some of the math was beyond even her knowledge.

In spite of the difficulties, the family experienced many blessings by living at the camp. The landscape was beautiful, and every evening there were gorgeous sunsets over the river. Jan liked to go down to the river by herself, sit on a fallen tree, and imagine she was in a novel.

The whole family loved to play in the water. Though their "beach" at the riverfront consisted mainly of red mud, they could reach a beautiful, clean, sandy beach by boat—a perfect place to swim and play. The caretaker's children soon became their friends and often joined Jay, Jan, and Jeff in their play at the waterfront. Dixie marveled to hear Jeff, who had never wanted to speak Portuguese in Campinas, as he chattered away with the caretaker's children.

The children, and especially Jay, still felt like they were living in the Wild West and loving every minute of it. They certainly had some wild experiences. On one occasion, they heard a strange, horrible noise in the front yard. Upon inspection, the family found that a snake had caught a frog by its hind leg and was trying to pull it into its hole. Max stomped on the snake's head with his heavy boots. It quickly flipped out of its hole, but it was no match for a 200-pound man. Unfortunately, the frog was killed in the battle along with the snake.

Another time, Max and Sr. Antonio found a poisonous snake in a stalk of bananas they were harvesting. There were many snakes in the area, and they learned that most of them were poisonous. Thankfully, no one in the family was ever bitten. Jay collected the snakes they had killed, which he kept in jars of alcohol. He lined them up on top of his wardrobe, eventually accumulating 26 snakes and lizards, most of them different kinds.

In addition to Jay's snake collection, the family began to "collect" live animals as well. Max bought a horse for the camp, and all three children enjoyed riding it. Sometimes they rode the horse to town to get the mail. While exploring the river, the family found an island that was full of guinea pigs, and the kids brought a few of them home as pets—much to their mother's dismay!

On another occasion, Max took the children to a market to buy more pets. The day was cold and rainy, but it couldn't dampen their excitement. They took the ferry across the river and drove to the city of Três Lagoas in the state of Mato Grosso. Their main goal was to buy a monkey, Jay's dream pet, but the market was full of all kinds of animals and other interesting things. They walked by one booth with ostriches for sale.

"I wonder what Mother would say if we came home with one of

those?" Max joked. The next booth was full of colorful parrots, all squawking and talking.

"Oh, how beautiful!" Jan exclaimed. "Daddy, can we get a parrot?"

"Hmm, I don't see why not," Max said.

"Yay!" Excited, the kids examined the parrots, dialoguing as best they could with the seller. In the end, they selected a beautiful, tame, green parrot. Max paid for it, and the seller held it out and let it climb onto Jan's shoulder. She grinned proudly.

"What should we call it?" asked Jay as they walked.

"How about Poppy?" Jan said.

"I like that!" declared Jeff.

"Me too," Max said, smiling.

Poppy would remain a favorite family pet for several years. The children tried to teach it many words, but in the end, it would only learn two: "Mother!" and "What?"

Finally, Max and the children reached the monkey seller. The man was surrounded by shaking, chattering boxes—wild monkeys brought directly from the jungle. The boxes were nailed shut, but the kids were able to peer in at them through the slats.

"All right, kids," said Max. "Time to choose a monkey!" They took their time; Jay, especially, wanted to choose the perfect monkey. Finally, they made their selection and paid for it; the seller handed Jay one of the chattering, screeching boxes. The children were excited the whole drive home, as they talked to and about their new pets.

"Now remember," Max told them, "you kids are responsible for taking care of these animals."

"I'll be in charge of the monkey," Jay said. "Jan can have the parrot."

"Fine with me!" said Jan.

"And I'll help with both!" exclaimed Jeff, not wanting to be left out.

When they arrived home, they were greeted by jealous dogs. Max and Jay worked quickly to make homes for the new pets where they would be safe. Poppy was quite tame, but the monkey was a different story. With Sr. Antonio's help, they filed the monkey's teeth and put him on a chain so he couldn't get away. Max soon set aside some time to try to train him.

"I will never have a child or a dog that won't obey me," declared

Max. "That applies to monkeys too." Unfortunately, the monkey won the first battle, and Max received a nasty bite on his finger. The next day Jay went out to try a different approach. He wanted to teach the monkey to be his friend. To his dismay, Jay received the same treatment as Max and left with a bite as well.

Soon after, this monkey became very sick and died. Jay was so disappointed. Even worse was the news that Max and Jay needed 14 days of rabies shots. The vet said that the monkey showed signs of rabies, so they sent the body to a facility to be tested. However, because it had already been more than a week since Max and Jay were bitten, they couldn't afford to wait for the results.

So, they began going to the pharmacy regularly for their shots. The man there said that the shots needed to go into the stomach, right under the skin. Max and Jay watched as he would boil the syringe and then run it under tap water to cool it before administering the injections. Max knew that running the syringe under tap water unsterilized it, but what could he do? They had to get the rabies shots, so they continued to go back. Both Max and Jay got itchy red welts on their stomachs, which didn't completely heal until years later.

When the monkey's test results came back, they learned that it did not have rabies. But Max and Jay had one of their first "Wild West Brazil" experiences!

~*~

We know so little, can communicate so little, but want God to use us and this spot.
—Dixie, in a letter home

The first year at the camp was rough for the Edwards family, not only because of the house remodeling and the new environment, but also because of the challenge of developing a camping ministry. Max knew that God had called him to Panorama to reach out to youth through camps, and when he arrived, he was excited about the possibilities. However, getting started proved to be more difficult than he expected.

The first camp meeting that took place that year was in the first week of February, right after they returned from language-school graduation. This camp had been planned and organized by another church group. Max's job was to buy supplies, fix things that weren't working, and do other logistical tasks. At the same time, he was shuttling workers back and forth from town every day to work on the remodeling of their house. As it turned out, only five or six campers came to this first camp. In fact, there were more camp counselors than there were campers. Even though Max had not organized this camp, he found this to be discouraging. What had made him think that he could develop a camping program that would attract youth? He ended the week dispirited and exhausted.

The next camp, later in February, was organized by a Presbyterian group. This camp had about 80 to 100 attendees, which was much more encouraging. The camp kept Max hopping, as he tried to keep everything functioning. They had not yet done much remodeling on the camp, and many things were broken or installed incorrectly. However, the attendees seemed to enjoy the camp. The 3Js sang for them and were instant stars.

Finally, Max began to organize a camp of his own. Renewing his optimism, he hoped to fill the camp to capacity; he wanted 70 campers. They advertised mainly in the nearby city of Dracena. The Edwards family visited English classes in high schools to advertise. The 3Js would sing in English, then Max would speak in his broken Portuguese and invite students to the camp. Max talked to the youth about the camp at every opportunity he had and advertised in every way that he knew. He worked hard to overcome the barriers between himself and the local people. People were somewhat leery of the Edwards family, as there were very few Protestants and even fewer foreigners in the area. By visiting English classes and connecting with people, Max did his best to win their hearts and overcome their suspicions. But it was an uphill battle. The whole family prayed and worked as hard as they could in preparation for their first camp.

The camp was planned for the beginning of April—Easter weekend. A few other OMS missionaries and their teenage children came from out of town to help with the leadership of the camp and to participate. The Edwardses thought they needed the dorm rooms near the house for these guests, so they hurried to get into the house before the camp began. They moved in just a day before camp began.

In the end, 37 campers attended. It was not as many as they had hoped for, but it was still a good-sized group. Overall, the camp went well. Missionary Charles Elkjer spoke in the sessions, and the free time was packed with activities such as swimming, boating, horseback riding, and volleyball. Everyone was divided into two teams, and they competed throughout the two days. Max even made all the boys do chin-ups in the morning before breakfast. By the end of the camp, eight of the campers had made decisions to become Christians, and many seemed hungry to learn more. So the Edwardses counted their first camp to be a success. Max had just needed to know that he could do it—and found that he could.

Enthusiastically, they planned an "Echo Day" in May, when the attendees of the April camp could come back for one day of camp activities. Max also started a weekly Bible study in Dracena to follow up with the youth who had accepted Christ at camp. They had learned at the camp that many of the young people in the area didn't even know any *crentes*—people who followed Christ in their daily lives. Max wanted to do everything he could to give them that Christian influence.

Unfortunately, Echo Day was another disappointment—only seven campers came. Again Max was discouraged. What had he done wrong? The April camp had seemed like such a success, but could it really be called a success if no one came back? Was this really what God had called him to do?

And so, for the first months and even years at the camp, things went up and down; sometimes they felt like they were successful, and sometimes they didn't. News spread about the camp, and attendance at the camps gradually increased. They held one in July 1971, one in December, and another the following January.

Max had some difficult learning moments in those early camps. Many of the youth who came were rough and rowdy, and he didn't always know the most culturally appropriate way to respond. Sometimes the language also impeded him. One time some unruly boys were leading the rest of the campers in a water fight late at night. One of the counselors came up to the house and asked Max to come get them to settle down. As Max left, Dixie could hear the noise of the water fight; it sounded like a circus to her. Then she heard Max yell, and all became quiet. Later Max told her, "I told them to stop. They did and looked at me, and then every word of Portuguese I knew left me!"

On another occasion Max had trouble with a certain boy named Davi, a local youth from the town of Panorama. Max had given the young man multiple warnings, but he didn't seem to listen or care. At a loss to know what to do, Max watched him carefully. After supper one evening, campers were taking showers, brushing their teeth, changing their clothes, and getting ready for the evening service. Seeing an opportunity to make mischief, Davi ran into the girls' bathroom with a tube of toothpaste, squirted it over the stalls, and smeared it on the girls who were at the sinks.

Max saw Davi run into the restroom and was waiting when he ran out. As Davi tried to speed by Max, Max grabbed him by the arm and smacked him once on the back. Suddenly the boy stopped and looked at Max in disbelief.

"You hit me!" he said. Max instantly realized that what he had done was culturally inappropriate.

"I … I'm sorry," he said. "I didn't know what else to do."

Several of the girls had followed Davi out of the restroom, and they hit him as well. "You deserve a lot worse!" they said.

However, Davi was quite offended at Max. "I want to go home," he said.

"I can take you back to town tomorrow," Max replied. "Not tonight."

"Then I will walk home!" Davi exclaimed. He huffed to his room, packed his things, and began the five-mile trek to town.

The camp was a small one, and soon everybody knew what had happened. The campers were stunned that Max would apologize in front of everyone, and all agreed that Davi should have accepted the apology and stayed at the camp. So they decided to go after him and bring him back. When they caught up with him, one of the girls rebuked him loudly for ruining the camp. Everyone was talking at once; some tried to calm the girl down, and others tried to convince Davi to stay.

Finally the girl said, "If I were *Tio*[9] Max, I would have hit you 10 times!" She whirled around and walked back toward the camp buildings on her own. The other campers tried a little longer to convince Davi to stay, but to no avail.

---

9   *Tio* (uncle) and *Tia* (aunt) are terms often used by young people to address adults in Brazil.

"He humiliated me," he said. "I can't go back." Davi continued walking toward town, and the rest of the youth returned to camp.

Meanwhile, Max was in the camp office, wondering if this was the end of his camping ministry. He knelt at his chair.

Lord, he prayed, *I don't know what to do. I don't want my failure to follow a cultural norm to hinder the good work that You want to do here. Please help me and give me wisdom.*

When the campers returned, some of them went to see Max in the office. "We think you should go get Davi and bring him back," they said.

Max nodded. "I'll try," he agreed. He got into the jeep and drove slowly down the lane and out onto the road. Among the rest of the campers, a spontaneous prayer meeting broke out in the dining hall over the whole situation.

Max apologized to Davi again and tried to convince him to stay, but he still refused. So Max drove him home. When they got there, Max went in with him and tearfully apologized to his parents. They accepted his apology, but Davi still wouldn't return to camp.

When Max returned to the camp, he got everyone together and formally apologized for what he had done. "I should not have responded in that way," he said. "I will try to do better in the future."

The campers, one after another, expressed their support for *Tio* Max. They felt he had done the right thing. This was a turning point in the camp. Max's readiness to apologize to this rude young man touched their hearts. That evening, campers gave testimonies saying how they were impressed by *Tio* Max's humility. Many accepted Christ as their Savior at that camp.

In the end, Max saw God bring good out of his mistake, and it did not end his camping ministry. However, it was one of several difficult learning experiences for him during those first camps. Davi returned to later camps and eventually became a Christian as well. But in those early camps, when attendance was up and down, the facilities were still subpar, and language and cultural mistakes were abundant, it was difficult to see the long-term benefits. The Edwardses clung to their faith. Some days, they felt like they had little else, but they knew that it was enough.

~ * ~

Excerpts from tonight's prayers. Jeff: "And dear Lord, help
Mother's baby to come out all right." Jay: "Help us through
these next few weeks as everything is all scrunched up
with the baby coming, youth camp, and Grandma and
Pa coming." So, I think if we can get "unscrunched" and
the baby comes "out all right," that all will be well here!
—Dixie, in a letter home, July 1971

By June and July 1971, things were getting a little easier for the Edwards family. They had settled into their home and felt more comfortable at the camp. They scheduled a camp for the end of July, and the local youth seemed interested in it. In June, Jay and Jan went to Londrina to have their school progress evaluated by the teacher who was working with the missionary kids (MKs) there. She told them that they were doing well and could take the month of July off. For the kids, this was very exciting news—they hadn't had a real summer vacation since 1969.

Even more exciting was the fact that there was a baby on the way. The family prayed for a girl and planned to name her Joy Anna. Their doctor in Dracena told them to expect "her" at the end of July or the beginning of August. Dixie was hoping for August 3, her birthday. Dixie and Jan enjoyed planning and collecting little girl baby things. Some of their friends and supporters in the U.S. were incredulous that Dixie was going to have a baby out in Middle-of-Nowhere, Brazil, but the Edwardses weren't worried. Dixie said, "I'm depending on the same God I had for the other three." Having a baby on the way gave her something wonderful to look forward to.

The time for the July camp came, and they were pleased to find that they had 60 campers. Everything was going smoothly. A couple of days into the camp, on Saturday morning, Dixie felt a familiar tightness in her belly. *Is that what I think it is?* she wondered. *During the one week-end when there isn't time for a hospital trip.* As the minutes and hours ticked by, the contractions came closer together and grew more painful. Finally, Dixie sent Jeff to go find Max.

By the middle of the afternoon, Max was helping Dixie out to the car. When the counselors and campers saw her leaving, they all hurried to come and see her off.

"Goodbye," they said. "Good luck in your delivery!" One by one, they came forward to kiss her on the cheek. Dixie smiled and thanked them, trying not to show her discomfort. Greetings were very important in Brazilian culture, and she wanted to be polite. *But oh,* she thought, *I wish I were at the hospital already!*

After the goodbyes, Max and Dixie headed to the hospital in the nearby city of Dracena. After several hours and an emergency cesarean section, Max and Dixie welcomed another son into the world. Though the family was expecting a girl, they all fell in love with little Joe Russel the moment they saw him. He was named after his two grandfathers, Joe Brumfield and Russel Edwards. Jan came to stay at the hospital with Joe and her mother and cared for them until they were able to come home. Dixie was very sore from the operation but so thankful to have a healthy fourth J to care for.

Despite the disruption, the camp went well. Of the 60 campers, 26 accepted Christ as their Savior while they were there. The counselors visited Dixie at the hospital and teased her for not following the schedule; she was supposed to wait until after the camp to have her baby.

After Joe was born, many neighbors and friends came to the Edwards' home to bring gifts. On one occasion, a neighbor brought Dixie a live chicken. She had its feet tied together and was carrying it upside down.

"Thank you so much," Dixie said to the woman. "Won't you come in?"

Jay, who was nearby, watched as they came inside and the woman laid the chicken on the living room rug.

Wow, thought Jay. *I'm barely allowed to walk on that new rug, and Mother just let that lady put a chicken on it!* The chicken lay there while the ladies talked, occasionally flapping its wings on the rug. Soon the neighbor got up to leave, and Dixie saw her to the door. After the woman had left, she turned around and saw Jay.

"Jay," she said, "please take that chicken outside."

Jay obeyed, thinking to himself, *I guess even though Mother wants to keep the rug clean, it was more important to her to be kind to our neighbor.* He never forgot that experience.

After having a baby in Panorama, Dixie sensed that it was easier to connect with the local Brazilian mothers than it had been before; she was one of them now. As she had children from the ages of almost 14 all the way down to newborn, she was able to relate to the different mothers and families that she encountered. The Edwards family had the opportunity to demonstrate to the people they encountered, both inside and outside of the church, what a loving Christian family looked like. Everyone could see the love that Max and Dixie gave their children, and they noticed how well-behaved, friendly, and God-fearing the children were. People were always impressed with their family, and Max and Dixie had multiple opportunities to share with others about godly parenting.

~ * ~

That August, Dixie's parents, Joe and Pauline Brumfield, and two of Dixie's nephews, Tim and Scott Terrell, came to visit them. A little later, in November, Max's parents, Russel and Maud Edwards, visited. These times were great blessings to the Edwardses as they were able to show some of their family members their new home in Brazil. At a time when their only regular communication with relatives was through written letters, it was wonderful to see and talk to them in person. It was also good for both sets of parents to see Brazil, so they could better understand Max's decision to move his family there for God's work. After visiting, they felt more at peace about their children's situation.

There were times during that first year when Max and Dixie felt great exhaustion and depression. As Dixie looked at the chaotic state of their home, the children's education, the camp, and their ministry, she wondered, *Lord, Lord, what have we done with our lives and our family?* Even after they moved into the house, it seemed like the problems were never ending; the roof was full of leaks, the toilet didn't work, and everything Dixie tried to plant outside was eaten by insects. They were short on funds, and the language still felt difficult. Mail delivery was inconsistent, and they struggled with homesickness, especially when letters didn't come for weeks at a time. Yet they could also see great needs and opportunities for ministry. Many of the youth who came to the camps knew so little about God and were hungry to learn. One of the teenage boys Max worked with told him, "You are the only person I've ever known who made me want to read the Bible." He gave him an orchid plant in thanks. When he looked at the flower, Max felt encouraged. It reminded him why he was there.

Chapter 10

Protection and Provision

"Have I not commanded you? Be strong and courageous.
Do not be afraid; do not be discouraged, for the LORD
your God will be with you wherever you go."
Joshua 1:9 (NIV)

*M*ax ran his finger along the page and tried to remember what he had been saying. In his right hand, he held the stuffed owl he was using as a sermon illustration, while managing his notes on the pulpit with his left hand. He looked up at the sea of faces that filled their small church. The group was a mixture of people from the town and those from the country, both young and old. Sometimes the tension between different groups was so strong he could almost feel it. However, in this moment, all were listening to him intently. Many smiled encouragingly, and Max smiled back. He loved these people; he wanted to serve them, to help them grow, and to teach them. He prayed every day for the wisdom and strength to be a good pastor. But right now, he just wanted to remember the Portuguese word for "wise."

"It's like …" He struggled to describe his thoughts. Suddenly, members of the congregation began calling out words. Soon he heard the right one.

"Yes!" he said, pointing at the young man who had suggested it. "*Sábio.* Wise." He went on with his sermon.

The church members would soon make this a regular habit, suggesting words to help their pastor get through his Portuguese sermon. Due to some necessary personnel changes in the ministries in the Panorama area, Max became pastor of their little town church in April, 1972. He would continue in this role until he and his family left for furlough in 1973. Sometimes Max became disheartened with the lack of love and tolerance that he saw in the church; however, as the pastor, he was now in a better position to make some changes.

Max's primary response was to spend time investing in relationships. He visited people in their homes, received people at the camp, and brought youth members with him to various ministry activities. Dixie did the same, investing most of her time with the women and children. Dixie and Jan started a Bible club for teenage girls called Girls Alive (*Moças Vivas*). Max held various Bible studies and meetings at different times with youth in the church. He came to be well respected, and the teenage boys frequently came to him for counsel.

In addition to local ministry, they continued to work on developing their camping program as well as the camp's facilities. They hosted more work crews from the U.S. who came to help with the remodeling.

Max was also put in charge of OMS' church-planting ministry in their area (named Every Creature Crusade at the time, now called Every Community for Christ [ECC]). They would set up a tent in a town and hold revival meetings. If enough people in an area became Christians, they could start a church there. Young Brazilian pastors were the workers in this program; they led the services and lived near the tent while it was up. Max supervised them and oversaw the budget. These Brazilian pastors found Max to be quite different from their preconceived ideas about Americans. On one occasion, when Max was helping them set up a new location in Dracena, they approached him with a request.

"Please hire someone to dig a hole for our latrine," they said.

Max frowned. ECC was short on money, and this seemed like an unnecessary expense.

"You can dig it yourselves," he responded.

The young men were shocked. "No, we can't!" they exclaimed.

"Okay then," Max shrugged. "I'll do it."

The men just looked at him. Surely the American had the money to hire a digger?

"You decide where you want it," he said, "and I'll be back tomorrow."

True to his word, before their amazed faces, Max came back the next day with a shovel and dug a hole for their toilet. They never expected to see such a sight.

Over time, they saw growth in their ministry. A new church was planted in Dracena through the ECC ministry. Later, the tent moved across the river to a town called Brasilândia, and a new church was planted there. The Panorama church grew as well, and more of its youth showed interest in serving Christ. In June 1972, Dixie wrote in a letter home: "After two years of toil, tears, and frustration with the language, we're beginning to know the satisfaction of being used of God ... we're feeling accepted by the people and are quite burdened for the church—this thrills us! For this, we came here!"

One thing they encountered in Panorama that was new to them was visible spiritual warfare. They learned that in Brazil, spiritism—the practice of spirit-worship and witchcraft—was common, even among people who claimed to be Catholic. When people left spiritism and became Christians, they often found it difficult to disentangle themselves from their past satanic connections. In the Panorama church, people would often come forward for prayer for healing or for release from demon possession. The Edwardses saw many strange things, and sometimes they weren't sure what to make of it all.

Sometimes Jay wondered how much of what he heard was really "real." *Do demons really do these kinds of things?* he wondered. *Or are the people just faking or deceiving themselves?*

One day as Jay sat in church, a woman stood up and marched to the center aisle. She started talking loudly and barking. Thirteen-year-old Jay's eyes widened as he watched her. The barking sounded like that of a big dog. He had never heard a human make that kind of noise. He was sitting in an aisle seat, and the woman was so close he could almost touch her. Several of the church elders jumped up and hurried into the aisle to pray for her.

As the elders' voices rose in prayer, the woman collapsed right next to Jay. She closed her mouth, but the barking continued, coming right out of her chest. It was one of the most horrible things he had ever heard. Jay squeezed his eyes closed and prayed silently.

Oh Lord, he prayed, *never again will I doubt that demons do this kind of a thing, because it's happening right here, and I'm seeing it. There is no way that she could produce that on her own. Please free her from this evil spirit, Jesus, and send it out of this place.*

After what seemed like forever, the barking stopped. Jay opened his eyes. The woman had relaxed, and the elders were helping her up. Suddenly, he felt the evil presence leave, like the room felt lighter. Jay breathed a sigh of relief. He never forgot that experience.

Though the whole family would see these things in church, Max and Dixie did their best to protect their children from spiritual warfare, and they were careful never to sensationalize it for them. Common sense told Max that he should never go looking for those kinds of things but just deal with what came to him. He had little experience in handling such things, so when the situations arose, he had to rely on his instincts, his knowledge of the Bible, and the guidance of the Holy Spirit to know what to do.

Sometimes, the Edwards family had the privilege of witnessing miracles too. On one occasion, not long after they arrived in Panorama, Max was called to the home of an elderly woman who had recently accepted Christ. The woman was experiencing severe back pain, and she wanted Max to pray for her. Later, he told Dixie about his experience.

"I prayed for her," he said, "then she just stood up and said, 'The pain is gone,' and she reached down and touched her toes!"

"Amazing!" exclaimed Dixie. "Although, I guess we shouldn't be surprised. We know that God can do anything."

Max shook his head as if he still couldn't believe it. "That wasn't my faith; that was her faith that healed her. She just released it with that prayer."

The Edwardses also experienced God's protection on many occasions. Panorama was sometimes a scary place to be, out in the country with no other Americans and very few Brazilians nearby, far away from town without even a telephone if they needed help. When Max was away on ministry in the car, Dixie and the children were left without transportation, except for the horse and their bikes. But they knew that they were where they were supposed to be, and the Lord protected them.

On one occasion in August 1972, they were driving home from Dracena after attending an evening service at the new church there.

Before they left, the pastor of the church had prayed for their safety going home. It was dark, and there were no other cars on the road nearby. Max, Jeff, and Jay were sitting in the front, and Dixie and Jan were in the back with baby Joey sleeping on the seat between them. They were tired from the long day, and all was quiet.

CRASH!

The front passenger window shattered, spraying Jay and Jeff with glass. Dixie dove sideways over the baby, and as she did, she felt something graze her hair.

"Something just whizzed past my head!" she exclaimed. Max slowed the car down.

"Daddy, stop! Stop!" Dixie said.

"No, don't stop, Daddy! Don't stop! Keep going!" Jay yelled. He wasn't entirely sure why, but he felt it would be dangerous to stop there on that deserted road. Max continued to slow down.

"Is everybody all right?" he asked.

"Yes," they all responded. So, Max sped up again and they kept going. As they drove home, they discussed what might have happened.

"I've heard reports of holdups on that road," Dixie said quietly.

"Maybe someone threw a rock at our car hoping that we would stop," said Jay.

"If so, they were probably aiming for the windshield," Max said grimly. "We are fortunate that they missed."

They drove the rest of the way home without incident and soon were unloading the car. Jay opened the trunk door to get his guitar out of the back. There, sitting in front of his guitar, was a large rock—maybe half the size of his fist.

"Daddy, look at this!" he said.

Max took the rock and showed it to the rest of the family.

"Does anyone remember if this rock was here before?" he asked.

They all knew that it wasn't. The rock had evidently smashed the front side window and flown diagonally across the back, barely missing Jay on the side and Dixie by her head. It then flew into the rear and hit the tailgate on the inside, making a dent, which they found later. The Edwards family was amazed at God's protection. The rock could have seriously injured Dixie if it had been just an inch closer. If anyone had gotten hurt, or if the rock had hit the windshield, Max would have stopped the car, and then who knows what would have happened?

When they went inside, Dixie went immediately to her room to find her Bible. She opened to Psalm 91 and brought it out to the living room where the family was.

"Let's read God's Word together," she said. "Thou shalt not be afraid for the terror by night; … For he shall give his angels charge over thee, to keep thee in all thy ways" (Psalm 91:5, 11 KJV).

"God protected us tonight," she said. They gathered in a circle, held hands, and thanked the Lord for his care.

~ * ~

February 1972

Dixie pulled the car into their driveway and got out. She looked around. *Jay's gone,* she thought. She knew he would be gone when she returned. She had said goodbye to him before she left to take a group to the train station, but with all the people and chaos and hurry, she hadn't really had time to focus on sending him off. The week had been a busy one with many people coming and going. They often had busy weeks, but this was the first time one of her children was the one leaving. Sadly, she knew it wouldn't be the last time.

This was the time she had feared and dreaded ever since Max felt the call to be a missionary—the moment she had to send her children away to school. She knew this was what was best for Jay; studying alone at home just wasn't working for him. He needed a classroom, classmates, and a teacher who could give him more time and attention. So Jay was going to a boarding school for missionary kids in the city of Maringá. It was the best option for him, but knowing that didn't take away the ache in Dixie's heart. She just prayed that God would take care of her son when she couldn't.

And God did take care of Jay at boarding school. He was so glad to be with other kids rather than in his room with only his books and his kerosene lamp to keep him company. The school was small and tight-knit. Jay was the youngest boy, and he thought the other guys were so much fun. They had some great times together, and Jay was able to do better in school.

Jan also wanted to be in a classroom, but she was not ready to study away from home. She and her parents discussed options and decided that she would try attending the local Brazilian school. Just a month after Jay left for boarding school, Jan began her adventure at the local Panorama school. Overall, she enjoyed it. Jan liked studying and interacting with other kids her age.

However, Jan's school year was interrupted when, at the beginning of September, she became very ill. It appeared to be some kind of virus with stomach problems and a fever. She was so sick that when Max and Dixie took her to the doctor, he told them that she needed to stay in the hospital to receive fluids through an IV. So they took her to the hospital in Dracena, 45 minutes away from Panorama Camp.

Jan had to stay in the hospital for three days to replenish her fluids. She was put in a room with another 12-year-old girl, who didn't seem to be sick at all! The girl was full of energy, jumping on her bed and bounding around the room.

At one point, the girl looked at Jan's IV and said, "I can make this go much faster!" With that, she bounced over to Jan's bed, reached up, and opened the clamp at the top of the IV. Jan, barely able to move, could feel the fluid throbbing into her arm.

"Please close it!" she begged weakly. Finally the girl agreed. This was just one of several interesting hospital experiences for Jan. The nurses at the hospital rarely checked on patients, and when they did come in, they always brought Jan tea and dry bread. Jan didn't like the tea, and her bed was near a window that was always open. So when the nurses left, she would lean out the window, check to see that there was no one below, and pour the tea out. The nurses were none the wiser. They assumed she was drinking all her tea, so they kept bringing her more. Needless to say, the hospital was not a very pleasant experience for Jan!

When Jan returned home from the hospital, she was feeling better; however, a few days later, she became ill again. She lost a significant amount of weight. Eventually, her skin and even her eyeballs turned completely yellow. At the time, Max was out of town, and Dixie had no car or telephone to be able to get her to a doctor. When Max returned, he knew as soon as he saw Jan that she was a sick girl. They took her to the doctor again, who this time immediately diagnosed her with hepatitis. He told her not to eat any fat and ordered bed rest for four to six weeks. They never knew if she had hepatitis from the beginning, or if she acquired it in the hospital.

Following the doctor's orders was difficult for Jan, especially after she felt better and had more energy. She spent a lot of time listening to music and was able to do some embroidery, crochet, and other handwork. Eventually, Max and Dixie decided that she had missed too much school to be able to go back to Brazilian school that year. So they dusted off Jay's old seventh-grade textbooks, and Jan spent her time reading. Though she had enjoyed Brazilian school, she became anxious to get back to an American education system and to study with her MK friends. They sent in an application for Jan to join Jay in boarding school.

By the end of October, the doctor declared Jan well, and she left for Maringá. The goodbyes were hard for all of the family, but at this point, it was the best option for Jan, just as it was for Jay. Like Jay, Jan enjoyed the school immensely, though it was difficult to be away from home. All the students lived in one house with the boys upstairs and the girls downstairs. During certain hours, Jan could go up to Jay's room, and they practiced music together. They appreciated getting to be with other MKs and learning in a classroom.

Throughout this time, Dixie continued to teach Jeff at home. This system worked well for him, as he was still too young to study away from home. His schedule was flexible, and Jeff and Dixie could still engage in their other activities. Jeff enjoyed playing with the caretaker's children and helping his daddy in ministry and camp work. He loved being out in the country. He would ride all over on his red bike, imagining it was a horse, a motorcycle, or a car. He also spent many hours playing with his slingshot and his pellet gun. Panorama was a wonderful place for an eight-year-old boy.

Jeff's grandma had given him a pair of black flippers for swimming. He loved using these flippers to swim in the Paraná River because he could swim fast with them. One day, when he was out swimming with Max and Jay, he kicked a little too hard, and one of his flippers came off.

"Daddy! My flipper came off! Help me find it!" Jeff exclaimed. In the murky, reddish-brown water of the river, he couldn't see where it had gone. Max and Jay both helped him look for it, but to no avail. Saddened, Jeff walked back up to the house with his one remaining flipper. Dixie, who was near the house, saw him approaching.

"What's the matter, Jeffie?" she asked.

"I lost my flipper," Jeff told her.

Dixie put aside what she was doing and walked over to Jeff. "Jeffie," she said, "let's pray, and maybe God will help us find your black flipper." So, together, they bowed their heads and prayed that the flipper would be found.

The next time he went swimming, Jeff thought, *Maybe we'll find my black flipper.*

But they didn't find it. Nor did they find it the next time, or the time after that. Eventually, Jeff stopped thinking about his flipper. He left his other one in the house and swam without them. Then one day, when they were out swimming again, Max stepped on something that felt funny.

"Jay!" he called. "Come feel down where my foot is." Jay swam down and pulled out the object stuck in the mud. It was Jeff's flipper!

"Yay!" Jeff exclaimed.

As he was headed back up to the house, Dixie saw him with flipper in hand.

"Jeffie, is that your lost flipper?" she asked.

"Yes!" Jeff said. "We found it!"

"That's wonderful! Let's pray and thank God for helping you find your flipper." So once again, they bowed their heads and thanked God for His help.

And so, with daily exciting adventures and following the example of his parents, Jeff continued to grow in faith and maturity. In May 1972, he was baptized by his daddy in the river, along with several other people in their church.

Joey, the newest addition to the Edwards clan, was a joy to the family as he grew and developed through his baby stages. The Brazilians all loved him too; everyone wanted to hold him and play with him. He was an energetic, active baby, getting into everything he could reach, and he had a strong personality to match. He kept Max and Dixie on their toes.

Whenever Jay and Jan were home on breaks, The 3Js were a popular attraction, singing at camps and other special events. They had developed a repertoire in both languages. In early 1972, they decided to make a record of their singing to sell to supporters and fans in both the U.S. and Brazil. So in May of that year they recorded their singing in missionary Mike Murphy's studio in Londrina. They sent the tape back to Dixie's parents in the U.S., and by the end of the year, The 3Js had a record!

Jay and Jan participated in their parents' ministry as much as they could; Jeff also became more involved as he got older. They were all an immense support to their parents, not only with their singing but also in building relationships, participating in physical work, and setting an example for others.

Max was often away from home, especially in the evenings, for services and other ministry activities. However, when he was home, he did his best to prioritize time with his family. Sometimes when it was raining or the car broke down, they were stuck at home and enjoyed their time together by playing Rook, dominoes, chess, or even Twister. If it was a Sunday evening, they would hold a family church service at home. Whether Max was home or not, Dixie continued to have devotions with the kids every night, and together they prayed over every challenge that came their way.

~ * ~

For the Edwards family, life in Panorama meant new adventures every day. One day in March 1972, the caretaker, Sr. Antonio, asked Max and Dixie if they had noticed that the water was tasting funny. They had noticed, so Max decided to go up to the water box and take a look. When he opened the manhole, he found the source of the problem—a decomposing snake. This was the water that they drank and used for all their other needs. They were horrified but thankful that no one had become seriously ill. The water was also full of little frogs, which Jay and Jeff enjoyed catching. Max drained the water, cleaned the water box, and filled it up again. All in a day's work at Panorama Camp.

Max labored constantly to improve the campground. There was always something new to build and many things that needed to be fixed. Even after the Edwards family moved into the house, they still had problems, especially with the roof when there was a lot of rain and wind. As Dixie wrote in a letter home, the roof and ceilings were leaking "like sieves," so the roof had to be replaced. The electricity would frequently go off, often needing repairs after storms. They still battled with "critters"—insects, rats, and bats. Throughout the camp, they did extensive painting and some remodeling; they also built a shuffleboard and a basketball court. Many of these improvements were made by MFM work crews, who would come for a week or two to help. The rest was done by local workers, the caretaker, and Max himself. The place finally started looking nice and feeling pleasant.

Besides the work crews, the Edwardses occasionally hosted evangelistic teams from the U.S. and other missionaries and workers. Sometimes the camp was very quiet, but when they had guests, there was always plenty to do. Dixie learned to cook and wash for large groups, and Max coordinated activities and escorted guests as they traveled around Brazil. They also hosted Brazilians at the camp on many occasions. It took Dixie some time to get used to some aspects of Brazilian culture. Their Brazilian guests usually brought extra people with them. Dixie learned to make big meals and be flexible.

As Max worked at the camp and in ministry, he continually practiced his Portuguese. His vocabulary grew in three directions: as he studied the Bible and prepared sermons, he learned Christian vocabulary; because he was a farmer and was doing some minor farming at the camp, he learned farming terms; and as he worked to build the camp, he learned vocabulary for materials and construction. When he first went to the store for materials, he would go behind the counter and pick out what he wanted. Then the workers there would tell him the Portuguese word. They always looked forward to Max's visits because they liked to teach him. Eventually he learned the words for the things he needed.

The Edwardses also worked toward expanding their camping program; they tried to hold camps during the times when youth would be on vacation from school. The camps were still small, but those who came enjoyed it and often returned. Many seeds were planted in hearts, and several accepted Christ each time. It was a rewarding ministry; however, Max couldn't help but wonder if it was God's will for him to run these camps by himself. To really reach Brazilian youth, he felt it would be better to have a Brazilian director of the camping program. He prayed that God would provide someone to fill this need.

In addition to the Edwards' camps, other church groups used the facilities for their camps. One of these church groups was the Brazilian branch of the Japanese Holiness Church, which began to hold their annual youth convention at Panorama Camp. On one such occasion, the director of the programming for this convention was a young seminary student named Mitsuo. Max came to know Mitsuo throughout the course of the camp and was very impressed with his work.

One day he invited Mitsuo to go with him to purchase camp supplies. At one point while they were out, Max parked the truck and shared about some of the battles he was having. He told Mitsuo how he had been questioning, before God, if he should really be the camp director. Max explained that he didn't know if directing the camp was God's continued plan for him and for his family. Max asked Mitsuo if he would consider being the director of programming for Panorama Camp, and Max would stay on as the vice director.

Mitsuo was surprised and humbled by this offer. He later commented, "This gesture of confidence in me and of humility on his part surprises me to this day. A man of his experience and status and with all the decision-making power relegated to him by the mission, and yet, he offered to place me over himself in the camp directorship. This gesture on his part decisively contributed to my formation and preparation for future ministries. Because of this opportunity to work with Uncle Max, I was able to go on and help train other camp leaders and several who would go on to become pastors."

Mitsuo began leading the camp programming in 1973, and in 1975, after he graduated from seminary, he became the camp's official director with Max as vice director. He continued in this position until 1982, after the Edwardses left Panorama. He, along with his wife, Sizue, later launched new camping ministries in other parts of the country.

As they neared the end of their first missionary term, the Edwardses could see how God was working in and through their lives. The decisions that Max had made in response to God's call—leaving the farm, going to Brazil, moving to Panorama—that had seemed so senseless at the time, started to make sense. And Max knew God had much more in store.

The Monsters Come Out at Night
By Jeff Edwards

My childhood years were at Panorama Camp, the best place ever to grow up for a little boy with a slingshot, hunting knife, pellet gun, and boxer dogs. I also had a great imagination, which worked well with these. Sometimes my little red Schwinn bike was a galloping stallion, sometimes a flashy, fast motorcycle, and sometimes just a simple red bicycle. My parents let me roam the forested, river-bordered camp-grounds, and I had a blast hunting, exploring, and scaring all sorts of critters with my wild shooting.

My best friends were sons of Mr. Antonio and Mrs. Maria, who helped us care for the grounds at the camp. They had 10 children, but the 3 sons closest to my age were Nenê, Daví, and Bebete. I'd play with them any time I could, once I finished my homeschooling. I was a common commodity at their simple house (three small rooms, a small kitchen, and a small living room for 10 kids).

Since the camp was so big, my parents invented a simple but effective way to call me home from whatever far corner of the camp I happened to be in at the time. They used my dad's old military police whistle. They'd step outside our house, give it a long, shrill rap, and then wait for my hollered response: "Coooooommmminnnnngggggg!" That seemed to work. Whether I was down close to the Paraná River, by the creek bed fishing, or at the caretaker's house, the whistle reached my ears, and my lungs were healthy enough to echo back a response.

One night, I was playing with Nenê, Daví, and Bebete at their house. It was about 150 meters from our house. I heard the whistle; it was time to go home. I duly answered with my strong vocal cords. I usually didn't play at their house at night, and I think I now know why. I started out, headed down the long, dirt lane that connected one house to the other.

At first, it was no big deal. Their house was lit with a few simple light bulbs. However, 50 meters into the walk home, the darkness enveloped me. I was too far from their home to be splashed by light, and the light from my home was still 100 meters down the lane and very, very faint—just a glimmer at best. My imagination kicked in big-time. I walked faster, outpacing the anacondas and alligators that were creeping up on me. Then I jogged. There were also bears and tigers. Before I knew it, I was in an all-out, do-or-die race for my life. Running as fast as my eight-year-old legs would carry me, I sprinted for all I was worth. Then it became even more precarious. There were all sorts of other creatures with gleaming eyes, dripping fangs, and sinister intentions, nipping at the heels of my worn-out canvas tennis shoes. I rounded the house at a frantic sprint, heart exploding in my little chest. I had to reach the screen door and leap into the protective safety of my home. As I rounded the last corner, just two meters from safety, there he was— the monster with outstretched claws ready to grab me. My forward momentum hurled me directly into its belly and into the grasp of its powerful arms. It seized me and lifted me up. I screamed, and I knew I was about to meet my Maker.

For a split second, utter terror overcame me. Then utter calm came as I burst into tears of fear and relief all at the same time. The "monster" was my dad, standing there right in front of the back screen door to surprise me with a big bear hug as I came home. He was so sorry to have scared me. I was so relieved to be safe in his arms. He carried me outside in the still night for a few minutes as I settled down, choked back my tears, and blurted out my near-death experience. It was so good to be in his strong, safe arms.

There are times when we are scared. Sometimes this fear comes because we let our thoughts take us to worst-case scenarios. We play the "what if" game, and it never ends well. Sometimes it's because life is hard; tragedies happen, our world is broken, and we experience the brokenness in real life—and it is scary. We must always remember that God is there, waiting for us with outstretched arms to console us, hold us, comfort us, allow us to cry on His shoulder, and tell us He's sorry for our pain. Regardless of our pain, imagined or real, He is and will always be there for us with outstretched arms. We are never alone in the darkness if God is our dad. We only need to run to Him.

My Brazilian School Experiences
By Jan Edwards Dormer

My education was unconventional to say the least. I began school in rural Indiana and graduated high school in a class of one in Londrina, Brazil, through a correspondence course. What transpired in between was 12 different schools and many types of schooling: from American public school to national Brazilian Christian and public schools to boarding school to Christian international school and finally to distance education. Such a school life could only have been orchestrated by God to provide me with experiences both great and challenging, which would equip me for the educational roles God has placed me in today.

My school life, as that of my brothers, is documented throughout this book. But my Brazilian school experiences stand out to me as life-directing moments, and it is those that I want to share here.

While my parents were in language school in Campinas, the decision was made to place Jay and me in a private Christian Brazilian school so we could learn Portuguese. Back in 1970, people generally believed that children just "soak up" language, and the prevailing thought in missions was to immerse kids in the local school where they would learn the language quickly. I'm sure I embraced this decision. I had been excited about going to Brazil and was eager to learn Portuguese.

Then came the first day of school. I remember it well. Arriving at the school, I stood in the courtyard in my cute little navy skirt, white blouse, and red belt, which I had proudly donned that morning for this momentous occasion … and was engulfed by fear. For the first time, I could understand nothing around me. I had been hearing Portuguese since our arrival, but now I was all alone, hearing no English at all. Some girls yelled something at me, but I didn't know if they were asking me to join them or telling me to get lost. I knew that Jay was somewhere, but I didn't know where. Our recess times were different, and I never saw him.

The classroom was even worse than the courtyard. The teacher yelled, and I thought she was yelling at me. (I discovered later that this was simply a typical teaching style in Brazilian schools, and it was not directed at me.) The teacher must not have known any English because she never spoke a word of English to me. I had been a good student in

American school, and I loved to learn. But here, I saw strange words on the board and on worksheets. Even the handwriting was different, and I struggled to decipher some of the letters. I didn't know what to do. I tried to copy some of the words into my notebook, but didn't know what I was writing down. Another American missionary kid, a boy, joined my class at some point. But the teacher didn't want us to speak in English to each other. Plus, he got in trouble a lot, and that's the last thing I wanted to do!

I cried many nights. For a while, my parents didn't know how hard it was on me. And my teacher never knew. I'm sure she thought I was learning and was fine. But I wasn't fine, and thanks to parents who cared more about their little girl than about what was considered the best thing to do to help children learn the language, they soon took us out of that school. There was nothing wrong with the school or the teachers; it's just not possible to grow and learn as a fourth grader should when you have no means of communication.

We found a Brazilian tutor to help us kids learn Portuguese at home. And I made a happy discovery: I loved learning Portuguese! Now things made sense. The teacher would draw pictures and write the corresponding words. We practiced simple phrases: *Bom dia! Tudo bem? Tudo bem!* I felt successful in Portuguese for the first time since arriving in Brazil.

Then came our move to Panorama and the quandary of what our education would look like there. We tried homeschooling and going back and forth to Londrina for a while. Eventually, though, my parents looked at the local Panorama public school as perhaps being the best solution for me, now in fifth grade. I was anxious to try Brazilian school again. This time I had a friend to go with—Clarice, the caretaker's daughter who was my age. But more importantly, I now felt quite confident in Portuguese.

The poor, public school in Panorama was very different from the private Christian school in Campinas. Our "school bus" was a dump truck. Apparently, this was the only vehicle the town could find to pick up the country kids and take us into town for school. Girls had to wear skirts, but we had to step up on the high tires of the dump truck to get in. After a while, I learned that the boys weren't letting the girls go first out of chivalry.

The dump truck couldn't be spared to take us home after school though. So Clarice and I walked the five miles home. We sometimes were able to catch rides on horse carts or tractors. But other days we played a rock-throwing and skipping game all the way home to pass the time. The time I spent with Clarice during our school days is one of my cherished memories from Panorama.

Our classroom was a far cry from modern classrooms. There were about 40 kids, and we sat two to a bench at rough wooden tables on which decades of students before us had made their marks. There was nothing on the walls and nothing but a rough chalkboard in the front of the room. Students didn't have textbooks or worksheets. We had notebooks for each subject, and school consisted of the teachers coming in with the textbook of a subject, writing the text on the board, and us copying it into our notebooks. There was no real "teaching" that I can recall. However, I did well in copying and memorizing for tests, so I made good grades. And I did learn some things. To this day, I can sing all the stanzas of the Brazilian national anthem, and I can still see in my mind's eye my beautiful colored maps drawn into my geography notebook.

Unfortunately, after a few months in that school, I developed joint pain that was eventually diagnosed as juvenile rheumatoid arthritis. In addition, I came down with hepatitis and had to be out of school for six weeks. By the time I recovered enough to resume school, I had missed too much to return to Brazilian school, so I went to be with Jay in boarding school.

My two Brazilian school experiences no doubt helped to lead me into the profession that I love today. I regularly train teachers in meeting the needs of English learners in schools. Every time I speak with teachers, I remember being that frightened fourth-grade girl who just needed a chance to learn some Portuguese before being immersed in Brazilian school. I also tell about being in a poor school that had nothing, but being able to actually learn something and enjoy it in that environment because I had the crucial piece for learning: language.

As I look back on my educational life, I see God's hand at work. He never let me go and has used all the twists and turns in my educational narrative for His good in preparing others for educational service.

Chapter 11

Two Worlds

LORD, you alone are my portion and my cup; you make
my lot secure. The boundary lines have fallen for me in
pleasant places; surely I have a delightful inheritance. I
will praise the LORD, who counsels me; even at night my
heart instructs me. I keep my eyes always on the LORD.
With him at my right hand, I will not be shaken.
Psalm 16:5–8 (NIV)

Over time, the Edwards family grew familiar with the world of
Panorama and felt at home there. Max and Dixie became acquainted
with all kinds of people—from their rich neighbor to the townspeople
to the poor country folk. They frequently visited people's homes to
encourage them to come to Sunday school and church. Most of the
people they visited were those who lived in the country and worked at
the brick factory. These people were uneducated and usually had small
homes and many children.

On one occasion, when they were visiting a family, the mother told
Dixie, "We can't afford for all of our children to go to junior high and
high school, so the girls stay home." Their girls only went until fourth
grade; then they stayed home to work while the boys continued in school.

Many adults had no schooling and couldn't read or write. Furthermore,
even among those who could read, most had never been taught to read
and study the Bible on their own. So Dixie started a Bible study with

some young mothers and was excited to see their enthusiasm. She also tried to encourage more Bible study in the women's group at church.

Max took every opportunity he could to become involved in the local culture. As "the American," he was invited to many events, and sometimes the people he met invited him to do activities with them. On one occasion, he helped a man butcher a hog; on others, he went fishing in the river. And of course, he always invited the people to church. He also traveled around the area whenever he could and established preaching points along the river. Gradually, the family became established in the area.

Max worked hard to learn the local culture and forge good relationships with people, both in ministry and in business. However, it wasn't always easy, and sometimes there were difficulties in spite of his best efforts.

One time a gardener came to Max looking for work. "I was working for the neighbor," he told Max, "but now I'm done over there, and I'd like to work here." There was plenty of work to be done on the campground, so Max hired him.

When the neighbor found out about this, he came over to the camp to see Max. Furious, he yelled at him for hiring his worker and called him names that Max had never even heard before.

"I didn't know he wasn't done working for you," Max said.

"Of course you did; you just paid him more money," the neighbor retorted. He had his mind made up and wouldn't hear anything Max tried to say. He then went home, still angry.

Max tried several times in the next few days to visit this neighbor, but the man wouldn't receive him. Max was troubled by this broken relationship. One day when he and Jay were out in the truck, they met the neighbor's foreman. They talked a little, and the foreman explained what had happened. The gardener had lied to Max about being finished at the neighbor's; he was just tired of working for a difficult man and quit. But the neighbor would not believe that Max hadn't purposefully hired his worker away from him.

"I'd like to go see him and apologize," Max told the foreman.

"He won't talk to you," the foreman responded.

"Well, I'd still like to go sometime," Max said.

Eventually, Max did go to the neighbor's place to apologize. He and Jay went to the man's property to look for him. They went in, opened the gate, and drove down a lane to the house. The neighbor and his foreman were standing outside, so Max and Jay got out of the truck. Jay took a few steps and stopped, unsure of what he was supposed to do. Max went up to the neighbor to talk to him, but the neighbor responded as he had before, voicing his opinion very loudly. The foreman stood back, clearly uncomfortable. Finally, Max got down on one knee.

"I never intended to wrong you, but since you feel that I did, I want to apologize. I'm sorry."

Max's apology was met with silence. The neighbor simply turned and walked away, leaving Max kneeling alone and the foreman standing uneasily in the background. Max got up, went back to the truck, and left. He had done all that he could do to mend the relationship.

Later the foreman came to Max and told him that he had quit his job. "I'm not working for a man who treats a gentleman like you like that," he said. "You didn't need to do that. That guy doesn't deserve to have anybody bowing down to him."

Max drew comfort in knowing that his behavior was a witness to the people who saw it, even if the neighbor chose not to forgive him. Later, this neighbor did change his attitude toward Max. He visited and initiated a friendship with him.

People were impressed by Max with his friendly, outgoing attitude and continual humility. Gradually, he won the hearts of almost everyone he knew. The Edwards' ministry continued to grow and blossom.

~ * ~

When the Edwardses went to Brazil, the OMS policy was for missionaries to follow a regular schedule of living four years on the field and then spending one year back "home" on furlough. The year of furlough was a time to connect with the people and churches who supported them financially and to raise additional funding, if necessary. In Max's case, he needed to raise quite a bit of additional funding for the camp. OMS had given him the responsibility of raising the money to finish paying for it, and they needed continual funding for their renovations and building at the camp.

The Edwards family had arrived in Brazil at the beginning of 1970, so they expected to return to the U.S. on furlough around Christmas of 1973. However, at their Brazil mission meetings in January 1973, their superiors decided that it would be better for them to leave in June 1973, six months early. This would allow the children to participate in a full school year in the U.S. Furthermore, OMS would then have Brazil missionaries "fresh off the field" for their national convention in June.

The family rushed to get everything in order so they would be ready to leave in June. In addition to the general packing and preparations, Max and Dixie wanted to be sure to leave their ministry in good shape. Therefore, during these months they put extra effort into their work. The people were sorry to see them go. The church was in a better place than it had ever been before, the camp had seen much improvement, and everyone loved Max and the family. They wanted to be sure that the Edwards family would return to Panorama after their furlough. Max and Dixie told them that was the plan. While they were gone, another missionary family, the Scotts, would take over their responsibilities at the camp. Then, they would resume those responsibilities upon their return. Shortly before they left, the young people of the church threw a surprise going-away party for them. The family left encouraged; they knew they were loved and that they were making a difference.

Filled with nervousness and excitement, the family returned to Indiana in June 1973. Reentry into the U.S. and furlough were difficult for the family. They weren't the same people they had been when they left the farm; they had all matured and developed in many ways. Jeff barely remembered living on the farm, and Joey had never been to the U.S. at all. America was a whole different world from their home in rural Brazil.

As is usually the case with missionary furloughs, they spent a considerable amount of time traveling. Over the summer vacation and on weekends, the whole family traveled. They visited many places, mostly small country churches, and ate at many church potlucks. Jan was always amazed at all the good food at the potlucks. On weekdays during the school year, Max traveled alone. He was hardly ever home.

To complicate this scenario, just before Christmas, Max slipped on the ice and broke his kneecap. The doctors fitted him with a heavy foot-to-hip cast, but Max didn't let it slow him down. He continued to drive and kept his speaking engagements. The whole family was very busy and hardly had time to adjust to living in the U.S. Dixie felt like she was floating, just getting through things without really knowing what she was doing.

In each church, they presented slides with pictures from Brazil, shared about their ministry and experiences, and showed curiosities that they brought. Max's story of how God brought him from the farm to Brazil continued to touch hearts everywhere the family went. Most of their supporters came from the rural communities of Indiana, Illinois, and Ohio—people who could relate to Max's background.

Just like before, The 3Js were an instant hit everywhere they went. Churches liked to have the Edwards family visit because they were so unique; singing children were a definite attraction. Jay and Jan sang beautiful harmony, and Jeff sang a strong lead. People were amazed to see so much talent in such young children. They sold copies of their record in every church they visited. When they sang, Jeff would look up and tap his foot to keep time. Two-year-old Joey, who always wanted to do whatever Jeff did, noticed this. On one occasion, Joey was permitted to stand and "sing" with his siblings in front of the church. However, instead of singing, he just energetically stomped his foot. He stole the show. Jay, Jan, and Jeff laughed so hard they couldn't finish their song. Needless to say, Joey didn't join the singing trio again until he was older.

American public school was also a different experience for the Edwards children after several years in Brazil. Jan faced a particularly challenging situation in her eighth-grade English class. One of the books she was supposed to read for class was *Frankenstein.* Because of Jan's experiences in Brazil with spiritual warfare, she felt strongly that she should not read that book. She determined that she would not read it and would take a failing grade in the assignment if she had to. She talked to her teacher, explained her position, and asked for an alternate assignment. Her teacher was an atheist and could not understand why Jan had a problem with the book. She gave Jan a hard time about refusing to read the book, which contributed to Jan having a difficult school year.

However, at the end of the year, the teacher stood up in front of the class and said, "I finally have come to the position where I think this was a brave thing for Jan to do—to refuse to read that book." Though the teacher could not understand Jan's perspective, she came to respect her character. More than 10 years later, Jan ran into that teacher again and found out that she had since become a Christian.

Jan and Jeff both joined the band in their public school and learned to play new instruments. Jan played the clarinet, and Jeff played the trumpet, which he enjoyed for years to come. The children all missed Brazil, but there were some positive aspects of the year as well. They spent time with their grandparents and other friends and family, and Jay enjoyed getting to work on the farm.

Their fundraising efforts were successful. They raised enough money to finish paying off the camp as well as enough for various other needs. The family experienced God's blessings as they visited their supporting churches. The people loved and encouraged them. They went back to Brazil in June 1974, tired but knowing that they had many faithful supporters praying for them as they returned to the field. They were ready to return to the world that they had learned to call home.

Chapter 12

Growth

We can provide the place, but we depend upon God's Holy Spirit to minister to hearts. Our prayer is that His purpose may be realized daily here at the camp.
—Edwards prayer letter, January 1975

*A*s the bus pulled into a rest stop, a familiar, sweet scent wafted through the air. Max and Dixie looked at each other and smiled. Tangerines! Max hurried off the bus to find the fruit stand where they were being sold. In his typical communication style of Portuguese-plus-hand motions, he bought three full bags of the huge, sweet tangerines. Happily, he carried them back to the bus to share with everyone. Brazil had the best fruit!

It was June 1974, and they had just arrived back in Brazil. Everything seemed to be just about the same as when they left. Within a few days, they were back home in Panorama. As they drove up, Dixie thought of how different it was from that day when they had first visited the camp almost four years ago. As they drove down the long lane back to the house, instead of tall, unkempt grass, she saw a beautifully cut lawn and trees laden with fruit dotting the property. They passed the buildings, now nicely maintained and painted, and the cement court. The once-tiny trees they had planted around it had grown and now shaded the court. Max parked the car, and they entered the house. On the inside, it was a little run down. Walls still had cracks, and the roof retained its never-ending problems. But it was livable, and this time, it felt like home.

The Edwards family got right back into their ministry, working on the campground, running a full camping schedule, hosting American groups, and getting involved in their local church and Sunday school. As they pressed on in their ministry over the next few years, they saw their long-term work at the camp grow and bear fruit. At the same time, they encountered many challenges with some of their ministries and within their personal lives as well.

~ * ~

When Max had first visited Panorama Camp in 1970, he had seen what it could be—a beautiful campground with all kinds of facilities that would provide a space that could be used to reach youth, from the little town of Panorama to the large metropolis of São Paulo. Now they were finally seeing those dreams become a reality. Throughout 1974 to 1976, the Edwardses hosted a slew of MFM work crews and other groups from the U.S. Many of these teams came to continue improving the campground. Numerous new construction projects were completed, including a new girls' dormitory, restrooms, a recreation building, and a chapel. They also drilled a new well for the camp's water supply. Some of the American groups completed additional projects, such as painting fence posts, remodeling and doing maintenance on the Edwards' home, and creating a mini-golf course that formed the letters *P-A-N-O-R-A-M-A*.

With all of the groups visiting to work on these projects and participate in ministry, the Edwards family became accustomed to having new "family members" coming and going all of the time. They enjoyed each person that came, and each group shared in whatever adventures they were having at the time. This made for many memories for both the Americans that visited and for the Edwards family.

In July 1975, Brazil had one of the worst winters it had experienced in years—temperatures were below freezing, far lower than usual. Coffee plants froze throughout the countryside, which created a national disaster for Brazil. At Panorama Camp, youth camps were being held during students' winter break. Campers walked around in blankets and huddled around the big fireplace in the dining hall. There was no heat in the buildings, and no one had brought enough blankets. The Edwards home had a fireplace, but they were cold too.

This year, as they did every year during this second term of ministry, the Edwardses hosted a group of American college students who stayed with them and participated in ministry during the American summer months, which was winter in Brazil. They were called NOW (Novice Overseas Worker) Corps groups. One particularly cold evening, Dixie was cooking a big pot of rice and hamburger for their dogs, as was her regular custom (dog food was not available in Panorama). The NOW Corps kids, along with Jay and Jeff, were spending the evening together in the living room by the fireplace. They were playing games, singing songs, and talking.

As Dixie waited for the dog food to cook, she turned around and started talking to Jan, who was on the other side of the room. She leaned back close to the gas stove to absorb a little bit of its heat. All of a sudden, she felt exceptionally warm. She took a few steps away from the stove, and the polyester jacket she was wearing promptly burst into flames. Jan reached for her, but she kept walking. Dixie was scared, but she didn't know what to do. She walked to the doorway of the living room and said rather calmly, "Somebody help me."

As the kids looked at her, they could see flames coming up behind her shoulders. Jay and Scott, one of the college students, ran to her. Jay and Dixie both tried to get her melting jacket off, but it had buttons that were difficult to open. Scott grabbed her, threw her onto the hardwood floor, and smothered the flames. The fall hurt, but Dixie knew it was better than the alternative. She told Scott later, "You saved my life!"

Once Dixie knew she would be okay, the burns began to hurt. Jeff ran to get Max, who took her to the doctor. She had a few second-degree burns and multiple first-degree burns on her back and arm. She realized that it could have been much worse; her hair had just begun to catch fire.

When they returned from the hospital, they found all of the NOW Corps students in their bedroom, crying and praying together. The event had made them all a family. Though her burns hurt, Dixie was thankful for God's protection and for the way He used the experience to touch hearts.

The Edwards family made time for play as well as for work, especially when groups were visiting. When it was warm, the kids especially enjoyed playing in inner tubes and floating in them down the river. One time, when there was a work crew with them, they decided to float down to one of the islands in the river. They would enjoy some time there, and then Max would bring them back to the camp in the motorboat. The kids had done this many times before, and this time they wanted Dixie to come along too.

"It's so easy, Mother!" Jan said. "Anyone can do it!"

"I don't think so," Dixie replied. "You kids know, I can't even swim! I'll come along with Daddy in the motorboat."

"You don't have to be able to swim," they answered. "You just sit in the inner tube and float."

Some of the American crew members smiled and joined in. "We've never done this before either, Dixie. You can't be any worse at it than we are."

At last, Dixie consented. "Okay," she said, "if all I have to do is float, I guess I can do that."

"Hurray!"

They distributed the inner tubes, and Jay gave some brief instructions. "Just make sure you get into the inside current of the river," he said, "and it will take you right to the island. It only takes about half an hour to float down. Don't get over into the water that flows around the outside of the island, 'cause then you'll just float out, away from the island."

So they all got into their inner tubes and headed out. Some of the Americans were with the Edwards kids, and a few were with Dixie. It was a beautiful day for a float; the sun was shining and warm, but the water was pleasantly cool. The big black inner tubes dotted the mile-wide river. The huge blue sky stretched above them. It was a great break for the whole group, who had been laboring on construction all week. They talked and laughed with one another. What an experience, floating down a huge river in Brazil. Dixie smiled and talked with her companions, trying to relax. This was okay. She would be okay. She could do this.

Though the river looked calm and peaceful, the floaters could feel the current pulling them along fast. The two groups—those with the kids and those with Dixie—lost track of each other. Before long, the kids' group arrived at the island. As they approached it, they jumped out of their inner tubes and dragged them up onto the sandy white beach. The Americans with them followed suit.

"How'd you like it?" Jay asked one of the men.

"It was fun!" he responded. Suddenly, they heard one of their companions call from further down the beach.

"What's that?" he exclaimed, pointing. Jay squinted and saw a little group of black dots—inner tubes with people in them!

"That's Dixie," someone else exclaimed. "She missed the island!"

It was true. Dixie and her group were floating by, helpless. Dixie saw the island and everyone waving to them, but she didn't know what to do.

Jan's jaw dropped. She didn't think it was possible to miss the island. Everyone in their group talked excitedly.

"What should we do?"

"Maybe we should go after them?"

"How would that help? Better to send Max after them in the motorboat."

Soon after, Max and the motorboat arrived with their picnic lunch. Quickly they told him what had happened, they unloaded the boat, and he set out again after the group.

Meanwhile, Dixie and her companions were getting nervous. *Surely Max will come after us soon,* Dixie thought. *This whole group counted on me to get them to that inside current, and I didn't!*

They kept floating. Jungle and small rural dwellings slid by on the far-off banks. Dixie didn't know how to get back or even how to get to dry land. The huge river stretched all around them—in front, behind, and on both sides. The island that she "couldn't miss" was getting smaller and smaller behind them. *Oh, Lord,* she prayed silently, *please bring Max to come take us back soon.*

After a while, they saw a speck in the distance. Max! Dixie had never been so glad to see him. He soon caught up with them.

"Now, where do you folks think you're goin'?" Max called good-naturedly. Attaching the inner tubes to the boat, he managed to pull them all to safety. One of the Americans would later recall feeling like there was an angel sitting in the inner tube with them. Boy, were they glad to set their feet on dry land again! That was Dixie's first, and last, attempt at floating to the island.

Even on work days, little Joey learned to find the advantages of having an enlarged family when work crews were there. One time, when he was three, one such work crew was occupied with some of the new buildings. The men were outside laboring, and the women were inside doing housework. Cleaning, cooking, and doing laundry for large groups was a full-time job, and Dixie was always glad when there were women in the groups to help her.

One of Joey's favorite things was to have stories read to him. So on this particularly busy day, he brought a book to his mom.

"Will you read me a story, Mommy?"

"I'm sorry, honey, I'm too busy right now," Dixie responded. Joey tried asking the other women and got similar responses. So he tucked the book under his arm and went outside. Squinting in the sun, he looked around until he found where the men were working. They looked busy too, but Joey had a new idea. He walked up to one of the men and tapped him on the shoulder. The man looked up at Joey and smiled.

"Can you read me just one page of this story?" Joey asked. The man put down his trowel and read one page to Joey. Thanking him, Joey moved on to the next man with the next page. Going one by one, he eventually got his whole story read. The men told the women about it that evening.

"All of a sudden, I looked, and there was Jack, reading to Joey with his trowel laid aside!" Max laughed. Yes, Joey knew how to persist and "work the system" to get what he wanted!

Joey was certainly a handful. Though Max and Dixie knew that he was safe at the camp, they found that they needed to keep an eye on him to make sure he stayed out of mischief. On one occasion, Joey saw his daddy baptizing new Christians down in the river. It was a wonderful, happy occasion. They all sang songs and celebrated the commitment of the new Christians. It was explained to Joey that these people were publicly declaring that they were Christians, and that they would go to heaven.

Soon after, their boxer dog, Ginger, gave birth to three little puppies. Three-year-old Joey loved those puppies so much and wanted to make sure they went to heaven too. So he found Ginger's big water bucket and brought the puppies. He tried to baptize them just like Daddy had baptized the new Christians. They were not very cooperative, but he knew he was just trying to do what was best for them. Joey learned the hard way that day-old puppies are not yet ready for baptism by immersion. Sadly, one of the puppies died. But at least it died a "Christian" puppy!

Max worked tirelessly to improve the campground and add amenities. When they didn't have the tools or supplies to do the maintenance and projects that he wanted to do, he would find a way. He was constantly hunting down equipment, talking to suppliers, and making things himself when the items he wanted couldn't be found. His farmer's ingenuity and easy way with people enabled him to do the work that needed to be done. Abimael, his Brazilian worker, also worked regularly on the camp's facilities. Max was thankful to have found a talented, trustworthy Brazilian to work by his side.

Once the grounds were well maintained, there were fewer snakes, toads, and rats around to bother the camp's occupants. It was really a beautiful and comfortable place, and the Edwards family felt privileged to live and work there. Dixie wrote in a letter home: "The camp is so pretty and well cared for now. You'd hardly know it—it's changed so much."

On spare land at the camp, they grew some of their own food—rice, beans, corn, garlic, lettuce, potatoes, watermelons, bananas, pineapples, and more. Max and Sr. Antonio worked together on these crops with Jay helping anytime he was available. It was very different from farming in Indiana, but it was farming nonetheless. They were able to produce enough to sell some for profit and donate some to other OMS ministries that needed food. They also decided to invest in chickens—fryers to eat and hens to lay eggs. In addition, Sr. Antonio raised hogs. These homegrown foods allowed them to save money on meals for the groups that flowed in and out of the camp. Max was delighted to find that he could put his farming knowledge to good use.

These farming endeavors at the camp led to more new experiences for some of the Americans that visited, especially those who were from cities in the U.S. and had never done farm work. On one occasion, Max and Dixie had the privilege of teaching a group of young adults from the U.S. how to kill and dress chickens. That morning the plan was to kill and clean 50 fryers and put them in the camp freezers. The men were to catch, decapitate, scald, and defeather the chickens. The women were to clean and cut up the birds, bag them, and lay them on the kitchen table. Then the guys would carry them out to the freezers.

The men made two substantial fires under two half-barrels of water. The water was brought to a rolling boil, and the first four to six chickens were beheaded and blanched for 10 to 15 seconds and then defeathered. Jeff and Jay carried these first few into the kitchen and plopped them in the sink. Jay was curious to know how to cut up a chicken, so he stayed around for a few minutes. The girls swarmed around Dixie at the sink, and Jay leaned over the stove, looking on from the side.

Dixie sat the chicken on its front, leaving the rear in the air. She then cut it open below the tail. Reaching her hand in, she gently pulled the guts away from the cavity walls and pulled them out, most coming out all in one pull. One of the girls gasped in horror and declared in a statement that would live in infamy for the rest of the summer, "Oooooh, the chickens in the U.S. don't have that on the inside!"

~ * ~

Dixie sank into her chair at the dining room table. At last, the day's work was done, and she had a moment to write a letter. This was Wednesday, so she would write to Max's parents. Every week she tried to write to her parents on Sunday and to Max's parents on Wednesday. With how busy she was, it was hard to keep the schedule at times, but she did her best. Now the house was quiet; the only sounds she could hear were the wind blowing outside and the ticking of the clocks. Max and the children were all asleep. Even their pet parrot, perched in the lighted dining room, was dozing off. Dixie smiled at it. *I think my late-night writing is an aggravation to him,* she thought. *Oh well. Someday I'll get a cage cover made.*

She picked up her pen to write:

Jan. 28, 1976

Dear In-Loves,
    Greetings from you-know-where and you-know-who!
(I get tired of the same ole' beginning all the time).
    Would you believe that it is <u>cool</u> here, and the
wind is really blowing? We <u>might</u> need to sleep with
a sheet tonight! Have had such a miserable heat
wave that this change is a blessed surprise.

As she wrote about family news and various other items, she thought about the week they'd had. Foremost in her mind was the fact that she had only three more days with her kids before they went back to school in the far-away city of São Paulo. Today was Wednesday; they would leave on Saturday to take the long train ride back. The most recent camp had ended Sunday; both Jay and Jan had been counselors. Jeff had run the canteen.

Dixie relived Saturday night. After shutting the canteen for the night, Jeff had come into the house and gotten ready for bed. When he was ready, he had asked Dixie to come pray with him. She did so gladly. As she left his room, a realization struck her. Next Saturday night, he wouldn't be here. She wouldn't be praying with him, listening to him tell about his day, or cooking for him. She wouldn't have his dirty clothes to wash or his things scattered around the house to clean up. All three of her "big kids" would be gone. Against her will, the tears came. Dixie went to her room and got her Bible. That night, Max was still out with the campers, so she had the house to herself. She could hear Satan whispering in her ear: *This camp doesn't matter. Why stay here to host these campers—other people's kids—if you have to give up your own? You're paying someone else to cook and clean and care for your kids, all so you can care for others. Is it really worth it?*

Was it worth it? It was a question Dixie faced every time her kids went away. It never got any easier. Dixie had spent two hours that night crying and praying.

God had given her His answer on Sunday morning during the camp's last service. Now she smiled as she put her pen to paper, ready to describe it to her mother-in-law.

Our last camp was a really great one. Had 75 kids who all acknowl-edged Christ as Savior before leaving. On Sunday morning, we thrilled to two hours of spontaneous testimonies from the kids. All but maybe three or four went to the front and said a few words. Many cried. They were so grateful—so thankful to have met Christ personally. Can't you imagine how humble and grateful Max and I felt? How privileged we are to share a part in the salvation of so many precious kids. So many said: "I didn't know one could have Jesus personally in his life … I feel so different inside … I don't understand what has happened to me"—phrases similar were said all morning. Sunday afternoon all but one counselor left and we received a whole new "batch" for these next two camps.

As Dixie had listened to the youth sharing their testimonies, tears streamed down her face. She had God's answer. This was why they were here—to give these young men and women a chance to meet Jesus. She had to trust that God's will for her and Max was God's will for their children too.

Dixie continued her letter, sharing more family news and asking questions about the goings-on back home. She finally wrapped it up. Had to get to bed. This was summer break for students, which meant camping season. They had back-to-back camps for most of January and February, with counselors staying on for two or three camps at a time. It was tiring, but they were pleased—especially Max. This was his original dream, to have constant camps during break times with counselors staying over. They did the same in July over winter break. They now had separate camps for younger kids and for youth, as well as church retreats and other events. Some of these events were small; others filled the camp to overflowing. When the Japanese Holiness Church had their annual youth camp, they usually filled it beyond capacity. Often they had 12 to 13 people in rooms for 10. Everyone who came loved the camp. The beautiful, peaceful campground was a retreat for those from the city and a luxury for those from the country. On one occasion, a visitor told Max, "I'd rather stay and die here than go back home."

Since Mitsuo had taken over the camp's leadership, the camps were better organized and flowed smoothly. Max and Dixie could see that God had specially anointed him for this ministry. Dixie wrote in another letter, "Mitsuo is quite a guy … when I think back to the early days and camps, ugh … so much has improved, thank God." Max was thankful that God had sent them an excellent director to run the camps. He was very happy to stay in the background and let Mitsuo take the leading role.

They were privileged to see God use these camps to touch many lives. Often during altar calls, almost everyone went forward. The campers would pray and worship late into the night in the chapel or in their dorm rooms. It was not uncommon for all the campers to leave at the end of camp professing Christianity. One of the best parts of the camps was the testimony time, such as the morning Dixie described in her letter. Usually, this was on the last morning of camp. Camper after camper would come forward and tell about how their lives had been transformed by the Holy Spirit.

Every camp was the same and yet different. The Edwards family saw God's work in both big and little things throughout. On one occasion, they had a camper who was a drug addict; he even brought drugs with him. By God's providence, he was placed in a room with a counselor who had himself been a drug user. The boy's life was transformed, and he even turned in the drugs that he had brought. They saw little miracles such as this every day at the camps. In a prayer letter, Dixie wrote, "Only One who sees all and knows all could have dovetailed the lives and situations of so many in order to bring lost youth to himself."

Sometimes the Holy Spirit would move in an exceptional way. During one such camp, after the Saturday evening service, Max, Mitsuo, and Jeff sat on the grass in front of the house, looking up at the starry night sky. In hushed voices, Max and Mitsuo shared together about the way that the Holy Spirit was moving and changing lives. Even young Jeff could feel that this camp was different, more intense than usual. At this late hour, they could still hear people crying and praying throughout the grounds. How privileged they felt to see such an outpouring of the Holy Spirit. It was a reminder of why they had come to Brazil and why they had come to the camp.

The Edwardses knew that there was only so much that youth could learn about God during a four-day camping experience. Nevertheless, they also knew that the decision was the first step, and many youth made that first step at the camp. Mitsuo started Bible clubs in some of the surrounding cities to provide follow-up for new Christians after the camps. Many campers also returned to future camps, learning and growing more with each visit.

Chapter 13

500 Miles

Well, it's over—and it is the hardest thing we've passed through for a long, long time. Jeff left this afternoon with the kids for São Paulo. Think I know just a wee bit of what you felt (and feel) to have us gone from sight. Jay and Jan were older, and I guess I was "more ready" to have them leave. I hope we've done right. God knows we made the decision hardest to make thinking only of Jeffie and his best ... God knows my heart. I'm not rebellious, and I want His will more than anything in this world—not only for me but for all of them also.
—Dixie, in a letter home, March 1975

One of the most difficult challenges that faced the Edwards family during this time was the kids' education. The little boarding school that Jay and Jan had attended had closed. They knew of a good Christian international school in the large city of São Paulo, Pan American Christian Academy (PACA). However, it was almost 500 miles from their family home of Panorama, and it was not a boarding school. Nevertheless, PACA seemed to be the best option they had, so they looked for a family that would be willing to host their children during the school year. Throughout the next two years, the children would live with a variety of families, and though they stayed with a lot of nice people, it was never the same as being at home with their own family.

Jay and Jan began at PACA in August 1974. Jan was a freshman, and Jay was a junior in high school. At first Max and Dixie decided to keep Jeff at home; they felt that he was too young to go away. Dixie would homeschool him, as she had done before. However, homeschooling proved as difficult as it had always been due to the constant activity at the camp. Dixie did her best, but she feared that whenever Jeff transitioned into a "real school," he wouldn't be at the same level as the other students. She also saw Jeff's longing whenever they visited Jay and Jan at PACA—not to be away from home, but to participate in a classroom and school activities. So on one of their visits to São Paulo, Dixie had a talk with the sixth-grade teacher at PACA.

"We'd like him to begin seventh grade here in the fall," she said, "but I'm not sure if he'll be ready academically."

"If you'd like, he can join us for the last couple of months of sixth grade," the teacher offered. "I can evaluate him to see if he is ready for seventh."

Dixie smiled and nodded. Jeff was only 11. Could she really send him away? Did she have a choice?

After much thinking, praying, and discussing as a family, they decided that it would be best to send Jeff to PACA for the last part of sixth grade. The family that was keeping Jay and Jan agreed to take Jeff too, so he would be with his siblings. Jay and Jan were anxious to look after him, so the family decided that Jeff would leave with Jay and Jan after Easter.

The weekend came. There was an Easter camp at Panorama. Jay and Jan had a couple of days off from school, so they came home for the weekend. Dixie was excited to see them, but at the same time dreaded the weekend, because it meant that Jeff would be leaving home for the first time.

It was a weekend of activity. Jay and Jan arrived with several other MKs. They both served as counselors, while Jeff participated as a camper. The camp was small but good—everyone who was not a Christian when they came, left professing Christ. As always, the Edwards kids were busy and involved. Jeff played his horn in several of the services; Jan spent every spare minute writing a book report that was due on Monday; Jay enjoyed his counselor role—and happily left his pile of books untouched! The camp ended Sunday morning. Originally, the kids had planned to stay over until Monday so the family could have some time alone together. However, Jay and Jan told their parents that they didn't think it was wise to miss school on Monday.

"I have soccer practice," Jay said, "and Jan has a whole bunch of stuff."

"Yes, I have drama practice and an English test. Also, the art fair is on Monday. I have to be there to enter the skirt and hat I made."

Max nodded. "Okay, then," he said. "You can leave on Sunday afternoon with the others."

Dixie's heart sank. She had so counted on a quiet morning of family time. *Oh well,* she thought. *What's one morning anyway? The kids are right—it's not worth it to miss so much school.* She began to pack Jeff's things; he didn't have much to say. What was there to say? Dixie could tell that he was anxious to go but sorry to leave at the same time.

They packed all of their things into the car and headed to the train station. Though the truck was full of teenagers—the Edwards kids plus four other MKs—all were quiet, exhausted from much activity and little sleep. They arrived and slowly unloaded their things.

They walked out onto the little platform. Max went to the window to buy their tickets, while the others stood and waited. The train station was on the edge of town, and when there wasn't a train pulled up, they could look out and see wide-open fields and the big, blue country sky. It was a beautiful day. Nature never knows when it is time to be sad.

At last the train pulled up, making far too much noise. Max, Dixie, and Joey first said goodbye to the other MKs. Then they turned to their own.

As Dixie looked around their little circle, she could see tears in every eye. Oh, her big family, going so far away! And Jeff looked so small, standing on the train platform, bravely holding his big suitcase. They all hugged, and Max said a prayer for their safe travels. Dixie was hardly listening. She didn't want to let her kids go. *Lord, give me strength,* she prayed as she hugged them again.

Then they got on the train and were gone—just like that.

Max and Dixie were quiet as they drove back to the camp. Joey chattered away. Though he had said goodbye, he hadn't yet realized that Jeff had really gone too. Dixie struggled to compose herself, knowing that she would have to teach Sunday school when they reached camp.

Sunday school went by in a blur. Dixie was thankful that she already had materials prepared to help her share the Easter story, as her mind was far away on that train with her kids. When Sunday school was over, Joey went to play with the caretaker's kids, and she finally had a moment to herself. Quietly, Dixie went into her house through the kitchen and back to their bedroom. When the bedroom door was safely closed behind her, she threw herself on the bed and sobbed.

The little Panorama train station came to hold many bittersweet memories for the Edwards family—memories of tearful partings and joyful reunions. For the kids, that train became full of memories too. The ride was 16 hours long, and Panorama was the end of the line. It was always so hard to get on that train in Panorama. At the beginning, there would be very few passengers, so they would sit separately for a while, each crying by themselves. After a few hours though, they started feeling better. By the time they arrived in São Paulo, the train was crowded, and they had rallied themselves for the tasks at hand. They really did love the school; they enjoyed the academic challenge, they made good friends, and they could participate in all kinds of extracurricular activities. But it never got easier to be away from their home and their family.

Heading back to Panorama from São Paulo was always a much happier occasion, but that trip had its own set of challenges. By the time they got out to little Panorama, the train was mostly empty. But it was always very crowded when they got on in São Paulo. The train company didn't limit the number of tickets they sold to the number of seats on the train, so sometimes it was hard to get a seat. Eventually, The 3Js devised a plan. When the train pulled up and everyone crowded around the door, they would run up to a window. They lifted little Jeff inside and sent their luggage in after him. He quickly spread their bags over three seats, and he held those seats until Jay and Jan could join him inside. The trains were so crowded, there would be people everywhere—on the tops of the seats, sitting in the windows, in the aisles, and lying in the luggage racks. Even the bathrooms would be filled with people. Once, Jan went 24 hours without using the restroom! Such were the adventures of MK life.

The kids continued to work together on their music, even while they were away. They became more creative, writing their own songs and medleys. On one occasion, they came home with a special song prepared. Their train pulled in at noon, and Max was at the station to meet them. As The 3Js stepped off the train, they smiled to see him standing there—tall, strong, and tanned, wearing his familiar cowboy hat. His blue eyes twinkled when he saw them.

"Welcome home!" he called.

"Daddy!" They ran up and gave him big hugs.

"Mother, Joey, and the work crew are at home eatin' lunch," Max informed them. "I told her I figured you'd want to eat too, so I'd better come get you!" They laughed and followed him to the car.

Jay, Jan, and Jeff were tired from the long trip, but seeing home always gave them a surge of adrenaline. They enjoyed watching the familiar countryside roll by the car windows as they talked the whole way home. Well, mostly Jan talked. She liked to update her parents on all the latest news.

Finally Max turned down the long lane of the camp. They were home! As he pulled up to the house, they jumped out and hurried to greet their mother, Joey, and the MFM work crew who had just finished eating; they were still seated around the table.

"Come have some food!" Dixie urged.

The three kids looked at each other and smiled.

"Before we do that, Mother, we have something we want to play for you," Jan said.

"Before lunch?"

"Yes!"

Quickly, Jay got his guitar and Jan her mandolin. They tuned their instruments and began.

> I'm sittin' in a railway station
>> Got a ticket for my destination
> Drenched with rain, alone I stand
>> And my suitcase and guitar in hand
> Waiting for the train to pass
>> To take me where I wanna go at last

Homeward bound
    I wish I was homeward bound
Home, where my family's waitin'
    Home, where the sun is shinin'
Home, yeah, that is where I wanna go

A hundred miles, a hundred miles,
    a hundred miles, a hundred miles
Lord, I'm five hundred miles
    Away from home

If you miss the train I'm on
    You will know that I am gone
You can hear the whistle blow,
    A hundred miles.

Lord, I'm one, Lord, I'm two,
    Lord, I'm three, Lord, I'm four
Lord, I'm five hundred miles
    Away from home

I am riding on this train
    There are tears in my eyes
I'm trying to read a letter from my home
    If this train a-runs me right
I'll be home Saturday night
    For I'm five hundred miles
From my home

And I hate to hear the lonely whistle blow.

Well, this train I ride on
    Is a hundred coaches long.
You can hear the whistle blow,
    A hundred miles.
If this train a-runs me right

I'll be home Saturday night
For I'm five hundred miles
   From my home

And I hate to hear the lonely whistle blow …

Oh, there's no place like home
   No place like home
I can't stand it any longer away from home
   Away from my home

   Home
I wanna go home
   Let me go home
Please, Lord,
   I wanna go home

I spent my time in a place where you have led me
   I've gone away to a place that I didn't know
You gave me strength to go on when I was lonely

But now, Oh Lord, I wanna go home
   Yes, I am going home (the whistle's blowin'!)
Going back on a train
   Yes, I am homeward bound!

The room erupted in applause. Dixie sat with her mouth open, her eyes full of tears. What a beautiful, touching piece—and done all without her help. She had taught them to sing, but now they were taking their talent to new levels on their own. They explained to her that this new song was a medley – some parts adapted from other songs, and some their own. They had blended these into something that really expressed the way they felt on those long train rides. Later they would title the song "500 Miles," but for now, they simply called it their "Home Song."

On New Year's Day, 1976, The 3Js recorded their second record. Unlike the first record, which consisted mostly of music taught to them by their mother, the second record was mostly their own work—songs they had found, written themselves, or learned on their own. Dixie couldn't have been prouder. They made "500 Miles" the title song of this new record, and they took their picture for it at the Panorama train station. It seemed only fitting.

~ * ~

Early 1975

Max took another bite of rice and beans as he mulled over what Pastor Vicente was saying. He sat in the little dining area of the pastor's home. Though the family didn't have much, the pastor's wife had laid out a beautiful tablecloth and had offered Max the best food she could make. Max appreciated it.

Outside the window, Max could see the town of Três Lagoas—which was even more "Wild West-like" than Panorama. The dusty red streets held as many horses as cars. Whenever Max came here, he felt a discomfort in his spirit, as if Satan himself owned this town. He knew that spiritism was rampant in this area, and this town was a law unto itself, which led to the problem that Vicente was presenting to him now.

"The orphanage is in terrible condition," Pastor Vicente continued. "The woman who runs it doesn't care about the children at all; she just wants to use them for her own purposes. She even sells them for sexual services."

Max swallowed his food. "Why doesn't the city government do anything about it?"

"The mayor wants to do something, but so far he hasn't been able to," Pastor Vicente responded. "The woman who runs it is a highly respected spiritist medium. She has too many connections, and people are afraid to cross her. But," Pastor Vicente leaned forward, looking earnestly at Max, "if you go to the mayor and ask for permission to take control of the orphanage, I think he will give it to you."

Max looked out the window again. There was so much work to be done in this city. If only it wasn't a three-hour drive from Panorama.

Pastor Vicente was still looking at him, waiting for a response. Max nodded. "I want to see it," he said.

So that afternoon they went to visit the orphanage. Max's heart was broken by what he saw. The orphanage housed 53 children of all ages. The facilities were extensive but were coated in a layer of filth. The children were not even trained to use the bathrooms. Furniture and food were sparse. The orphans were dirty, malnourished, and barely clothed. There was no discipline or love. Overcome with grief, Max didn't know what to say or do. He talked a bit to the kids. A little two-year-old boy approached him. The boy was filthy and wore nothing but some ragged shorts. Max picked him up.

"What's your name?" Max asked.

"Pelé," the little boy answered. As Max looked into the boy's dark eyes, he knew that he would never be able to forget that place.

Max was quiet as they left.

"God can give us this orphanage, and we'll take it over," Pastor Vicente said. "That is city property. If the mayor says you can have it, no one can say otherwise."

Max thought and prayed about it as he left. He pondered it as he drove, as he rode the ferry across the big river to the Panorama side, and as he took the familiar road back to the camp. All he could think about was little Pelé. He knew that his plate was full, but after seeing conditions at the orphanage, he just couldn't walk away from it.

On his next visit to Três Lagoas, Max went to the mayor, who, as Pastor Vicente had predicted, gladly granted his permission for Max to take lead of the orphanage. Putting the orphanage formally under their church would require some legal work, but Max and the mayor agreed on a date when he could take possession of it. In the meantime, Max and Pastor Vicente set about looking for families to move into the orphanage and care for the children. Max shared the need at the Panorama church, and two of their own families, people who had come to Christ under the Edwards' ministry, felt God's call to go. Their church took great interest in the orphans at that time. A third family, converted through the crusade ministry in another city, volunteered to go. Max and Pastor Vicente thanked God for His provision.

On the appointed day, Max went to the orphanage to take possession of it. However, when he showed up, he found everything to be "business as usual"; the woman had not left and was not preparing to leave. When she found out who Max was, she began swearing at him and threatening to put a hex on him. Max wasn't all that concerned about a hex, but he wasn't sure what to do about the woman refusing to leave. So he went to the mayor and told him about the situation.

"The police didn't go?" the mayor asked.

"No," Max responded.

"Well, the police have to go and get her out of there." So the mayor made the necessary calls, and eventually the police went with Max and took the woman out of the orphanage. Pastor Vicente followed with members of his church, and they began immediately to clean the place. They knew they needed to do as much as they could as fast as they could, so if anyone complained to the mayor about the change, he could show them how much better it was under the new management. They took a power washer and washed the whole place; then they brought in paint to make it look like new. The three families moved in and gave the children the care that they needed. As they cleaned out the medium's room, they found children's clothing, dishes, and important documents hidden there—things that should have been used for the care of the children. They also found many adults and children, relatives of the medium who were not even orphans, living there. They worked to remove the people who didn't belong and group the children into families for their care.

Noting that all the children had diarrhea, Max went to the store and bought several cases of cola. He brought them to the orphanage and told them to drink all they wanted, certain that this would help to "dry 'em up a little bit." The kids certainly enjoyed the treat.

The medium was irate. She worked her connections to stir up trouble for the families that had moved in, for Max, and for Jorge, the Brazilian who was temporarily in charge of the orphanage. There were so many threats against the orphanage and the volunteer families that the army stationed men there for their protection, less than a week after the new leaders took possession of the orphanage. Once when the Edwards family visited in the camp's pickup truck, they were advised to take the signs off of the truck and go straight home without driving through town. Thankfully, they had no trouble. On another occasion, Jorge was hung in effigy in front of his house. The Edwardses realized more every day what a hold Satan had on this town. Max saw that the devil had been stirred by their work at the orphanage, but he also knew that God was stronger.

The families and the orphans lived in cramped, uncomfortable quarters while the rest of the facilities were being cleaned and remodeled. They also had to teach the children how to live and behave in a proper manner. When they first started having meals, the malnourished children would just stuff themselves until they could hardly walk. Eventually, however, they became accustomed to their new way of life. A doctor came in to examine the children and treat them for worms and other health problems. In spite of all the chaos and hard work, the families that moved there were peaceful and happy to be doing God's will. Unfortunately, their trials were only beginning.

Max continued to work on the legal aspects of giving full control of the orphanage to their church. They had some prominent people on their side, but they also faced a lot of opposition. Max worked with a pastor to put out a radio broadcast in Três Lagoas, explaining what their church stood for and why they had entered the orphanage. They hoped not only to ease the opposition but also to rally the people of Três Lagoas to help the orphanage financially.

Seeing that Max was unintimidated by her threats, the medium decided to put a hex on him—one that was common in that part of Brazil. She took a toad, stuffed its mouth with dirt, and sewed its mouth shut. Then, she put the hex on it: "As the toad goes, so go you. When the toad dies, you die." When the people at the church in Três Lagoas heard about this, they were afraid for Max. A relative of someone in the church had died just a few years ago from the same hex. So the church prayed over Max and told him that he should probably stay away for a while. Max was still not very concerned; he was confident of God's protection. He went home, and nothing happened to him. He came back the next week, and the church rejoiced.

"The other man died," they said, "but she can't touch God's servant."

So Max continued to visit the orphanage regularly, supported them, and helped out as best he could. When Jay, Jan, and Jeff were home from school on breaks, the whole family went to help. Max put a lot of miles on his little white VW bug car, as he made the drive to and from Três Lagoas. He made an impression on everyone he met—the big, strong American, always wearing his cowboy hat.

He usually visited on weekends and often preached in the Sunday evening church service there. On one such occasion, Pastor Vicente approached Max after the service.

"Max," he said, "I had a revelation during the service that you were going to die. I think it was from God." He paused. "There are more and more rumors," he said, "of plots to harm you. It's not safe for you to drive home at night. I don't want you to go home tonight; stay with us."

"Well," Max responded, "Dixie is expecting me. If I leave within the next 30 minutes, I can make it to the ferry and get home by late tonight, which is what she's expecting." Panorama Camp still had no phone, so Max had no way to contact Dixie and tell her if he changed his plans.

"Max, I'm telling you. I think you should stay here, and I think it's from God."

Finally, Max relented. "Okay," he said. "If you feel that strongly about it, I'll spend the night with you." So he spent the night at Pastor Vicente's place and went home in the morning. And that was that, as far as Max was concerned.

The next time Max visited Três Lagoas, he learned some disturbing news. On that Sunday night, the night he had intended to drive home, a German farmer had been killed on the road leaving Três Lagoas. He was driving a white VW bug and reportedly wearing a cowboy hat. The man was killed, and the car was burned. It was presumed that Max was the intended target for this assassination. The medium had realized that the hex was not working, so she resorted to the "old-fashioned way" of hiring someone to get rid of him. Max solemnly realized that God had protected him yet again.

Max continued to visit and to do everything he could for the orphanage in spite of the opposition and the threats. For several years, the church was able to keep possession of the orphanage and give the children there a better life. Unfortunately, however, they ran out of funds to keep it going. The families who were working there left, and they were unable to find others who were willing to staff it. Max's time was spread too thin with all of his different ministries, and he was unable to give extra time to it. The Três Lagoas church did everything they could to keep the orphanage open, but they were no longer able to find other churches interested in helping. Eventually, they lost control of the orphanage, and it went back to the people who had run it before. The Edwardses mourned deeply the loss but hoped that some children had been touched and helped during the years that they were able to work there.

This still hurts today, 30 years later. I will never understand why God's other local servants would not pick up the ball and do their small part to keep it open. Lack of finances closed this important ministry.
—Jay Edwards, 2017

~ * ~

The Edwards family also faced challenges as they continued their other ministries. They received a mixed response from the local people on their return from furlough. In some ways, they were greeted with enthusiasm. They had some of their highest numbers ever in Sunday school attendance in the months following their return. Dixie restarted her girls' club, and a similar club was begun for boys. And of course, the camping ministry continued to grow, especially under the directorship of Mitsuo.

In the town of Panorama, Max continued to be an influential local figure, admired and respected by everyone he met. When a hospital was built in town, he was asked to be on its board of directors. He and Dixie both did a great deal of visiting in local homes; they prayed with people, encouraged them to come to Sunday school, and shared the Gospel with them.

However, the local church seemed to always have problems, and it was hard to know how to respond. Eventually, the pastor of the Panorama church suggested that they stop hauling people to and from town every week and recommended holding a regular Sunday service in the new camp chapel instead. Max and Dixie heartily agreed with this idea; they felt it was a good way to try to reach the rural population. The attendance at their services was high, even though only a few of those who attended were Christians. Max was glad for the opportunity to share the Gospel with so many people.

Their Sunday school and other local ministries also yielded mixed results. At times people responded eagerly, while at other times it seemed they just weren't grasping the message. Max and Dixie experienced many ups and downs, sometimes feeling like they were making real progress, and other times feeling that the people came to Sunday school only because they enjoyed the campground. They had to remind themselves that the results were not up to them; they were called only to be faithful and to trust the Holy Spirit to work.

As Max's parents in the U.S. aged and experienced various health challenges, he sometimes felt torn between his ministry on the mission field and his duties as the only son of a farming family. He experienced firsthand the fact that obedience to God's call sometimes involved sacrifice—not only his own sacrifices but also sacrifice on the part of his parents and family. However, as he wrestled with these realities in prayer, he knew that all he could do was continue to obey. He had to trust that God would take care of his loved ones—from his children away at school, to Dixie and Joey often at home alone while he traveled, to his parents back in Indiana. No matter what challenges they faced, Max knew that the center of God's will was still the safest place to be.

> We have prayed and feel God has called us here. So we have to have faith to believe that God will help you have the strength to go on without my help ... I would gladly come home and be your hand, but I fear being out of the will of God. This is the most important thing in my life.
> —Max, in a letter home, October 1975

Chapter 14

Changes

For who is God besides the LORD? And who is the Rock except our God? It is God who arms me with strength and keeps my way secure.
2 Samuel 22:32–33 (NIV)

May 1976

*M*ax climbed back into the car, rubbing sleep from his eyes. Fellow missionary Mike Murphy got in the other side.

"It just doesn't seem quite right," Max said, staring at the piece of land before them.

Mike nodded. "On to the next one then." He put the car into reverse and headed back to the main road.

They were in the countryside just outside of Londrina, a small city where Mike and many other OMS missionaries worked. As the site of the OMS Brazil headquarters, and the center of the OMS-affiliated national denomination, it was an ideal location for a new campground. For several weeks now, Max had been making trips to look at pieces of land. They wanted to take their time and make sure they found God's choice; at the same time, they knew that land prices were rising. Mike was flying to the U.S. in a matter of weeks, and he would meet with a farmer friend[10] of Max's who had offered to help finance the land purchase. Max was running out of time to make a decision.

---

10   At his request, the friend's name is not mentioned. He told Max, "God knows, and that's enough." He initially connected with the Edwards family through MFM trips and was a faithful friend and supporter throughout their ministry.

Max had come to Londrina the day before, Sunday evening, after preaching in the Panorama church in the afternoon. He had to be back in Panorama by the following night so he could pick up Dixie and Joey and drive with them to São Paulo.

Mike turned off the main road again, this time onto a dusty lane of red dirt. As they bumped along, he said to Max, "This area is pretty out of the way. We're probably wasting our time, but since you're here, I thought we'd best check it out. This road leads to a large coffee plantation. Some open pieces of land border it."

Max nodded and hung on to the car door. His stomach lurched as the car went up and down the hills. This area was so different from flat Panorama.

They had gone about four miles when they saw a large field on their right. Mike slowed the car as both men stared at it. Max's heart stirred. Suddenly, he and Mike said in unison, "Could this be what we are looking for?"

Mike stopped the car, and both men got out. Though the sun shone brightly, the wind was cold as it stirred around them and bit their cheeks and hands. The grass and weeds of the field rustled. It was empty, except for a few sheds and a small wooden house. Max folded his arms as he stared at the field.

The 36-acre piece of land was triangular with roads on two sides. One of these roads, where the missionaries now stood, was on the high end of the property. From there it sloped downward, until it reached a little creek that ran along the bottom of the property. The other road ran on Max's right side; the left side was bordered with more fields and farmland.

Max's mind kicked into high gear. He no longer saw the open field, the grass, and anthills, undisturbed by anything but the wind. Instead, he saw the creek at the far end dammed to make a small lake. Above that, there was a soccer court, basketball court, and swimming pool. Dorm buildings climbed the hill along each side of the property. Farther up, there was a dining hall and recreation building. Higher still was a residence for the camp manager, a chapel, and various other buildings. The property was lined with trees and sidewalks; and it was abuzz with laughing youth. It was perfect.

A nearby cow mooed; Max blinked. The bright-blue sky and waving grass came back into focus. "This is it," Max said.

Mike nodded. "Okay, then. Let's see if we can get it."

On the way home, they discussed financial options.

"How much of it do you think your friend will want to cover?" Mike asked.

"Don't know. I guess we'll see what he gives, then try to raise the rest."

They tracked down the owner of the land and managed to negotiate the price down to $32,000. Max headed back to Panorama on Tuesday, thankful that God had led them to the right piece of land. *Okay, God,* he prayed, *now it's up to you to provide the finances.*

Max smiled to himself. *Missionaries have big ideas,* he thought, *sometimes good, sometimes poor—but always without money!* Raising money for a big purchase like this would be hard. However, Max knew from experience that if God wanted a camp built, He would provide everything they needed.

He decided to contact his friend and let him know that they had found the piece of land they wanted. At his request, Max told him how much it cost.

Less than a week later, that summer's NOW Corps group arrived. They came with a surprise for Max—a check for $32,000 from Max's farmer friend.

Max completed the land purchase as soon as he had the chance. They managed to negotiate the man down even further and got the land for $29,000. Immediately, Max contacted his friend to offer to return the extra $3,000.

"No," he replied, "get electricity."

Max was happy to comply. A power line crossed one portion of the property. With the remaining $3,000, he was able to set two poles, one of which held the electric transformer. He also laid 3 copper wires, each 38 feet long and buried 3 feet deep.

Max recruited a Christian couple from the Panorama area, Seu Miguel and Dona Lucila, to work at the camp as caretakers. They moved to the new camp with their family and began to clear the land to prepare for building. With land, electricity, and caretakers, the new spot was well on its way to being a camp. It was the beginning of a vision to reach hundreds of youth in the Londrina area and beyond.

The missionaries discussed the future of this camp and what they would call it. Mike's wife, Lorena Murphy, suggested the camp name. "How about *Shalom*?" she asked, using the Hebrew word meaning "peace." "It describes what we want to happen in the lives of the campers—that they will find God's peace." The others heartily agreed, and the spot was soon christened Camp Shalom.

~ * ~

The Lord didn't tell us the way would always be easy, did he? I praise Him anyway, knowing that where He guides, He provides ... all that we need to serve Him effectively.
—Dixie, in a letter home, October 1976

1976

Changes! They seemed to be the order of the day.

The hardest change was watching Jay graduate from PACA and leave for the U.S. His last year of high school had been a good one. Some close friends of the Edwardses, the Owsley family, had kept Jay and Jeff at their home for the year. This had been a real blessing to the Edwards children; the Owsleys made them feel like part of their family. They also had a son, Dan, who was in Jay's class and a friend to all three of the "Js."

Now, it was hard to believe that both Jay and Dan were graduating! Jay planned to go to the U.S. right after graduation. He would work with his Grandpa Edwards on the farm throughout the summer and fall, then start at Asbury College in January. His parents were so proud of him, but they knew that his departure would leave a "Jay-shaped hole" in their home.

The graduation was beautiful. Max and Dixie, who had been delayed by São Paulo's infamous traffic, walked in just in time to hear Jay's class singing,

Through it all
    Through it all
I've learned to trust in Jesus,
    I've learned to trust in God.
Through it all
    Through it all
I've learned to depend upon His Word.[11]

Dixie felt tears prick her eyes; it was so beautifully appropriate. Yes, through all of the changes and hardships, they learned to trust God and depend upon Him more.

The next few months went by in a blur with NOW Corps, camps, traveling, and working. They started building a pool at Panorama, which would be inaugurated with a baptism in September. At Camp Shalom, they cleared weeds and set the poles for electricity.

Another big change for the Edwards family came in August. They decided that they had had enough of sending the kids away to live with other families during the school year. So they rented a home in São Paulo, and Dixie moved there with Jan, Jeff, and Joe. This allowed little Joey to begin kindergarten at PACA. Max would spend that school year commuting between Panorama, Londrina, and São Paulo with the whole family living at Panorama during school vacations. Max carried responsibilities in all three of these cities. In Panorama, he maintained and improved the campground while running camps there with Mitsuo. In Londrina, he worked on the new camp. And, in São Paulo, he was appointed business manager for the mission. Sometimes Dixie and Joey went with Max to Panorama when there were work crews or other visiting groups. When Jay surprised them by showing up with a work crew in September, Jan and Jeff skipped school and went to Panorama too.

It was a year of new challenges, growth, and experiences. Though Dixie loved being able to care for her own children in her own home, they sometimes found city life confining and difficult. São Paulo was crowded, polluted, and colder than sunny Panorama. Furthermore, it seemed like Max was always away on trips, especially when there

---

11   By Andraé Crouch.

were problems at home. This new kind of separation was hard on the whole family.

On one Saturday in late October, Jan and Joey huddled closely together as they hurried down the street toward home. It had been rainy all day and showed no signs of slowing. Jan clutched her umbrella in one hand and Joey's hand in the other, her purse clamped awkwardly between them as she tried to keep it from slipping off her shoulder. The umbrella seemed to be doing little good. Between the water escaping around its edges and the splashing from the puddles below, Jan supposed they would be soaked before they got home. The water ran merrily over the streets, forming little rivers that Joey watched intently as he walked.

Jan glanced at him. Joey seemed deep in thought. Was he thinking about the child-evangelism event they had just left? She hoped so.

Shaking her thick strawberry-blond hair out of her eyes, Jan looked around. The streets of their neighborhood were fairly empty; she supposed most people preferred to stay dry in such weather. Though she was cold and wet, Jan found it refreshingly peaceful. Their family had had a rough week. Max had been gone for almost two weeks; he was in Panorama at a pastors' retreat. They couldn't go with him because they had school; the whole family felt cooped up in the big city, especially on rainy days like today. The electricity had been off and on since the rainstorms had started. Just this morning, a thunderstorm had sent a surge of power into their little TV and killed it. At almost the same time, the refrigerator plug had begun to melt, and Dixie had to move it to a different outlet on the other side of the kitchen. Dixie was tired, frustrated, and missing Max—Jan could tell. Jan had not been feeling too well either.

And yet, maybe something good would happen this week. Jan had been watching Joey closely, and she wondered if he might be ready to choose the Christian faith for himself. She turned to him and smiled.

"How did you like the Bible club?" she asked.

Joey nodded. "It was good," he said—a little too seriously for a five-year-old. Jan continued to talk with him about the program, the songs, and what the speaker had said. Their little house came into view. Jan got out her keys and unlocked the gate. Joey went inside, and Jan followed, locking the gate again behind her. It looked like their mother and Jeff were out somewhere. She unlocked the door and ushered Joey inside. They were still chatting as they removed their wet coats and shoes.

"Joey," Jan asked, "do you have Jesus in your heart?"

Joey's forehead scrunched up. "Well, no," he said. "But, I'd like to."

Jan smiled. "Do you want to pray right now to accept Jesus into your heart?"

"Yes!" Joey grinned and nodded. Jan went over to the couch and knelt, and Joey followed suit. They folded their hands and closed their eyes. Jan recited a simple prayer of salvation, and Joey repeated it after her.

"Dear Jesus," they prayed, "thank You for dying on the cross for me. I'm sorry for my sins. I want You to come and live in my heart. Amen."

Jan and Joey opened their eyes at the same time and smiled at each other.

"I'm so proud of you, Joey. Now you're a Christian like the rest of us," Jan told him. Joey beamed and gave Jan a big hug.

Soon after, Dixie and Jeff arrived home.

"Mother!" Joey exclaimed, bounding to the door. He flung his arms around her waist. "I accepted Jesus into my heart!"

Jan smiled. "It's true," she said.

"Wow, that's wonderful," Dixie exclaimed.

"That's awesome," Jeff agreed, grinning.

Joey was glowing. "Now we are all Christians!" he said.

Yes, something good had happened that weekend—something so very good. The days were long and a bit boring, cooped up inside with no TV, but the Edwards family made it work, as they always did. On Sunday, after a delicious lunch, they opened all the curtains in the living room because they had no electricity that day; they played dominoes on the floor all afternoon. Outside it rained hard and even hailed, but they had a good time anyway. Dixie didn't feel up to driving to church in the storm, so family devotions replaced church that night for the Edwards family.

Dixie woke up Monday morning feeling 100-percent better. God took care of their family, even when everything went wrong and Max wasn't home. And what better way for God to show His presence and blessing than to draw little Joey into His kingdom? They were an all-Christian family now, and Dixie was so grateful.

Another new experience for them during this year in São Paulo was their first time being robbed. Early in November, they came home from a family trip to Panorama to find the back door kicked in and their TV, clock radio, and several other electronic devices missing. They were shocked and disappointed. However, as they surveyed the damage, Max commented, "Everything that was taken was 'pleasure' stuff. They didn't take anything essential or anything that we need for ministry."

It was true—the kids' instruments, which were valuable items, were all untouched, as was Dixie's sewing machine and even money hidden in the house. The family thanked God once again for His protection.

By the time December rolled around, the Edwardses were ready to head home to Panorama for the hot summer months of December and January. They enjoyed the usual summer season of family time, mission meetings, and January camps. The new swimming pool was a favorite spot for all! The kids especially loved the water, and Jan taught Joey to swim using fun games to help him practice.

The camps, some for children and others for youth, went relatively smoothly, and as always, many accepted Christ while they were there. The Edwards kids enjoyed participating in these camps, but sometimes the constant activity left them feeling worn-out. This was especially true for Joey, who as a little child received a lot of attention from the older youth. Though he often enjoyed this attention, eventually he would become impatient with the affectionate demonstrations of the Brazilian girls and women who were constantly trying to hug or kiss him.

On one such frustrating day, the wife of the local doctor, a family friend, visited the camp with her two children. When she saw Joey, she tried to hug him and pinch his cheek affectionately, as was customary. But five-year-old Joey had had it; he couldn't take one more pinch that day! He promptly kicked her in the shin and ran off.

When Max and Dixie heard what had happened, they wasted no time in sitting Joey down to talk about it. Max took a great deal of time explaining respect to Joey, showing him why what he had done was wrong.

"Sometimes," he said, "we have to endure things that we don't like because it's necessary. Do you understand, son?"

"Yes, sir," Joey said in a small voice.

"Good," said Max. "This afternoon, we will go to her house, and you will apologize for what you did." Joey nodded.

As promised, that afternoon Max took Joey into town to the doctor's house. Joey apologized to the doctor's wife sweetly; she cried in response. Joey learned a lesson about respect, and Max was able to share the story with the youth in his message that night in a way that touched hearts.

Soon PACA was back in session, and the Edwards family packed up again and headed back to their São Paulo home.

In April 1977, the family had some very special visitors: Dixie's parents, the Brumfields, came to see them. They were given a very enthusiastic welcome at the airport. Later that afternoon, the family had some free time, and Joey was still bubbling with energy from the exciting day. He approached his older brother.

"Jeff, will you play soccer with me?"

Jeff smiled and tousled Joey's hair. "Sure," he said, "let's play."

So the boys went out behind the house. Like most Brazilian homes in the city, their "backyard" was an outdoor cement floor, surrounded on all sides by high walls. Dixie did laundry and other outdoor house-work there. Still, Jeff and Joey loved to play soccer in this area. They used the household items in the yard as goalposts—the outdoor sink, the hose, and the washer. And if they kicked the ball out of bounds, it just bounced off the walls and came back. Joey thought it was a great place to play.

Today was no exception. They played a while, laughing, wrestling, and sweating. At one point, the little white-and-orange ball rolled out to the middle of the yard and stopped halfway between Jeff and Joe. Both boys ran for it and kicked it at the exact same time.

Jeff was small for his age, but at 13 he was quite a bit larger than 5-year-old Joey. The force of his kick went through the ball and rever-berated through Joey's leg. Joey flew backwards and fell to the ground, screaming in pain. Jeff bent over him.

"You okay, buddy?"

Joey felt his leg; it hurt so bad he began to cry.

Jeff's forehead crinkled in concern. "Stop crying! Stop crying!" he said. "If Mother hears you crying, she'll make us stop playing."

Well, Joey could not stop crying, and eventually Dixie, Grandma

Pauline, and Grandpa Joe came out to see what was wrong. They all helped Joey into the kitchen.

"What's the matter?" Dixie asked. The boys explained to her what had happened. Joey couldn't put any weight on his leg without crying. She was concerned. Could it be broken?

Grandma Pauline, who was a nurse, was concerned as well. "I think you should take him to the hospital," she said.

Soon Max came home from running errands. When he heard that Jeff had not even touched Joey, he didn't think there could be much wrong.

"Your leg's not broken!" he exclaimed. "Quit whinin'. It's a long ways from your heart."

Joey tried to quit whining but didn't feel any better the next day. Dixie and Pauline persuaded Max to take Joey to the doctor. "Just in case," they said.

After a doctor's visit and an X-ray, they found that Joey's leg was, in fact, broken. His shin was fractured in two places. Max felt so sorry for not taking him more seriously. The doctor put Joey's leg in a cast, which went all the way from his foot to the top of his leg. They gave him little crutches, but the crutches were too difficult for Joey to use. He found a much more efficient way to get around the house: scooting backwards on his bottom! He sat on the smooth tile floor and used his hands to propel himself around. Before the cast came off, he had worn through the part that had covered his heel, and also wore out a pair of shorts!

The family enjoyed their time with the Brumfields in spite of Joey's injury. The Brumfields visited Panorama during an Easter camp and were amazed to see what a beautiful place it had become, hosting such an important ministry. So much had changed since their last visit in 1971. They went home understanding even more of what their daughter's life had become in the seven years since she had moved to Brazil.

~ * ~

Start over again? Oh, Lord, I don't have the courage. This was my first thought. But as I reflected on my life and God's calling, my heart's prayer could

*only be Lord, we came to serve. Put us where we
can serve You and others to best advantage.*
—Dixie, in a prayer letter, May 1977

Before the Edwardses knew it, school was out, and it was moving-time
again—back to Panorama. They had decided that for the next school
year, they needed to be in Londrina so Max could really focus on developing Camp Shalom. But before that, they would spend the winter in
Panorama again, hosting the NOW Corps and the July camps.

June and July were a whirlwind of activity as always. On one occasion, Jan had the opportunity to go with a pastor and several Brazilian
youth on a weeklong houseboat trip up the river. They took items like
clothes and medicine to the people who lived close to the river, and
held evangelism events along the way. It was an unforgettable experience for Jan.

Another exciting thing happened that July—at least something that
was exciting for one little six-year-old boy: Joey got a little Dalmatian
puppy. While the family was in Panorama, Max went to São Paulo for
a few days on business. During his time there, a friend happened to
connect him to a businessman who was in a hurry to leave the country
and needed to find homes for his dog's last litter of puppies. Max knew
that Joey would love to have a puppy for a birthday present, so he happily accepted a puppy from the businessman. The only challenge was
figuring out how to transport it back to Panorama. Max was scheduled
to return via overnight bus, and technically pets weren't allowed on
those buses. However, with no other options, he decided to bring the
puppy in a little box and hoped that no one would notice. As he took his
seat, he slid the box carefully underneath and smiled at his neighbor.
He leaned back and tried to sleep.

However, a few minutes later, a little whimper came from below. Max
held his breath and looked around. Had anyone noticed? Maybe not.
He settled back again and almost drifted off when he heard a whine,
louder than the whimper this time. Max shifted in his seat. The whim-
pering and whining continued, and his fellow passengers looked around
with confused expressions on their faces. Finally, Max realized that he
couldn't hide it any longer. He stood up and addressed the whole bus.

"I'm sorry about the noise coming from over here," he said. "I'm bringing a puppy home to my little boy who wants a dog." His fellow passengers were all very understanding and supportive.

When Joey saw the puppy, he was ecstatic. He named her Snoopy, and she was his companion throughout the rest of their time in Brazil.

The move to Londrina was another big change for the Edwards family. Though they were hesitant to move again, they realized that three homes—Panorama, Londrina, and São Paulo—were just too much for them to manage. So, now they were down to two; they lived in Londrina and Max focused primarily on developing Camp Shalom; at the same time, they were still in charge of the maintenance of Panorama Camp. The kids would have a sort of group homeschooling situation with other MKs in Londrina; a teacher, Miss Joanne Cherry, came from the U.S. to teach them. She taught Joey and the other elementary school kids directly. Jeff, Jan, and the other high schoolers did correspondence school with Miss Cherry there to assist them if they needed it. It was hard for the kids to leave PACA, but this was a workable situation, and they would still be at home with their parents.

Londrina was the location of OMS' Brazil headquarters; OMS had an affiliated seminary there as well, and many missionaries lived in housing on the seminary compound. While the Edwards family loved their fellow OMS missionaries, they had lived in Brazilian communities ever since they had finished language school, and they preferred to continue that way. In 1977, one mission house was available on the seminary compound. Along with the Edwardses, another missionary family was moving to Londrina that year. They were going to be teachers in the seminary, so it seemed natural to the Edwardses that the new family would be the best fit to stay on the compound. Accordingly, Max and Dixie put in a request to find a house to rent in the community. However, the mission board thought differently; they decided that the Edwards family should live on the compound, and the other missionaries could rent.

Dixie was stunned. Surely the board had made the wrong decision. As if picking up and moving her family yet again wasn't hard enough, to be denied their choice in housing felt like an exceptionally hard blow. She had been so sure that their perspective was right.

Max understood her feelings, but he also knew that the board's decision was final. "Honey, you have to get victory over this," he said. "God is sovereign."

Yes, God was sovereign; Dixie knew it. She knew that He could have given them their housing choice if He had wanted to. She remembered the promise that God had given her when they first arrived in Brazil: "Christ, my Rock." Maybe she had slipped off her Rock a little. But she knew what she had to do, and she did it.

As she came before the Lord in prayer, Dixie remembered *Have We No Rights?*—the book they had read during their missionary internship. She still struggled sometimes with wanting her rights: her right to privacy … to her time … to her home—her right to make her own decisions for herself and for her family. While the desire for these rights may be natural, Dixie knew that God was calling her to give up every one of them for the sake of Christ and His work.

Perhaps it didn't really matter to God where they lived; He could work in them and through them whether on the compound or outside of it. But perhaps He had allowed the decision to go this way because He needed to address an attitude. Dixie was reminded that though people look at the outside, God looks at the heart. By God's grace, Dixie learned the lesson again; she could be flexible for Him! She became so flexible, in fact, that she moved again nine months later to vacate the home for others who needed it. They lived in another missionary's home for the last three months before they left on furlough.

And so, the year of 1977 to 1978 was spent with "only" two homes—Londrina and Panorama. It was still difficult for Max to be constantly traveling back and forth between the two camps. The family became involved in a new church in a poor community just outside of Londrina. It was good to be involved in local ministry.

Work on Camp Shalom continued to progress in spite of the usual problems Max ran into whenever working on a project in Brazil. At one point, he mixed cement with a hoe because the electricity was out. Max said to Dixie, "I don't know what the Lord is trying to teach me, but I hope I learn it fast!" He continually learned more about patience and how to make do when things didn't go as planned. Even though the new campground was still in progress, they began holding day camps as soon as they could.

In December, the Edwards family headed to Panorama for their last summer there. Soon they would be moving out of that home completely to focus their next term on Camp Shalom and other projects. They had a nice, quiet family Christmas, followed by the fun chaos of mission meetings. January was filled as always with camps, a work crew, and other visitors. Max and Dixie spent a great deal of time traveling between Panorama, Londrina, sometimes São Paulo, and even Rio de Janeiro, as they escorted groups of people and carried out various tasks. They were thankful to have Mitsuo at Panorama running the camps.

At the end of January, the Edwards family moved back to Londrina. By this time, several facilities had been completed at Shalom, including a recreation and dining hall, a cement ball court, and one dormitory unit that housed 32 people. They held their first real camp there in early February—a four-day camp for the youth from the Londrina churches.

In March 1978, the Scott family, other OMS missionaries, returned from furlough and were assigned to Panorama Camp. They took over the Edwardses' responsibilities there, so Max could focus on Shalom and on other ministries. Thus, the Edwards family moved out of Panorama for the last time. It was a bittersweet moment; they had put so much work into Panorama, and it had really become home to them.

However, by then even Dixie, who was more reluctant than Max to move on to new things, was ready. In a letter home, she wrote, "PTL, Panorama is off of us. I'm so grateful. It was time for us to leave and another step in. Max is an 'initiator.' He is a leader and can get things going. Sounds like married to [a man like this], I may not ever stay in one place very long, huh? He's worth every move. We've had a great life together."

It was an ending and a beginning. Their time in Panorama had come to a close. However, there was still much to do at Shalom, and they would find even more opportunities in their next term. In May, they wrapped up that school year with a graduation ceremony for Jan, who finished high school in a class of one via correspondence. Jan and Jeff flew to the U.S. shortly afterward, leaving Max, Dixie, and Joey to carry out their usual winter activities before following them.

That year, the routine of NOW Corps, activity, and camps was high-lighted by the fact that they met a special person: Kirsten Webster, who had been dating Jay for several months. She came as part of that year's NOW Corps group. Kirsten, originally from Oklahoma and Kansas, was interested in Latin American missions. She and Jay had met at Asbury, so Max and Dixie appreciated the chance to get to know her. At the end of the summer, she was able to travel back to the U.S. with them, and the whole family went to Disney World together.

So in August 1978, the Edwards family left for furlough again. They would have to wait until their return to see what God had planned for them next.

Now all the experiences we had in Panorama are history.
Am I glad I did it all? YES. Would I like to do it again? NO.
That's life: you pass this way but once; you must do the best
you can and move through the next door God has for you.
—Max

Chapter 15

Baskets and Rope Holders

I lift up my eyes to the mountains— where does my help come from? My help comes from the LORD, the Maker of heaven and earth.
Psalm 121:1–2 (NIV)

January 1979

The cold wind whistled outside, and clouds blotted out the stars of the evening sky. But the gym of the small Illinois high school was bright and warm as several local MFM groups gathered for an evening banquet. Max was there as one of the event's speakers, with Dixie, Jan, Jeff, and Joe accompanying him. They saw familiar faces among those gathered; these groups had sent quite a few people on short-term trips to work at both Panorama Camp and Camp Shalom. Max always enjoyed mingling with these missions-minded laymen. He was constantly in recruitment mode when talking to friends, both old and new.

"So, when are you coming to Brazil?" he would ask. "We could use a man like you on a work crusade." And as he flashed his handsome smile and shared about Brazil in his simple, straightforward manner, his listeners would begin to believe that they too could participate in God's work in Latin America.

After a delicious meal, Max's turn to speak came. He shared stories about how God was working, touching hearts and changing lives in Brazil. He told about the ongoing ministry in Panorama and the new vision for Camp Shalom. Fresh from a visit, he had some special stories to share:

"In December," he said, "I was privileged to accompany a group of 18 MFMers on a two-week trip to Brazil. Our goal was to build the chapel for the new Camp Shalom. But this group worked so fast that we were able to not just build the chapel, but also to pour the footers and floors for the director's residence and the recreation hall! Praise the Lord!

"We also heard some beautiful testimonies while we were there, of God's work in people's lives. I was excited to hear that the man who built the benches for the chapel had given his heart to the Lord! He had been the subject of prayer for a long time. I was also privileged to hold a baptism while we were staying there at the camp. On our last day in Brazil, we visited our OMS church in São Paulo and heard the testimony of a young man who had been on drugs before he met Jesus at Panorama. Now his life is completely changed, and he wants to attend seminary in Londrina to become a pastor."

Max paused and looked around at the crowd, his blue eyes piercing. "This is why we are in Brazil—to see people come to the Lord and to see them trained, becoming pastors and workers for the kingdom. After we built the chapel, we counted how many cement blocks we had used. The number was 3,800. We challenged ourselves to pray that God would bring one soul into His kingdom for every one of those blocks. Will you pray with us?"

Max had always been gifted in recruitment and fundraising, and as he spoke, many hearts were touched. Max humbly recognized that God was using him to bring the needed funds and workers to Brazil to complete Camp Shalom.

After the meeting, Jeff and Joey packed up their display table while Jan, Max, and Dixie chatted with those who remained. Though they had only been on furlough for six months, the kids had become experts at packing and unpacking the various curios from Brazil. There was the stuffed piranha, the crocodile head, the alligator head, the giant snakeskin from Panorama, the traditional musical instruments, their family prayer cards with their picture and contact information, and finally the big Brazilian flag that draped the table. As Jeff folded the flag and stuck it in the box with the rest of the items, he overheard one of the men talking to his daddy nearby.

"I heard that there is supposed to be bad weather this weekend in Indiana," the man was saying. "Think you'll make it home all right?"

Max shrugged. "Things seem okay on this end," he said. "I think if we leave now, we'll make it." He turned to Jeff. "Everything packed?"

"Yes, sir." Jeff straightened as Joey closed the lid of the box. Max nodded. "Then let's go."

Toting the box and other odds and ends, the family walked out into the cold wind and lifted their things into the trunk. They then piled into the car and headed out.

Despite ominous clouds, the first couple of hours of the drive passed without incident. Then it started to snow. The snow became heavier and heavier the closer they got to home.

"Do you think we should stop somewhere, Max?" Dixie asked. She was starting to worry.

"We can make it," Max insisted. "We're almost there."

They *were* almost there, but the snowstorm was developing into a full-blown blizzard. Looking out the front windshield, Max could see only a few feet of the road before it disappeared into a wall of white. Out the side windows were only snow and blackness. Only a few more miles though, and they would be home. Max turned from State Road 27 onto 500 South. This country road had even more snowdrifts across it than the previous one. Max did his best to navigate around, over, and through the snow, but the little car could only do so much. Finally, it met a snowdrift it could not overcome.

Crunch. The car stopped moving forward. In front, they could see snow piled all the way up to the hood. They were right at the corner of Bloomingsport Road—their road. Surely they could make it. Max revved the engine. The tires spun, but they weren't going anywhere. Finally, he turned off the engine and sighed. The rest of the family waited as the wind whistled around the little vehicle.

"Well," he said finally, "looks like we'll have to walk from here."

Dixie looked out the window again at the swirling snow. Though she had witnessed blizzards from the safety of her home, she had never been out in one. "Max, home is nearly half a mile from here!" she exclaimed. "Do you really think we can make it?"

"Sure we can!" Jeff chimed in from the back seat. "Half a mile isn't far."

"Well, in good weather it isn't," Dixie faltered.

"We don't have much of a choice," Max responded. "The Myers' place is about halfway there. Let's head there first."

So they did. Putting on all of the clothes and wrappings they could find, they climbed out of the car. They had never walked in a blizzard before. The snowy wind whipped around their faces and bodies, nearly knocking them over as they closed the car doors. Dixie gasped. *I can hardly catch my breath!*

"Joey," Max called over the howling of the wind, "I want you to hang on to my back belt loop." He took Joey's hand and helped him grab the belt loop. He then started forward, half leading, half dragging Joey. "Everyone follow me!"

By this time, the snow had piled up so high that they couldn't really tell where the road was. They stumbled across the snowdrifts, staying as close together as they could. They took big steps and tried to get through snow as high as their knees.

I hope Daddy knows where he's going, Jan thought. She couldn't see hardly anything. Oh, it was so cold!

Jeff was amazed by the power of the storm around them with the cold wind and snow. *This is cool,* he thought. It was certainly a new experience.

Joey was scared and cold, but he focused on hanging on to Max's belt loop. *I'll be fine if I stay with Daddy,* he told himself.

After what felt like hours, the family saw lights ahead, shining golden through the white snow. It was the Myers' house! Gratefully, they struggled up to the porch and knocked on the door.

Evelyn Myers opened it.

"My goodness!" she exclaimed at the sight of the Edwards family. "Were you out in this storm? Come in, come in!"

They hurried inside and felt the warm air begin to thaw their faces. Mrs. Myers fixed them hot chocolate while they told her their story. Max's eyes twinkled as he leaned against the window frame and looked out at the snow.

"Well, this is an experience we wouldn't have in Brazil!" he declared. They all agreed.

Soon after, the family decided they had the courage to walk the rest of the way home. The Myers invited them to stay the night, but the Edwardses knew that if the storm got worse, they would want to be home. So they went out into the storm again, this time more confident that they could make it. As soon as they arrived home, Dixie hurried to the bathroom and filled the tub with hot water for Joey. They were glad that they still had electricity. The family thanked God for once again bringing them home safely. It was good to know that His protection was covering them both in Brazil and in the U.S.

The following months saw more of the regular deputation routine. During the school year, it was more difficult for the whole family to travel, so sometimes Max traveled alone, or sometimes he took Dixie and Joey with him. Jan began college in January, 1979.

The biggest highlight of these months was Jay and Kirsten's wedding in March, 1979. They were married in southwestern Kansas at Kirsten's home church. Because it was just before planting season, their "honeymoon" was a road trip back to Indiana. After their wedding, Jay farmed full-time on the family land, while Kirsten finished her degree at Ball State University in Indiana. And so, the Edwards family gained an additional member.

The family stayed in the U.S. for a little longer this time, until after Christmas, 1979. By then, Max, Dixie, Jeff, and Joey were ready to go home!

As I've been studying the book of Acts, the Holy Spirit has called my attention to the time when Paul was let down over the wall in a basket. I considered then all those who were holding the rope as Paul was being lowered to safety. It may have been boring there in the darkness holding onto that rope. But think of what happened to the early church through Paul because he was aided to leave that night. Boring? Perhaps ... but worthwhile and rewarding.

How we do appreciate those who have been holding the

> *rope for us by praying and giving ... Recent reports from*
> *Brazil indicate we need to hurry back. There is so much*
> *to do and God has called us to help do it! Thank you so*
> *much for being rope-holders for us. It's our <u>privilege</u> to go.*
> —Max, in a prayer letter, April 1979

~ * ~

January 1980

"Laurinha,[12] wake up, wake up! We're here!"

Laura Mendonça groggily opened her eyes. Looking to her right, she saw a friend smiling back at her. Her friend's dark eyes were bloodshot; she was as tired from the trip as Laura was, yet brimming with excitement. Laura then turned to her left to look out the train window. There it was: the Panorama train station. They made it!

As Laura gathered her things and began to feel more awake, she became more excited, too. She always enjoyed going to Panorama Camp, but this time was special: this time she was going as a counselor, not just a camper. At 15, she was just barely old enough to work as a counselor, but she already felt like she had been waiting forever for an invitation. She had served as a counselor at the Japanese Holiness Church's day camps near São Paulo and loved it. Now Mitsuo had finally selected her to be a counselor for the entire camping season at Panorama.

Laura was a small girl with dark-brown eyes and dark, wavy hair that reached her shoulders. The bag that she carried with her things for the month of January seemed almost as big as she was. Following her friends, she stumbled off the train to the truck where the Scotts waited to take them to the camp.

The counselors were at camp four days early for counselors' training, led by Mitsuo. To Laura, it felt like boot camp. Mitsuo expected counselors to be disciplined and responsible; laziness and disobedience were not tolerated. Their days started with group devotions at 6 a.m., followed by prayer times, study times, and confession times. Though it was hard, Laura learned much about spiritual disciplines that would

---

12   An affectionate diminutive form of "Laura"

benefit her for years to come. There was a strong focus on holiness and personal growth. In addition to caring for the campers, the counselors covered the camps in prayer. They signed up for 30-minute time slots throughout each camp, so that at any given time during a camp, someone would be praying.

Many of the other counselors were people Laura knew, but some were not. Some she had seen at previous camps but had never met personally. One of these was Jeffry Edwards, the handsome American boy. He and his little brother, Joey, were spending a few weeks at Panorama while their parents took care of business elsewhere. Joey would participate in children's camp while Jeffry served as a counselor. Laura knew that they had just returned from a year and a half in the U.S.

Laura was assigned the task of collecting all the counselors' zip codes before camp started. This meant that she had to meet all of the other counselors personally. So one day between activities, a mutual friend introduced her to Jeffry. Laura gave Jeffry a friendly smile, and he couldn't help but smile back.

Jeff had actually forgotten some of his Portuguese during his time in the U.S. Laura didn't know much English, but she was happy to help in any way that she could. So they sat together at meals and activities, and when Jeff didn't understand something, Laura would do her best to translate. In this way, they quickly became friends. It was a strange experience for Laura because she had never had many male friends; all her close friends were girls. She knew that Jeffry was very popular with the girls, and she wasn't interested in getting involved in a competition for his attention. But she couldn't help but be attracted to his kind and genuine personality.

Jeff found himself immediately interested in this vivacious young girl with her beautiful smile. Jeff and Laura found their friendship growing in spite of themselves.

While Jeff and Joey spent the month of January at Panorama, Max and Dixie were in São Paulo, finding a home for the family and moving in. They had decided that for this term, they needed to be in the big city so the boys could attend PACA while still living at home. Max would be involved in the OMS' ministries and business in São Paulo in addition to continuing to develop Camp Shalom. The six-hour commute between Londrina and São Paulo was not ideal, but it seemed to be the best situation for the family at that time.

Max and Dixie were pleased to find a lovely little home to rent in a relatively quiet São Paulo neighborhood. They quickly started the process of bringing things out of storage, cleaning, and organizing. By the time they went after the boys two weeks later, they were well on their way to feeling settled in the new home.

They returned to Panorama a few days early so they could visit their various contacts in the area. While they were there, Max asked Mitsuo for the names of the two camp counselors who were from São Paulo, one of which was Laura. Max was thinking ahead to the next camping season; Camp Shalom should be ready to accommodate regular camps by July. Though many of the counselors were from cities close to Panorama, those from São Paulo could just as easily—or perhaps more easily—travel to Londrina. With this in mind, he approached the two of them.

"As you probably know, we've started a new camp in the Londrina area," he said. "I'm looking for counselors to serve there for the July season. Would you two be willing to spend July there at the new camp rather than here?"

Laura and the other counselor readily agreed. Though Laura loved Panorama, if her help was needed more at Shalom, she was just as happy to serve there. Besides, she had a feeling that that was where Jeff would be next season too!

~ * ~

Dixie carefully lifted the cookie sheet and slid it into the oven. Soon the house would be full of the sweet aroma of baking cookies. The kitchen already smelled delicious from the popcorn she had just made for Jeff. She could hear the boys munching on it in the living room as they played their new Intellivision game. Max was upstairs preparing a message. Sunday afternoons—the lovely calm between Sunday school in the morning and the service in the evening. Dixie sat down at the kitchen table with her pad of paper and pen and began a letter to her parents.

February 3, 1980. She wrote about family news and anything interesting that she could think about their Brazil life. They were becoming more settled in the big city. Dixie loved the house they had found to rent. It was certainly small and different from the country homes she was used to, but the architecture was lovely, and the kitchen was closer to an American style than anything she had seen before in Brazilian homes. It was a duplex, so they shared a wall with their neighbor on one side. But on the other side and around to the back of the house, they had a tiled courtyard, similar to their previous São Paulo home. There was a spacious maid's quarters in the back, which for the Edwardses made a perfect guest room. The neighborhood was nice too. Joey was already starting to get to know some of the neighborhood boys and would go out to play with them in the street.

The boys seemed to be doing well in school, though the adjustment was a little more difficult for Joey than it was for Jeff. Jeff was already involved in soccer and basketball, and he loved being back at PACA. Dixie was sure Joey would soon feel the same.

That morning Max and Dixie had taught Sunday school for the first time at their new church, *Planalto Paulista*. Dixie taught the children's class and Max the adults' class. They loved it. This church was lively and healthy—full of people who really wanted to grow in their faith. Dixie had missed teaching Sunday school while they were on furlough, and she was so happy to be back.

Besides church involvement and working on Camp Shalom, Max was also working with a telephone ministry, *Telemensagem*. This was a hotline for Christian counseling. When people called the number, they could hear an encouraging message, and they had the option of speaking to someone on the phone. Signs all over the city of São Paulo, even in prominent places like the subway station, advertised this service. The ministry had a little office downtown, and local Christians were trained to answer the phones and connect people to a Christian counselor if they needed it. Some people who called ended up coming to the office to receive counseling in person. Max visited the office as often as he could to provide training, assistance, and issue resolution. They were already seeing fruit from this ministry.

And yet, Max and Dixie could not help pondering what God's plans were for them in São Paulo. Nearing the end of her letter, Dixie wrote,

"Max and I are both wondering exactly how God wants to use us here—we seem so out-of-place being country people. Amazingly we are both content in a little place—no yard and neighbors all around. Contentment comes from within and isn't determined by the outside conditions."

Certainly, they were content. They could see how God was meeting all of their needs. But could it be that He had something more for them in this big city?

~ * ~

For now, Max was plenty busy with the tasks already assigned to him. His main focus was Camp Shalom. He traveled there almost every week, taking overnight buses there and back. Though there was still much that he wanted to do and build, the camp now had all of the basic facilities needed to host overnight camps. In March 1980, another MFM work crusade came to help with the construction. They made significant progress on the director's residence. The Edwards family was glad to hear this, since they knew that they would be living there from June to August.

Shalom hosted several small church camps and events over the months, getting ready for the first full season of three camps in July. In early June, the year's NOW Corps group arrived, and the Edwards family began the routine of traveling and working with them. They spent much of that winter at the camp, putting final touches on the residence. It was so cold at one point that they had to move all of the NOW Corpsmen out of the dorms and into the house, where it was warmer.

For the first camping season at Shalom, they held one camp for each age group: children, adolescents, and youth. The camps were difficult. It was still very cold, and during one of the camps, the new director for the Shalom camps, Toshiro, was ill. Max was traveling part of the time, and the adolescents, especially, were difficult to manage. Max and Dixie had to remind themselves to be patient; after all, the first camps at Panorama had been rough too. In spite of the problems, they appreciated having a fantastic group of counselors—including Jeff, and Laura Mendonça—who served as examples to the campers on a daily basis.

Everyone learned and grew through the experience, and in the end, a few of the campers made commitments to follow Christ.

In August, the Edwards family was blessed with a few more visitors from the U.S: Dixie's sister, Judy, and some friends, the Hinshaw family. Dixie had mentioned to Laura that the Hinshaws may be interested in hosting an exchange student in their home. When the Hinshaws met Laura, they liked her and officially invited her to come. It was decided that she would spend the spring semester of 1981 in Indiana, living with the Hinshaws and attending the local public school.

Laura was excited about this opportunity, but she was also nervous. She really had to learn English now! Dixie offered to help by giving her private lessons. So from then until December, Laura went to the Edwards' home a couple of times a week for English lessons with Dixie. On other days, she attended a local language school, and one day a week, she had a lesson with her pastor's wife, who spoke English. Dixie's lessons focused on learning about American culture and the Bible in English, while Laura's other lessons focused more on grammar and following formalized curricula. By the time Laura left in December, her English was much better, and Max and Dixie felt like she was part of their family. They knew they would miss her during her time in the U.S.

Chapter 16

The Devil's Mouth

We're busy—but that's the way we want it! I remember well when Max was quite frustrated in language school ten years ago. Seemed there was nothing he could do that contributed to the work—felt like dead weight. I remember hearing him pray, Lord, give me responsibility. As I recall this request I thank God for granting His desire. Sometimes, I have to admit, a sigh goes with the praise! The prayer has been fully answered.
—Dixie, in a prayer letter, June 1980

Max leaned against the doorframe and folded his arms, looking out into the deepening darkness. He glanced at his watch—7:45. He could hear Dixie and her choir still rehearsing inside. Soon it would be time for the evening service.

The rented building stood on a corner near the low point of one of São Paulo's many hills. If Max looked up the hill in one direction, he saw the road that they took into the neighborhood when coming from their home. If he looked up the opposite direction, he saw the winding street that eventually melted into the local slum, or *favela*. Most of his congregation would come from that direction. One could drive for a little while down that road, but eventually would have to park and walk to enter the disorganized slum of bare brick, tin, and wooden buildings. This kind of poverty was quite different from what they had seen in Panorama.

Max and Dixie had found that God did, in fact, have more for them to do in the great metropolis of São Paulo. They found it in this little neighborhood of São Savério, or as some of the locals called it, *Boca do Diabo*, "The Devil's Mouth." The area was certainly under the dominion of the devil. Beyond their own little congregation, Max did not know of a single church in the neighborhood—not even a Catholic one. Most residents were involved in spiritism, or *macumba*, which incorporated various kinds of witchcraft and devil worship. Sometimes, when they came to church in the morning for Sunday school, they saw dead chickens and burn marks in the ground in the empty lot across the street from the church—sure signs that a ritual had taken place there the night before.

Speaking of which ... Max's forehead creased. He could hear the beating of *macumba* drums beginning in the distance even as he stood there. Yes, the spiritual oppression in this area was heavy, so heavy he could almost feel it. And yet, he could not help but allow his frown to turn into a smile when he saw the first few church members approach, walking serenely down the road out of the *favela*. Though they were poor, they were clean and dressed in their best clothes, freshly washed. Their enthusiasm for God shone through every aspect of their being.

These people inspired Max. There was Dona Maria, the elderly woman who had once been a prominent medium in her community. She had become a Christian shortly before the Edwardses arrived, and Max had had the privilege of baptizing her. The spiritual forces that had once been a part of her daily life constantly sought to regain control, but Dona Maria never stopped fighting. She had a simple and beautiful faith; her life had clearly been transformed by God.

Not far behind her was Ivani, a teenage girl who was the only Christian in her family. They were heavily involved in the spiritist community; one of her brothers even ran a spiritist center. She constantly faced verbal persecution from family members for her Christian faith, but her face radiated the joy of Christ.

Though many in the congregation were new Christians and cer-tainly weren't perfect, they persevered in their faith when everyone and everything around them tried to hinder them. They sought to share their beliefs with their friends and family whenever they could, and they took initiative to grow their faith and their church. They were presently looking for ways to raise money so that they could purchase their building and remodel it into a real church. They also sought to serve their community. The church had services on Tuesday, Thursday, Saturday, and Sunday nights; on the remaining nights, the church youth used the space to teach reading and writing to the illiterate. Max was quickly finding this church to be one of the most rewarding as well as the most challenging ministries he had ever had.

The São Savério congregation was a new church plant, formed by members of the Edwards' former church, Planalto Paulista. Several of those involved in the plant were Christians who lived in this area and had a passion to reach their own community. In late 1980, Max was appointed as pastor of this new church, to shepherd the small congregation as they organized and grew. They had started with about 30 baptized members, but that number was growing.

Joey was upstairs, playing marbles with some of his new friends. He liked their new church, even though it was different. When they had first arrived in São Savério, Max had an idea to spread the word about service, and he recruited Jeff to help him. Joey had seen his dad open the back of their white station wagon and instruct Jeff to sit inside with his trumpet. He watched with envy as Dad drove Jeff through the neighborhood while Jeff played the trumpet. As people came out to see what was going on, Max called out in Portuguese, "Service at 8! Come to the service tonight at 8!"

Someday, I want to be good enough on the trumpet to do that, Joey thought. At any rate, the church services always had lots of visitors, so maybe Jeff's trumpet playing was working.

When they heard the choir finish practicing downstairs, Joey and his friends put their marbles away and headed down for the service. The building wasn't meant to be a church, but Joey thought it was fine. He entered the main hall and looked around. Dixie was up front putting choir music away, and Max was at the door greeting people who were coming in. Joey went with his friends to sit on the floor in front of the pulpit.

One thing Joey had noticed that was different about this church was that people would go to the front to ask the pastor to pray for them. Maybe this happened at their old church too, but he couldn't remember it happening this much. His dad always stayed after the service to be there for anyone who wanted prayer, and there was always a line of people waiting. Sometimes people would come forward even during the service. And sometimes strange things happened when Max prayed for them. Joey's parents said that this was because they used to be spiritists, and the demons didn't want to let them go.

Today was one of those days. Right in the middle of the service, a man came up to the front. Joey had seen the man before; he was a newer Christian, and like most of the new Christians, he used to be a spiritist. The man looked tired and upset, as if he was carrying something heavy that no one could see. Max began to pray for him, and other men came forward too, until there was a whole circle around him, praying. Then … there were strange sounds, like growls and roars. It sounded like a bear!

Joey craned his neck to see what was going on. When he lifted himself up a little, he could see over the heads of the other children and through the legs of the circle of men at the front. The man was acting like a bear, standing on all fours and growling. The men around him continued to pray with Max in the middle of them. Joey's heart beat faster. *Will this demon-possessed man hurt Dad?* he wondered. Then, right before his eyes, the man's hands raised up above the ground! He still leaned forward as though putting weight on his hands, but they no longer touched the floor. Joey watched with his mouth agape. He knew that there was a supernatural power at work—an evil one. It was confusing sometimes. These people at church were Christians, but so many of them still had problems like this. Dixie had told him that people who came from Christian families like theirs had no idea what it was like to have been involved with spirits and to try to break away from them. God was stronger, but Satan wouldn't give up easily. Joey silently thanked God that he had never been involved with demons and prayed that God would protect his dad and set the demon-possessed man free. After what felt like forever, the demon finally left, and the man relaxed. He looked so relieved! Joey was relieved too. God had heard their prayers.

In pastoring this church, Max often spent long hours counseling, visiting members in their homes, and talking with those who approached him after services. There were many stories represented by the members of the church; each story was individual, and yet so many were similar.

On one occasion a young man named Orlando approached Max a few minutes before the start of the Saturday evening service. This man had just accepted Christ at the Thursday service a couple of days before. He was one of the brothers of Ivani, the teenage girl who until this point had been the only Christian in her family. Orlando was a gentle, soft-spoken man, but he came to Max and told him he had some problems that were troubling him. Max nodded in understanding.

"Why don't we pray together?" he suggested. He led Orlando into a room to the side of the main hall; the room had no door and an open window, but it offered a small bit of privacy. They sat down together, and Max put his hands on Orlando's shoulders and began to pray.

Immediately the gentle young man before him was transformed into a different person. For the next half hour, Orlando struggled with Max: speaking in other voices, growling like a bear, even trying to choke Max and scratch his face. Max talked to the demons possessing the man, and they argued back. They said they wouldn't leave, but Max kept praying. After 15 minutes, another church member came in to help. Three different times Orlando relaxed; perhaps this was an indication of three different demons leaving him. After 35 minutes of prayer and struggle, he returned to his ordinary self.

Max sighed in relief. Though he had some experience with these things now, each time was different. He was thankful that God was always stronger than anything that opposed him.

The church continued to expand over time. They were able to rent another building behind their hall to have more space for Sunday school classes, which allowed them to have four classes instead of just two. When Laura returned from her exchange study, she attended São Savério with the Edwardses and helped with Sunday school.

In September 1981, the São Savério believers formally organized into a church. Though most of the people had little means, they tithed regularly and saw God's provision for their church. They were eventually able to do some remodeling to make their hall more "church-like" on the inside with a platform, pulpit, and pews. At one point they focused prayer on the young men who needed to find work. In the days following, 10 of those men were able to get jobs! The people were encouraged to see God working and providing in their daily lives.

And so, when he was not at Camp Shalom, Max found himself dedicating most of his time to the São Savério church. Sometimes he felt that he was not able to give it all of the attention it needed, but he was thankful for the opportunities that God had given him. He also became involved in some other local ministries, including a recuperation center for men addicted to drugs or alcohol, and a prison ministry. All of these different ministries were rewarding in their own respects, and Max felt privileged to see the many ways that God was working in São Paulo.

~ * ~

March 9, 1981

Dear Mom & Dad—and All
   Yesterday was quite a day, a good one, hurried
and varied with the routine and the unexpected.
   Left at 8:30 a.m. for S.S.[13] at S.S. (São Savério, remember? That's the name of a saint 'who-knows-who?' I'd never heard of him. That's the name of the bairro[14] of our rented hall where our congregation meets.) Went past Planalto to make sure the baptistery tank would be full for our baptism in the afternoon. It <u>wouldn't</u> have been. Pastor had forgotten ... On to S.S. for S.S. Kids dribble in—wish they'd come at 9. By 9:30 must have had 25–30 and by closing time we had 38! Well that's a <u>lot</u> of kids! Just like Panorama days. The <u>big</u> kids (ages 10–12 or so) bring their toddler brother or sister along. I have 'em all. Sure is different from a U.S. organized church! We've no room or we'd divide. <u>If</u> we get to buy that property, we will keep the bottom for social part and build a sanctuary on top. A great plan. We're praying for God to give us the property—enable us to buy it. For now, I have the children from 9–10 (while youth and adults make noise outside), then they go in and the kids go out (and make noise—ha!). A workable situation. I've seen worse. I'm doing the story of Esther. Using a seal per child

---

13   Sunday school.
14   Neighborhood.

per Sunday so will need some soon. Max's class went till 11:30. Always after _every_ service, there are people and/or business of church to treat. We didn't get home till 12:30.

Quick dinner—had till 2:30 at home. Baptism was nice. Three were a mother (of 8 and grandmother of 12) and her married daughter and her youngest, age 14. Another youth, girl of 18, and a boy 14. The older woman accepted Christ soon after we arrived. Had a smoking problem, which hindered her baptism. Said she had victory over it and was ready. Over at 4:15. Max always takes Polaroid fotos[15] of candidates. A real lembrança[16] for each. Left Jeff and Joey home to do homework. Left again at 5:45 for church. Had my 1st English class and a _lot_ showed—25 maybe. They know the NOW Corpsmen are coming, and that's what stimulated the beginning. They want to be able to communicate a little. Our youth are _really_ anticipating their visit. We plan a week's meetings nightly with the American youth calling during the day with Brazilian kids in the community. I began with the alphabet, verb "to be," then phrases, sentences. "_I love God. Do you love God? I am a Christian. Are you a Christian? My name is. What is your name?_"—plus _nos. 1–20_. It's fun. I _love_ it. Had some non-Christians there; that's good. Next week having Choir at 6 and English at 7, _hoping_ the visitors will stay for church.

Then we had our 1st Choir practice for S.S.! The other church is really sad that I left. I pray that God will give them a "lift" some way … These things are hard.

With Choir, I explained the notes, going up or down, showed each (voice) part where to "read" their notes. Three of my basses moved to tenor after a few minutes. Left 4 in bass, 6 in tenor, _2_ sopranos, and 5 altos. Brazilians don't sing high; I've found _few_. Well, we did an easy one, Battle Hymn of the Republic, here a favorite Christian hymn, and they did well. Had one tenor

---

15   Photos.
16   Keepsake.

*and two basses (Jeff) who already know parts from P.P.
I was pleased. They're "turned on." We'll have a choir!*

*Then church service. Hall was super loaded. It is an
unhandy arrangement for a "church." Has a big post in
middle, preacher looks around it to see everyone. There's a
toilet and sink to the side and back of "pulpit." You know
children. And we had <u>gobs</u>. Most of my S.S. class was there,
I think. I sat on front "row." Only about one yard between
me and the "pulpit" and that space was filled with children
on the floor. 10–12. They were "fairly" quiet (for kids!).
Every seat was full, and many stood. It's a little place; may
have had 80–90 there. Was to have been a long service (and
was) as was Communion. The 2nd hymn, the bass guitarist
chose, and I looked at him and frowned—"Battle Hymn."
He grinned at me, and we sang all five verses—what we had
just done for an hour! As I said, they like it. I do too. They
always raise their hands on chorus. We need to think of the
truth, power, and victory more. We are on the winning side!
After Vade (a super talented … boy, 18) sang a beautiful,
very modern Christian song, Max took the floor. Vade would
have led a half hour's singing of lively (I use the word for lack
of a more "lively" one —ha) choruses. If you haven't heard
Brazilians sing, you haven't heard volume. They put themselves in it—a solid half hour isn't unusual and most of that
time em pé (standing). Well, Max said the Spirit was right
to preach, so he began. Going through the Beatitudes. Did
3rd, "Blessed are the meek for they shall inherit the earth."
Excellent. Good attention in spite of the confusions. There
was a board (good size) put across entrance to bathroom so
no one would go. Well, when the first one tried it, took some
time and noise to scoot that thing back. Then the running of
water (everybody needs a drink!). The worst was the flush-
ing of the toilet right during a serious prayer of dedication
of new officers! Max kept his "cool" … Then, after the toilet
flushed, the water box had to refill, and it was above his
head—and is a "noisy filler." Oh well, all part of a family,*

huh? And our people are a family. Interestingly enough, no one smirked or giggled or anything. Was all so common to them. We had communion—Oh, before this, Max had the five new members … go forward. Each one in turn prayed for his pastor (he did this for all members when he began), and each was given a little notebook to use for prayer lists, etc. Then Communion. Forgot a "funny" during the message … Max was preaching away and using examples of people in the church when he said to our one, very simple lady, but very much a Christian, "And Margarida, you pray for that rebellious, backslidden daughter of yours" … and she arose (to her feet) and began. And pray, she did—for several minutes! The message continued after her Amen!

After church, there was a line of people to talk to or receive prayer from the pastor. This is normal. About the 3rd was Aura … She is unsaved (wife of the guitarist, himself a new Christian), and Max has talked with her on different occasions. She was at the baptism—her mother and two sisters were baptized. Max inquired about what she desired … She said, "I'm confused." Max got his oil out, anointed her, and began praying … suddenly she screamed, went limp, and fell to floor, leaning against his legs. Her body wretched and contorted. Max prayed once, no change, then prayed the 2nd time, expelling the demon, and she relaxed. Stood to her feet and didn't know what had happened. She cried and cried for happiness and relief (that was a first for Max to happen in that way). It was quite a service. Quite a day. We serve Quite a God. Rejoice with us in Him and pray for our faithfulness and sensitivity to God's voice.

Told Max I wanted to get it on paper before I forgot some of the interesting details.

Max is really tired today, has a headache. Wonders why; I think I know. A pastor has to rest sometime. He's trying that now—not succeeding because of phone. We did some running this morning to Korean

Church where seminary classes will begin April 7. Max is going to preach there Sunday night, the 15th.

He'll either preach in English or Portuguese (depending on the translator they find for him) and will be put in Korean. They want to take us out to supper first. Should be an enlightening evening. Jeff is to play a special on his trumpet. He uses the acompanhamentos[17] Jan made for him. He's good.

Today, we go to the school for parent-teacher conferences. I didn't receive the revealing "slip," so my boys are doing OK. Want to go anyway. Jeff has a term paper to do for Psychology by end of month. He applies himself well and makes A's and B's. Anxious for college—and soccer! (Who said that's not what college is for? ha) He even <u>dreamed</u> he was in training the 1st week of school! He's written and requested details about it but hasn't recv'd reply. I want him to play the horn and try out for stage band. He said, "Mother, soccer comes first. If I have time for both, I'll try out." Well, Mother wants him to play soccer, too!

Joey went for little league baseball Saturday morning. He enjoyed it. Got a ball in the eye. More praying.

We had an "American experience" Saturday! Went to the new, first McDonald's here in S.P. Was so much fun. Very similar to U.S.—efficient help, good food (maybe more expensive but been 1½ years since we were there)—even had apple pie (same wrapping) and soft ice cream! Was a real treat. We'll be going back.

Mom, we hope you are feeling <u>much</u> better. Pray daily for you. I pray that you'll feel <u>His</u> peace and presence—the most important.

Better sign off before the P.O. refuses this weight! This letter I want shared with Jay and Kirsten, Jan, and my folks. Want them all to know about the day we had yesterday. Share with any other interested people or person ...

---

17   Accompaniment.

Anxious for every word about you, Mom. Dad, I guess
"spring is just around the corner-field" —huh? Take care,
Lovingly,
Dixie
for
Max and boys

~ * ~

June 1981

"Happy anniversary to you,
   Happy anniversary to you,
Happy anniversary, Mother and Daddy ...
   Happy anniversary to you!"

Max and Dixie sat up in bed, bleary-eyed, and turned on the lights. Jeff, Joe, and Snoopy stood in the doorway in their pajamas, grinning. Jeff held a large, brightly wrapped package.

"Happy twenty-fifth anniversary!" the boys exclaimed.

"This gift is from all five of us kids," Jeff said. He brought it forward and set it on Dixie's lap.

"Oh, my!" Dixie exclaimed.

"Is it our anniversary?" Max asked, his eyes twinkling.

Dixie carefully unwrapped the gift. Inside she found a beautiful silver tray with an inscription and a set of six little silver cups made for *cafezinho*, or Brazilian-style coffee, with matching saucers.

"What a lovely gift! Thank you, boys!" Dixie and Max opened their arms, and the boys came forward for hugs and kisses.

"You boys had best go get ready for school," Dixie said. "I'll be down in a few minutes to make your breakfast."

"Okay!" Jeff and Joe headed out and back to their own room, and Snoopy followed along behind them. Max and Dixie looked at each other and smiled.

"Happy anniversary, honey." Max leaned over and gave his wife a big kiss.

They couldn't take long to celebrate though—not this morning anyway. Today promised to be an especially full day, mostly because Jeff's high school graduation was to be that evening. They were going to the school in the afternoon to help decorate. Max had been asked to give the keynote address. And if that wasn't enough, another missionary couple would be arriving that evening to spend the night and the next day with them.

So they hurried to begin the day's tasks. Just a few short hours later, Dixie was bringing the boys home after decorating to get ready for graduation and to eat a quick supper. Then they were off again—for the graduation of their third child! *My, how the years have flown,* Dixie thought.

Dan Owsley, who was living in São Paulo at the time, came with the family to graduation. Dixie was glad to have him there, especially when she thought about Jay and Jan so far away. Dan and Joey sat with Dixie in the audience; as the speaker, Max sat on the platform. On a large banner behind the platform was the chosen class verse:

"For I know the plans I have for you," declares the LORD, "plans to prosper you and not to harm you, plans to give you hope and a future."
Jeremiah 29:11 (NIV)

As Dixie read those words, she couldn't help thinking about the ways they had already been fulfilled in Jeff's life. As she had written in a letter home, "We've watched as Jeff grew up … the struggles, hurts, timidity, and dreams too intimate to describe. This one and a half years at PACA has been 'the icing on the cake.'" Jeff had matured into a confident young man, loved and respected by all. He had participated in every sport he could and was appointed either captain or co-captain for each one. He was recognized as a leader in other areas as well; for his senior year, he had been elected student body president and served in that role throughout the year. He had also been crowned homecoming king that October. As she saw him walk down the aisle in his bright-green graduation gown, Dixie couldn't have been prouder. *We're really going to miss him,* she thought. What a day—25 years of marriage and three children graduated to adulthood.

Fortunately, they would get to keep Jeff for a few more months before he left for college. Jeff stayed in Brazil during the winter months of June to August to assist with construction, camps, and the NOW Corps activities. That year, the NOW Corps had only three members, one of whom was Scott Terrell, Dixie's nephew. Laura Mendonça returned from her exchange study that June, and she also participated with the Edwards family and the NOW Corps in many of their activities. On July 4, Laura and Jeff officially started dating.

The group spent much of the winter at Camp Shalom. Though the facility was already hosting camps regularly, there was still a lot of work and construction to be done. Max also struggled with a lack of finances as various problems arose. One major problem that they faced in the winter of 1981 was difficulty with the camp's water supply. First, an official test on the water from their dug well found the water to be "unfit for human consumption." So they began work on a drilled well. However, before the drilled well was completed, the dug well began to dry up. Then they found they had no water, drinkable or undrinkable, and buying water was getting expensive. They were forced to cancel one of their youth camps, and Max and Dixie sent out a letter to their supporters requesting funding for the drilled well. They were getting discouraged.

One day, Dona Lucila, the camp cook, came to Dixie holding her Bible. Beaming, she showed her Exodus 23:25: "Worship the LORD your God, and his blessing will be on your food and water" (NIV).

"Don't worry," she encouraged Dixie. "God is going to bless the water at Camp Shalom." And He did. Eventually, the funds came in, and the well was finished, ready to supply the camp with good, clean water for years to come. Nevertheless, this was one of the challenges that slowed down the work at the camp.

One big project Max wanted to complete this year was an Olympic-sized swimming pool. Shalom had plenty of room for a pool; it was just a matter of getting the materials and doing the construction. Finances were tight, so Max decided they would try to pour the cement floor of the pool by hand, rather than hiring a cement truck. The NOW

Corpsmen, Jeff, Max, and some local workers spent one very long day mixing cement and hauling it in wheelbarrows to the pool site. Starting very early in the morning, they worked until it was almost dusk. They had poured about three-fourths of the floor by hand by that time. Max decided to hire a cement truck to finish the work before dark, since it all had to be poured in one day in order to set properly.

Jeff collapsed into his bed that night. He had never worked so hard in his life. He pulled out his Bible to read the Proverbs chapter of the day, Proverbs 24. His eyes fell to verse 10: "If you fail under pressure, your strength is too small" (NLT). Jeff smiled and underlined the verse. How appropriate for that day.

In spite of the hardships and difficulties, the group had a good winter and enjoyed each other's company. Jeff and Scott planned to room together at Asbury College that fall, so Jeff looked forward to that even as he dreaded leaving Brazil. It was decided that Jeff would fly back to the U.S. with a work crusade group that was coming in August. Max went along also to visit his parents for a few weeks and help Jeff get settled. It was a difficult day at the airport for everyone, but Max and Dixie knew that they could entrust Jeff to God's hands, just as they had entrusted Jay and Jan. He was faithful in caring for their kids, as He was faithful in caring for them.

That year, Laura entered PACA for her last year of high school rather than returning to Brazilian school. She was quickly becoming a member of the Edwards family. They helped her get settled into PACA, and she asked Dixie to teach her how to cook and sew. She and Dixie also met regularly to talk and pray together, and she attended the São Savério church and volunteered there. Max and Dixie loved her like a daughter. And of course, though they were far away, Laura and Jeff did their best to stay in touch. They regularly wrote each other six-page letters—the maximum number of pages for a letter before it became so heavy that it raised the postage cost.

The school year seemed to fly by. Max and Dixie saw Joey mature as he learned to get by without Jeff and his other siblings. Jan and Jeff both visited for Christmas, and the family enjoyed spending that time together. These "big kids" were maturing, too, during their time in college. At the end of the school year, Laura graduated from PACA and left to begin college at Asbury in the U.S. Several of Joey's good friends left PACA at the end of the year as well. Changes, hellos, and goodbyes—the life of missionaries!

The Steps

By Joe Edwards

Childhood memories are odd; they are a visual and emotional stew of images, sounds, and smells. Invariably, there are pictures involved, and you can't quite tell where the memory of the picture and the memory of the events begin and end. Maybe it makes those childhood memories more real and more vivid—memories that still elicit emotion and can change the mood of a 40-something adult so many decades later. The steps at the old international departures area at Congonhas airport in São Paulo is a place awash with these kinds of memories for me.

For decades, the procedure for international passengers flying out of the airport was to check in, check baggage, then walk with friends and family down the terminal to the base of a wide set of stairs that narrowed to a landing, then do a 90-degree turn behind a wall. After farewells, the people going would slip past a roped-off area where someone checked their boarding pass. They would walk up the first flight of steps, wave a final goodbye to the people staying behind, and start up the next set of steps as they disappeared behind the wall.

When I was a preteen, I was around those steps all the time. As the designated host family for OMS in São Paulo, we saw every missionary, MFM group, NOW Corps, or other visitor to Brazil come through our house and the Edwards shuttle service. But none of those memories are the ones that are burned into my emotions or induce melancholy at the mere mention of the steps. What stirs me still is the image of my brothers and sister disappearing up the steps and leaving me behind.

One of the first memories of my life is Jay leaving up those steps. I feel like I didn't see him for years after that (I don't really know if that's true or not, since time for a five-year-old is squishy). Everyone tells me I loved to spend time with my biggest brother, 14 years my senior, when I was very little, but I don't remember any of that. I do remember the steps swallowing him up, though, and leaving the airport with one less family member. I had a few more years with Jan, 12 years my senior, at homes in Panorama and Londrina. But soon her time came, and we traveled to São Paulo where those same steps took her away as well.

Finally, Jeff, eight years my senior, graduated from high school and, of course, by then I understood how things worked. When his time came, Laura also came with us to see him off, and I actually did okay, because I knew how the steps worked by now. I was 11 or 12 and was able to handle myself well at the airport.

We went home sad like always, but nothing was out of the ordinary, and I went about my normal bedtime routine. After the shower and pajamas, I bent over the bathroom sink to prepare my toothbrush. When I straightened up with my toothbrush in my mouth I looked in the mirror, expecting to see my big brother there with me like every other night... , but there was only a blank blue-tile wall. I lost it! Tears and blubbering don't go well with toothpaste foam, but that's what happened.

It's well documented that the MK life is a lot about departures, separation, leaving, or being left. As the youngest of four, being left was my lot in life. We had, and have, a very close family, and I love my siblings dearly, but we weren't given the time other "normal" families have to spend bonding. The Congonhas steps bring to mind swishy, foggy visuals and sharp, clear emotions; those steps hold an infamous place in the life of this MK.

Chapter 17

Cowboy Boots in the City

*As I consider Shalom I say thank you, Father ... for the
many MFMers who toiled and gave sacrificially to build it
... for an abundance of good water and for those who paid
for the well ... for the faithful giving of our share supporters who kept us going financially ... for strength for the day
(with much bus riding all night) for Max to keep up the necessary pace to see the construction completed ... for a beautiful pool so essential for a camp in Brazil ... for the Holy
Spirit Who will draw many to God at this dedicated place.*
—Dixie, in a prayer letter, February 1982

When Max and Dixie had started working at Panorama in 1971,
they had hoped and prayed that within 10 years it could be
turned over to Brazilian management. In June 1982, this goal was
realized as Max finalized the sale of Panorama Camp to the Japanese
Holiness Church of Brazil. Max and Dixie were thrilled; they knew the
church would make good use of the facility. As Dixie wrote in a prayer
letter, "This is progress in missions."[18]

They hoped that Camp Shalom would eventually be led by national
leadership as well. However, in this case the plan was for it to serve their
own national church, the *Igreja Missionária* or "Missionary Church."
Londrina was the heart of this denomination with the seminary there
and many of their churches spread throughout the area. So while Max
worked to build the camp's facilities, he also worked to arouse the interest of the local church leaders and gain their cooperation.

18   February 1982.

Some of the early camps were very small, but over time Camp Shalom increased in popularity. The camps at Shalom were somewhat different from those at Panorama. While Panorama had attracted many kids who were not from Christian homes, and many were saved at the camp, most of those who came to Shalom were from the *Igreja Missionária*. Therefore, though there were some conversions at Camp Shalom, the greater focus was on spiritual growth in current believers. Max and Dixie appreciated the opportunity to offer Bible teaching and encouragement to these youth who often came from difficult backgrounds in spite of the fact that they were "church kids."

In November 1981, the national church held its large annual conference for the first time at Camp Shalom rather than at Panorama. So Max had a deadline to get some of the major construction done. The pool and new dormitory units were finished just in time. The conference went well, and Shalom was used for more church activities in the following months.

Throughout most of this time, Max maintained a weekly schedule of spending half of every week in Londrina and half in São Paulo. Taking overnight buses, he usually left São Paulo Sunday night after church, spent Monday through Thursday at Shalom, and then traveled back to São Paulo Thursday night. He would then have Friday through Sunday to visit church people, prepare his message, and work with *Telemensagem*.

However, even this "regular schedule" was often thrown off by various events that he had to attend. The whole family generally spent the camping months of January and July at Camp Shalom. Sometimes Max found himself discouraged; though he loved the camp work, he loved the pastoring even more, and he wished he could stay in São Paulo and focus on the church. Later, he wrote that this time was "spiritually maybe one of the most rewarding times in my life, watching a congregation grow, and physically maybe one of the most difficult times." He was always on the go and sleep-deprived, so he and Dixie began to pray that he would have some kind of relief.

In January 1982, at the annual missions and church leaders' retreat, it was decided that another missionary family, the Mishlers, would move to Camp Shalom and oversee those camp activities. Though the Edwards family was sad to lose their "vacation home," they thanked God for this change, which took some of the burden off of Max. He would still visit frequently to attend church events and supervise construction projects, but he would not have to go quite as often, and he wouldn't have to worry about the management of the camp in his absence.

~ * ~

Great is Thy faithfulness
    Great is Thy faithfulness
Morning by morning new mercies I see!
    All I have needed Thy Hand hath provided
Great is Thy faithfulness
    Lord, unto me.[19]

June 1982

It was a quiet night on the Edwards' street of Rua Thebas. Max and the latest group of NOW Corps students were at Shalom for a four-day camp, while Dixie, Joey, and Snoopy slept soundly at home. The doors and the gate were locked tightly, and the house smelled of Dixie's freshly baked cookies.

All of a sudden, Dixie had a sense that something was amiss. Only half awake, she sat up in bed. Then, just as suddenly, she became very sleepy and lay back down. She slept soundly through the rest of the night—more deeply, perhaps, than she had ever slept.

The next morning, Dixie awoke at 6:30 as usual. She sat up and shivered. The house was cold. It felt like there was a draft coming in from outside. That was strange; it was June, Brazilian winter, so she had closed all the windows before they went to bed. Glancing around the room, she saw that her jewelry boxes were missing from the top of the dresser. Her heart dropped into her stomach. She jumped out of bed and hurried down the hall to the stairs.

From the top of the stairs, Dixie could see the front door and entryway. The area was in disarray; boxes and other miscellaneous items

---

19   Thomas Chisholm and William Runyan, "Great Is Thy Faithfulness," 1923.

were strewn about the floor. The front door stood slightly ajar. Dixie ran downstairs and walked through the living and dining rooms. All was a mess; drawers were opened, and things were strewn everywhere. The dining room table was covered in stuff that appeared to have come from Max's office upstairs. As she looked around, Dixie suddenly thought, *Joey!* She ran back upstairs as quickly as she could, her bare toes going numb from the cold marble floor. She hurried down the hallway and peeked into Joey's room.

Her youngest son lay peacefully sleeping in his bed. Dixie breathed a sigh of relief, thinking, *He is so much more important than things.* Convinced that Joey was fine, Dixie walked slowly back down the hall and sank onto the top step. *Oh, God,* she prayed, *I've been robbed!*

Dixie shuddered to think that thieves had been in her house, even in her bedroom, without her knowing it. She watched as the front door creaked slightly with the cold breeze and papers fluttered across the floor. She felt so helpless and alone, even though she knew that God was with her. Sighing, she got dressed, then went to the telephone and called the police.

Soon, a black-and-orange VW pulled up with two friendly policemen. When Dixie told them about her brief awakening in the night, they theorized that the thieves had sprayed her with some kind of sleeping drug.

"You'd better be thankful you slept," they told her. "Just last week, another woman was killed when she woke up during a robbery." Dixie thanked God for protecting her and Joey.

Dixie wondered if Snoopy had been drugged as well; she was acting sick. The policemen teased Dixie that she needed a better guard dog!

The thieves had taken most of Dixie's jewelry, some money, and some electronic items. They had found Max's important documents and dumped them all out on the dining room table but hadn't taken any. Thankfully, they failed to find the American money that Max and Dixie had hidden in the house.

While she talked to the policemen, Dixie organized the documents that were scattered around the table, checking to see if anything was missing. She came across an envelope of stickers she had left on the table the night before, intending to use them for Sunday school. The little books of stickers had been removed from the envelope, and a few were missing from a couple of the books.

"Look at this!" she exclaimed, showing the policemen. "A few of the stickers are missing. Do you think a child could have been involved?"

One of the policemen nodded. "That explains why there are no broken doors or windows," he said. Pointing toward the living room, he said, "They probably put a child through the high ventilation window in your living room, which doesn't have any bars on it. Then the kid opened the door from the inside for the adults."

Dixie shook her head. She hated to think of a child being used in that way; at the same time, it made her smile to imagine a little boy or girl standing there taking stickers while the adults did their thieving.

Joey came down the stairs. His eyes widened when he saw the mess. "What happened?" he asked. Dixie went to him and gave him a hug. "Joey, honey," she said, "we've been robbed. Some thieves came in last night, went through all of our things, and took some."

Immediately Joey's mind went to his most prized possessions. *My big men!* he thought frantically. He pulled out of his mother's arms and ran back upstairs to his bedroom. Opening his bottom drawer, he sighed with relief—his collection of plastic toy men was still there. They were his favorite toys, hand-me-downs from Jeff. Everything would be okay!

The policemen finished taking information. Dixie thanked them and saw them off at the gate. Coming back inside, she closed the door and locked it. *Well,* she thought, *this day is going differently than I had planned.* The church was holding a fundraising bazaar that day, and Dixie had promised to help. She had intended to get up early, bake a cake, and take the cake and the cookies she had made last night to the bazaar. Well, she could still make the cake and bring those things to church, if nothing else. Fortunately, her cookies hadn't been stolen! She mixed up the cake and put it in the oven. While it was baking, she and Joey tidied up the house and put documents and other items back where they belonged. Dixie wanted to call Max and tell him what had happened, but she knew that there was no phone out at Camp Shalom. Hopefully, he would go into town and call her at some point.

Dixie took her things to church and briefly explained to one of the women what had happened; then she went home. She didn't have the heart to do any of the other away-from-home activities that she had planned for that day. So she and Joey spent the rainy Saturday at home. Max called in the afternoon, and Dixie told him what had happened. He comforted her and told her that he was glad she hadn't awakened. Dixie wished he were home, but she knew that there was no point in asking him to cut his trip short; the damage was done. Besides, he had a great deal of responsibility for this camp; he was one of the speakers. But boy, would she be glad to see him tomorrow night!

Some of the church members visited that afternoon to check on her and comfort her. Many of them had experienced being robbed themselves; that was life in São Paulo. Though the whole experience was frightening for Dixie, she trusted that God was still in control. She wrote in a letter home: "God is good. What He permits, He has a purpose for. We don't need or depend upon our luxuries." That Sunday night, she shared in church about her experience and sang "Great Is Thy Faithfulness" in Portuguese. God was always faithful.

Yes, robberies were a part of big-city life. Besides this time at home, they had several experiences of robberies—or attempted robberies— when they were out and about downtown.

On one memorable occasion, less than a month after the house robbery, Max and Joey were downtown running errands. They wanted to buy materials for a go-cart they were building together, and Max also needed to exchange money. As the senior OMS missionary stationed in São Paulo, Max was once again business manager for the Mission, and he regularly went downtown to exchange money. Perhaps this had been noticed by the locals. Though São Paulo was much more diverse than the rural areas, Max remained a noticeable personality with his cowboy boots, strong American accent, and purposeful demeanor.

At any rate, on this day someone decided that he would make a good "mark." As Max and Joey were walking, someone came up and slammed into his shoulder from behind, spinning him around, while another man slipped his hand into Max's pocket. Max immediately grabbed the wrist of the hand in his pocket, then swung his other hand around, slamming the man with his briefcase and then grabbing him around the waist. The man had Max's money in his hand, but he couldn't get away.

Max had not been trained to tackle, but he thought, *If I can just pull this guy's pants down, he'll get embarrassed and leave.* So he kept his hand around the man's waist and tried to find the fastener on his pants. Meanwhile, the robber dropped the money that was in his hand, and his partner moved forward to hit Max on the head. By this time a small crowd had gathered to watch, although no one seemed particularly eager to help. Money was flying everywhere.

"I've got it, Dad!" Joey exclaimed. He rushed forward to pick up Max's fallen glasses and then darted around, gathering the money.

The thief shouted at Max, "You have your money. Now let me go!" Max did, and the man and his partner ran off. The crowd then came forward and helped Max and Joey pick up the rest of the money. Max had a bad cut on the side of his nose, and his ribs were hurting. Somehow, he and Joey both had blood on their clothes, so they went to a restroom to clean up before making their transaction. Joey was shaking, but Max figured it could've been worse.

"They didn't get anything," he reminded Joey. "Next time, maybe I should vary my route when I go to exchange money. Seems like maybe they were expectin' us." Joey was amazed that he could be so matter-of-fact about everything.

Over time, Max did start to take more precautions. Sometimes he would put his money in his boots where no one would expect to find it. He found that cowboy boots served a purpose even in the big city.

Fortunately for the Edwardses, 1982 held more for them than attempted robberies. In September, Max had his fiftieth birthday. Dixie threw him a surprise birthday party at church with approximately 130 people in attendance. They presented an overview of Max's life with some parts dramatized by members of the church. Joey played the part of 12-year-old Max accepting Christ during the thunderstorm. One of the ladies of the church made a huge cake and decorated it with the words *We love you, Uncle Max*. It was a very special celebration for Max, and the presentation of his story challenged many of the attendees in their lives and faith.

At Christmas, the Edwardses had a special treat: The entire family came to Brazil for the holiday! Jay and Kirsten came from Indiana, Jan came from Ecuador, where she had been doing her student teaching, and Jeff came from Asbury, accompanied by Laura. They all thoroughly enjoyed their time together. Jeff was able to do his practicum for his physical education degree at PACA. Joey loved having his big brother come with him to school every day for a few weeks. Soon after they arrived in Brazil, Jeff and Laura got engaged. Jay and Kirsten were able to visit Panorama, where Jay could share his memories with his wife, and introduce her to people he knew. It was an exciting holiday, and to top it off, Joey decided to be baptized. He was baptized along with three of his good friends from São Savério in early January.

Having finished her elementary education degree, Jan decided to stay and work in Brazil for a while, while her family was still there. She got a job teaching OMS' young missionary kids in Londrina, much as she and her siblings had been taught during their year there. Though she was in a different city from Max and Dixie, they enjoyed seeing her on some weekends and holidays.

So the Edwards family continued in their regular activities of ministry, school, and entertaining the various American groups that came through São Paulo. At one point, they had a boy named Walter stay with them. He was in the process of being adopted by a family in the U.S. Walter was Joey's age and stayed with Joey in his room.

At first, Joey had a difficult time dealing with Walter; he was from a rough background, and it showed. Joey found himself frequently needing to ask forgiveness of Walter after reacting to him in frustration. This habit of asking for forgiveness seemed to make an impression on the other boy. Walter had little exposure to the Christian message, but he heard a lot during the few days that he was with the Edwardses. One night he and Joey stayed up late talking about spiritual things. In the course of that conversation, Joey led Walter to accept Christ. Both boys were excited to tell Dixie about it the next morning! Yes, life and ministry were good for the Edwards family.

~ * ~

Smiling on the outside but crying on the inside ... but no, the crying gives way to praise and thanksgiving as we consider God's love and His guiding of our lives.
—Max and Dixie, in a prayer letter, July 1983

In many ways, Max was at the height of his ministry in Brazil. He had successfully built two thriving camps, one of which had already been turned over to the national church. He was pastoring a healthy, growing congregation, and he was involved in many other ministries. His preaching and his counseling had impacted many lives, and he was loved by all. And more opportunities seemed to be opening up—more places that needed camps, teachers, and leaders. He had also become one of the leaders among OMS' group of missionaries in Brazil, and it was expected that he would become the next field leader.

And yet, soon after they arrived back in Brazil for their third term in 1980, Max sensed that God was calling him to something else. One point of consideration was that his parents back in the U.S. needed his help. His mother was quite ill, and as the only son, Max felt it was his responsibility to be there for them. And yet, this feeling was more than just familial responsibility. Was God leading them to leave Brazil? Max began to pray for God's direction, knowing that, as always, the safest place to be was the center of His will. As he prayed, Max felt that God was calling him to work with Men for Missions in the U.S. By this time, Max had a strong passion for MFM. He loved seeing what laymen could do to advance God's kingdom. MFM groups had been the heart, as well as the hands and feet, of the work at both Panorama and Shalom; the men and women of MFM were the ones who worked, prayed, and gave to make those dreams a reality. The idea of working full-time for MFM excited Max, though he would be sorry to leave Brazil.

Quite certain that this calling was from God, Max approached Dixie. "God is done with me here," he told her simply. "I feel like He wants me in Men for Missions. I don't have anything else to do here."

Dixie was shocked. *Nothing else to do here? What about the church? What about Telemensagem? What about the opportunities all around?* Dixie had always thought that if a missionary stayed somewhere for three terms, they would stay there for the rest of their lives. This was their third term. Though it had taken a while for Dixie to get used to living in Brazil, she had now lived there more than 10 years, and it was her home. After carrying them through all of the trials and hardship, why would God call them away?

But Max was convinced. "Let's pray about this," he told Dixie. She agreed, reluctantly surrendering everything yet again. Dixie decided to do her best to adopt an attitude of gratitude and praise. God had been good to her and her family, and He would continue to be good. As she wrote in a letter home: "Max is needed here—but that is not the criteria for returning. We are torn between returning and staying. Pray for us to know His will."

In obedience to God's leading, Max called the OMS headquarters to connect with MFM and offer his services. His call was answered by a man he didn't know.

"Thank you for your offer," the man said, "but we don't need you."

Taken aback, Max returned to prayer. Again he felt clearly that God was telling him, *"I want you in MFM in the 20 eastern states."* So he called again.

"I believe God is calling me into MFM," he told the man.

He received the same response: "We don't need you."

Then Max was really confused. He prayed once more and still felt God clearly saying, *"I want you in MFM."* So, fearing God more than man, he contacted MFM a third time.

The director of MFM at that time, Harry Burr, knew Max personally but did not know that he had called to offer his services. This time, however, someone at MFM said to Harry, "Max Edwards thinks God is calling him to MFM." That very day Max answered an excited call from Harry.

"Get here as soon as you can!" he said. "We need you urgently."

His calling confirmed, Max and his family made preparations to move back to the U.S. He received his official acceptance letter from Harry in January 1982. As their term would end in June 1983, this gave the family a year and a half to prepare, physically and emotionally, for the move. It wasn't easy. Their roots in Brazil had grown deep, and it hurt to pull them up. Joey, who had been born in Brazil, had never really known another home. He was comfortable and happy in São Paulo, especially at PACA. Both he and Dixie struggled to accept the idea that they were really leaving.

Others were sorry to see them go. The São Savério church loved Pastor Max and couldn't imagine bringing in someone else. Their fellow missionaries were also surprised and saddened by their leaving.

However, Max could sense that his time in Brazil was complete, and he knew better than to stay when God was telling him to go. And so the Edwards family prepared for their next adventure—this time, back in rural Indiana.

Chapter 18

Go, Give, and Do

As I think about my life there (in the U.S.), I tend to worry. Pray for me that I'll accept it easily and not borrow frustrations and problems from the future. God's plan for me will be right. We're praying about many things concerning our move home—leaving here is really going to hurt a lot. I <u>must</u> be strong in my own personal life so His peace will be mine. Thanks for understanding—or for trying to. God knows. The adjustments will come, and we'll make it with God's help.
—Dixie, in a letter home, November 1982

July 1983

*D*ixie stood on the front porch of the "North Place," watching the road. The bright summer sun shone in the blue sky overhead, and the fields were green with ripening corn and soybeans. It was a beautiful day—a good day for moving boxes and furniture. Their shipment from Brazil should be arriving any minute now. Perhaps once the Edwards family had all of their things, the house would feel a little more like home. This house had been their home every time they had been in the U.S. on furlough, but that had always felt temporary. This time they really lived here; they needed to truly make it home.

The previous few weeks had gone by in a blur. Dixie had spent May, the family's last full month in Brazil, going through all of their things and deciding what to keep, what to sell, and what to give away. They had accumulated a lot of stuff in the past 14 years! A significant portion of it, including some new purchases, was packed in this shipment.

Leaving Brazil had been painful for the whole family. They loved their home, their church, and their fellow missionaries. Joey felt comfortable at PACA where he enjoyed playing soccer and connected well with the other MKs. Their departure had involved many tears on their part and on the part of those they left.

They sought to ease the pain of transition by taking some detours on the way home. They had visited OMS missionaries in Colombia and Ecuador, then gone on to Florida to spend a couple of days at Disney World. This helped some with the sorrow of departure but did little to ease the shock of readjustment to life in rural Indiana. Though they were glad to see friends and family, the Edwardses had become accustomed to a very different way of life, and it was hard to believe that they were here to stay.

The feelings were perhaps aggravated by the fact that they hit the ground running with events and activities, with little time to catch their breath in between. After just a week at home, Max headed to Greenwood for MFM staff meetings, followed closely by Dixie and Joey for an OMS retreat and convention. A couple of days after that, Max left to assist at the International Conference for Itinerate Evangelists in Amsterdam. And that brought them to this day … with Dixie standing and waiting for their shipment while Max was thousands of miles away in Europe.

In addition to their other belongings, Max and Dixie had purchased a large set of dining room furniture made of Brazilian wood and leather to ship to their home in the U.S. Dixie was anxious to get everything set up. Before long, she heard the rumble of an engine. The large truck pulled into view, emerging from among the tall cornstalks as it lumbered down the road.

The next few hours were spent in the hard work of unloading and unpacking. The truckers who brought the shipment unloaded it into the house for them. Dixie supervised the operation, telling them where to take the various items, and beginning to unpack whenever she had a spare minute. There were so many boxes and barrels, it would take her weeks to sort through them all.

Soon she realized that they were reaching the moment she had been waiting for—when her new dining room set would be unpacked. Excitedly, she watched the movers bring in the pieces of furniture; then she started to unwrap the cardboard that was protecting them. As she freed the first chair, however, she realized that something was not right. She groaned with surprise as she saw it—a greenish-white mold covered the chair. To Dixie's dismay, they found that the entire dining room set—a table, eight chairs, and a large hutch—were moldy. She had never had to deal with this kind of problem before, so she had to track down friends and neighbors for advice on how to clean everything.

Oh, how she needed Max! As she worked over the next few days to clean the furniture, unpack, and organize, it dawned on her that she was going to have to get used to situations like this. Max was now the director of the eastern region for MFM, in charge of coordinating MFM efforts in the 24 easternmost states. Though he wouldn't usually be at conferences in Europe, he would be on the road a considerable portion of the time, recruiting for MFM and encouraging local councils. He would also be leading many work crusades and other short-term trips overseas. Yes, she was going to have to get used to dealing with problems on her own. She was thankful to have family and friends nearby as well as Joe still living at home with her. Her mother, Pauline, and Laura came to help her clean the mold and finish other household tasks.

That fall Joe was starting sixth grade, and Max and Dixie had decided to enroll him in a private Christian school in the city of Muncie. They felt that being in a smaller Christian school rather than a large public school would help Joe transition from PACA. Muncie was a good 30-minute drive away, so it fell to Dixie to drive him to and from school daily. This was difficult for her as she had never enjoyed driving, and it took a considerable amount of time. Nevertheless, she wanted to do what was best for Joey.

Twelve-year-old Joe didn't think his new school resembled PACA at all. The student body of the conservative private school consisted mainly of upper-class American kids; and Joe, with his missionary-barrel clothing and "exotic" Brazilian background, could not find a way to fit in. He was not accustomed to restricting his speech to one language, and he developed a stutter, perhaps because he struggled to find the appropriate English words to articulate his thoughts. He missed

PACA and his friends, and he wished his family had never left Brazil.

Over time, however, the family began to slowly adjust to this new home and lifestyle. In addition to caring for their home and driving Joe to and from school, Dixie served as Max's secretary in the "Winchester MFM Headquarters," the new office they built onto their house. This role was something Dixie had been dreading ever since they had decided to move. When they first arrived, someone came from the OMS World Headquarters to bring the things they would need and to show Dixie how everything worked. Overwhelmed and freshly back from the field, Dixie broke down and cried. How could she manage everything?

Eventually she learned how to carry out the necessary tasks. Joe became accustomed to his new school too, even though he never really felt comfortable there. At first, he hoped they would someday return to Brazil. However, he came to realize that they were there to stay, so he sought to make the best of it. One of the perks of this new school was that it had a soccer team, which Joe joined his second year there.

Though it was a difficult summer and fall, the Edwards family rejoiced in welcoming two new members during this time. The first was Laura, who married Jeff in August 1983. Max officiated as he had at Jay's wedding. All went smoothly until the end when he proudly announced the couple as "Mr. and Mrs. Max Edwards." It was a story the family would laugh about for years to come. The second addition was Jason David, Jay and Kirsten's first son and Max and Dixie's first grandson. When he was born on October 4, on Jay's own birthday, Jay called Jan and told her, "I have my own cub!"

In May, 1984, Maud Edwards, Max's mother, passed away in her sleep. Max and Dixie were thankful that they were able to spend the last year of her life on earth nearby where they could visit and support her.

~ * ~

As MFM regional director, Max has presented to Christian laymen of 24 eastern states the challenge "to do anything God asks them to do, go anywhere God asks them to go, and give anything God asks them to give."
—OMS "Missionary Close-Up," September 1989

Max settled into his new role with Men for Missions quickly and easily. He had always had a special place in his heart for MFM. As someone who had none of the typical qualifications for service when he first became involved in missions, Max knew from experience that God could use anyone to accomplish His work—anyone who was willing to say yes to His call. He felt he could relate to the men involved in MFM, and they could relate to his background, too. After all, even though he had pastored churches and even trained other pastors in Brazil, he was still at heart a simple farmer.

The organization of MFM consisted of local councils of laymen all over the U.S. who were interested in missions. These councils met regularly and worked together to raise funds for missions as well as to send members on short-term trips overseas. As regional director, Max's duties involved visiting local councils, offering encouragement, organizing new councils, planning trips, and recruiting members to join those trips. He averaged 70,000 miles per year on his car as he drove among the eastern states that were his territory. This job utilized Max's exceptional recruiting and fundraising skills, and he thoroughly enjoyed it. The only part that was difficult for him and his family was that he was so often away from home. He tried to organize his schedule so that he was there at least half of the time, but this was easier said than done.

In his overseas travel with MFM groups, Max was able to visit many new places, including Haiti, Spain, Ecuador, Japan, and more. His favorite place to visit, however, was the South American nation of Brazil! One of the rewards of taking trips to Brazil was seeing the seeds he had planted there continuing to bear fruit. On one occasion, his Brazilian handyman friend, Abimael, witnessed to another Brazilian worker who was assisting an MFM group with a project. While they stood inside waiting for rain to pass so they could work, Abimael convinced the man to become a Christian on the spot. What an exciting thing to see a man who had worked with Max on countless occasions follow his example in witnessing to others.

Max was convinced of the power of MFM mission trips. He believed that these trips impacted both the people on the field and the lives of the MFMers who went. Sometimes people would ask him, "Why do you take groups overseas? Wouldn't it be better to just send the money?" In response, he would tell stories like this:

> "Last February, 21 of us worked on the Astorga Church in Brazil. The footers were dug and the material was on hand when we arrived. After one week, we raised the church to the bond-beam above the lower windows. Since that time the congregation has continued on to the present state … While we were working, the state TV station reporters interviewed us. As a result, our project was shown on prime-time news along with a clear testimony of our love for Jesus Christ. During that same week, we were on local radio for a 30-minute interview … and by the end of the week, there was a full-page story in the local newspaper, complete with pictures and a strong witness for our Lord.

> "Unknown to us, there was a local carpenter who saw all the publicity but didn't visit the building site or meet us personally. After we left town, he went to the site to inspect the workmanship of *the Americanos.* He was favorably impressed! … so much, in fact, that he began attending services at the church and has since been saved and baptized! He is now an active member in the church and spends all his extra time helping with this ongoing project! This is just one of the many examples."[20]

To illustrate the impact on the MFMers themselves, Max would share stories like this:

> "Let me share one outstanding testimony. One man found himself on the crusade, accompanied by another crusader to whom he hadn't spoken for five years because of harboring a grudge. In obedience to the prompting of the Holy Spirit, the grudge-bearer went to his brother, confessing all … then proceeded to enjoy the crusade! After two

---

20   Excerpt from a prayer letter, November 1988.

weeks of constant challenge and missions exposure, he
felt the need and saw the spiritual benefit of sharing this
experience with the whole group. When he finished, there
probably wasn't a dry-eyed crusader. I surely wouldn't
know, because my eyes were 'sweating' too much! No, I
don't <u>like</u> to travel, but yes, I <u>will</u> travel till Jesus comes in
order to see transformed lives and broadened visions."[21]

By all standards, Max was one of the most successful recruiters and
fundraisers MFM had ever had. Through his work, many new councils
were formed, dozens of people were moved to visit the mission field, and
a great deal of money was raised. God worked through him to inspire
others to do all that they could for His kingdom. The people he worked
with inspired Max, too, to continue to serve and give all he could to the
work God had given him to do.

~ * ~

August 1986

Joe followed Max into Winchester Community High School, taking it
all in. He was starting high school, and his parents had decided that it
was time for him to be in a school in his own community. In a general
sense, Joe didn't mind changing schools. Despite spending three years
at the Christian school in Muncie, he had never felt comfortable there.
But that school had something that the Winchester public school did
not have: soccer. Joe had found the one highlight of junior high days
to be playing on the soccer team, and the coach had already told him
that he would start as a freshman on the varsity team. This made it hard
for Joe to accept moving to this country public school where he felt he
would be lucky if anyone had even heard of soccer.

Max, however, thought that there could be a place for Joe in this
school's sports, even without a soccer team. So they visited a football
practice.

They walked onto the field to find the team already engaged in

21   Excerpt from a prayer letter, September 1989.

practice. Max strode up to the coach and shook his hand. Then he motioned to Joe.

"This is my son Joe," he said. "He's starting here this fall. He can kick a soccer ball, and I'm just wonderin' if he might be able to kick a football."

"Hi, Joe. I'm Coach Osborn," the coach said, shaking Joe's hand. "Let's see what you can do."

Max and Joe followed the coach out to the field, where another boy was practicing field-goal kicks.

"This is JW, our current kicker," the coach said. "He'll help you try it out."

JW nodded and set up a football on a large plastic tee. The boy jerked his chin toward the goalposts at the end of the field. "See if you can make a field goal," he said.

Joe looked at the ball. Though he had watched football on TV, the idea of kicking a football felt so strange. The ball was a weird shape, and the goalposts so high. On the other hand, the goal was huge, and the ball was just sitting there, not rolling around as a soccer ball usually would be. Confidently, he ran forward and kicked it, easily making the goal. It was so simple it almost felt like a trick.

JW worked with him a little while longer, moving the ball closer and farther from the goalposts. Eventually, the coach came up and stopped them.

"Well, JW, I don't think you need to be here anymore," he said.

"Okay," JW responded. Looking somewhat relieved to no longer be kicker, he ran off to join the rest of the team in practice. Coach Osborn smiled at Joe.

"Welcome to the team, Joe," he said. Max beamed at Joe from behind him.

As Joe and Max walked back to the car after practice, Joe began to think about the other changes happening in his family this year. Jan was engaged to a Canadian named Rod Dormer. She had moved back to Indiana for graduate school in the fall of 1984, and at that time, she and Jay had begun to produce their own music together. They made several tapes and held concerts in local churches. One of these concerts happened to be at a church where Rod was working as a youth pastor.

One thing led to another, and by April 1986, they were engaged. Jan's engagement had perks for Joe too; Rod invited him to join their youth group for some events where he met a pretty girl his age named Sharon Hanson. He and Sharon had dated all through that summer.

Thinking about Sharon made Joe smile, but he also felt unsure about what to do. He didn't have a car; in fact, he was barely old enough to drive, and she lived in Anderson, 40 miles away. Soon Jan and Rod would be married, and they were moving to Canada, so he wouldn't be able to join Jan on trips to Anderson anymore. When would he be able to see Sharon?

Well, first things first. Joe had to focus on his move to Winchester High and his new position as a football kicker. The coach and team were amused at how little he knew at first, but the school had a good football program, and he caught on quickly. He was placed almost immediately on the varsity team, and in time he came to enjoy the game. His background in soccer made him a successful kicker. By the end of his high school days, he held all of the school's kicking records, which he would continue to hold for decades. He even earned the nickname "Joe the Toe." Though Max continued to travel extensively throughout these years, he made a special effort to attend Joe's football games, sometimes driving many hours at a time in order to make it back by a Friday night.

Jan and Rod were married at the end of September 1986. Sharon was at the wedding, so Joe took advantage of the opportunity to break up with her. After all, he didn't know when he would see her again! The family continued to grow and change. Jan and Rod moved to Canada, and in January 1987, two new babies were born—Katie Cristina to Jeff and Laura, and Aaron Jonathan to Jay and Kirsten. At the end of 1987, both Jay and Jeff moved with their families to Brazil to work as missionaries. By this time, the Edwardses were more comfortable with Indiana life. Joe found high school to be a better experience than junior high had been. Dixie became accustomed to the bookkeeping and correspondence and to living in the Indiana countryside again. They attended New Liberty Church where the people felt like family to Max and Dixie. In April 1989, Rod and Jan had their first daughter, Danna Jo. When Sharon heard about it, she sent Joe a card of congratulations on becoming an uncle again. With this, Joe and Sharon renewed their communications and were soon dating again. When Joe applied to colleges in his senior year, he was offered a football scholarship at Valparaiso University. So, he made plans to begin there in the fall of 1990.

Max was in his element working for MFM; he could see God working in and through him every day. He was thankful that he had followed God's call.

Chapter 19

Mountains in Mexico

To refuse consideration is to deny possibility.
—One of Max's favorite quotes

September 1988

$\mathcal{M}$ ax put his fork down and looked up at Bob Erny, the vice president of Field Ministries at OMS. Bob and his wife had invited Max and Dixie to have lunch with them in Indianapolis.

"What did you say?" Max asked.

Bob's eyes twinkled. "I said we'd like the two of you to pray about beginning OMS' work in Mexico."

Max and Dixie glanced at each other. They had always thought that if they moved to the mission field again, it would be back to Brazil. This suggestion came as a complete surprise. Max swallowed.

"Obviously, I'm honored to be asked," he said. "But I don't think I'm the right man for the job. You'll want to start a seminary, of course, and I don't have the qualifications for that."

Bob shook his head. "We're not asking you to run the seminary long term," he said. "We just need someone to get things started—to find out what is needed, to raise funds and interest, and to recruit the people who will teach in the seminary and run other ministries too." Bob looked Max in the eye. "I think you're exactly the right man for the job. Pray about it."

Later, Max and Dixie sat quietly in the car as they drove home, pondering the proposition they had just heard. Finally Dixie spoke.

"Us in Mexico! Can you imagine?"

"Not really," Max responded.

"It just doesn't seem like a good fit for us," Dixie continued. Max nodded.

"I agree," he said, "but if this is an open door from God, I don't want to ignore it. Let's take some time to pray about it like Bob suggested."

Dixie nodded. "Okay."

Over the following days, Max and Dixie prayed, talked, and thought about the proposition. Max consulted with four of his close friends and asked for advice and prayer support. He felt torn. On one hand, he could see how God was using his gifts for work in MFM, and it seemed illogical to leave. On the other hand, he saw every new opportunity as possible direction from God; the last thing he wanted was to be outside of God's will.

Finally, one morning after his devotions, Max felt the need to talk to Wesley Duewel about the matter; he was president emeritus of OMS and a much-respected man of prayer. By the end of that conversation, Max felt he had his answer. He and Dixie would *not* make the decision. They were too biased; they wanted to stay where they were. They didn't see how they could be qualified to do the kind of work that was needed to open a new field for Mexico. Therefore, it would be better if some key players of OMS—namely Ed Erny, Terry Schaberg, Wesley Duewel, Dick Capin, Harry Burr, Warren Hardig, Bill Spate, and Bob Erny—could get together and form a united opinion about how OMS would best be served by the Edwards' gifts.

This group of men was a combination of MFM and OMS leaders. Max trusted that they could decide on the best placement for him and Dixie. He talked to Dixie about this plan, and she agreed. They felt peaceful. Max wrote a letter to Bob Erny, explaining their position and stating that they would submit to whatever decision was reached by this group. "As always, we will place our entire efforts into what is decided for us," he promised.

Within a few weeks, Max and Dixie got a call from Bob Erny, telling them the final decision: OMS leaders decided that their gifts would be best used starting the work in Mexico.

"Max," Bob said, "I believe that in five years you can find a property and the personnel to start a seminary. After that, you can return to MFM ministry."

And so in January 1989, the OMS board officially voted to begin ministry in Mexico and appointed Max as the field director. Immediately plans were made to conduct additional survey trips to decide where and how OMS could best serve Mexico. Missionaries would begin moving to the field as soon as they had decided on a location, raised funds, and if necessary, attended language school. The Edwardses were embarking on another new adventure.

~ * ~

If you lose the desire to learn, you give up the right to teach.
—One of Max's favorite quotes

Mexico, 1989

The CEO leaned forward and folded his hands, his eyes meeting Max's in a penetrating gaze. "If you want to help Mexico," he said in his heavy accent, "come here with plans to stay and train Mexican leaders."

Max nodded. "I'm glad to hear you say that," he responded with a smile, "because that is exactly what we hope to do."

As he left the meeting, Max shook his head in amazement. On this survey trip to Mexico, he had met with many business people, Christian and non-Christian, and all had told him the same thing: Train local leaders. Another businessman, an evangelical Christian, said:

If you are coming here to train Mexican leaders for the Christian community, the door is wide open to you. We need a mission that is willing to work at training national leadership and one that is not hung up on big numbers.[22]

This was exciting to hear because leadership training was one of OMS' specialties. Though they usually started with evangelism and church planting, they always quickly added discipleship and seminary training.

22   Edwards prayer letter, December 1989.

Max knew that if God was going to reach Mexico, it would be primarily through Mexicans, not through missionaries. OMS' main job would be to establish a place where Mexican believers could learn and grow in their faith.

Hand in hand with the question of *what* OMS would do in Mexico was the question of *where* they would do it. Mexico was a huge country. Max and his colleagues interviewed people in several different parts of the country. He also enlisted prayer support from his close friends. As they considered their options, Max became convinced that Mexico City, the capital, was the place to be. As one of the largest metropolitan areas in the world, the city was a center of both great need and great potential. They decided to begin by focusing on the growing middle class, which had previously been resistant to the Gospel. From what Max could see, a combination of economic crisis and the emptiness of worldly pleasures was softening their hearts. It seemed that God was bringing OMS there at just the right time.

As Max surveyed the possibilities and started making plans, he was struck by an overwhelming need to see that this new venture was covered in prayer from day one. Certainly, there was great potential, but there was also great opposition. The majority religion in the nation was Roman Catholicism, as it was in Brazil. However, the people, or perhaps the Catholic establishment, seemed to be hostile to evangelicals in a way that Max hadn't seen in Brazilian Catholics. Beginning a new Protestant movement in this environment would be difficult.

Considering all of this, Max sought permission from OMS to form "intercessor crusades." These would be trips similar to MFM work crusades, but the focus would be on learning about Mexico for the express purpose of praying for the country and the OMS work there. Max also hoped that these trips would be a way to get more churches involved in the Mexico ministry, both in prayer and in finances; perhaps they could even recruit missionaries to move to the Mexico field.

Permission granted, Max and Dixie organized their first crusade—a five-day trip to Mexico City, which they led themselves. As Max wrote in a prayer letter, "The crusades are designed to expose people to Mexico's past, Mexico's present, and then to visualize the future as pertaining to OMS' ministry."[23] During their time there, they visited Aztec pyramids and Catholic cathedrals as well as local Christians' and missionaries' homes. They learned about the political and religious situation in Mexico and about the plans for OMS' work there. This experience deeply impacted all those who went on this trip and future trips, and the Edwardses won many prayer warriors for Mexico. Beginning with this first group in February 1990, Max and Dixie led four intercessor crusades to Mexico before they moved there in January 1991. They continued hosting these groups over the years, and by 1993, 300 people had visited Mexico City and been challenged to pray for their ministry. They saw many prayers answered, and Max would always believe that these trips, or more specifically the prayers that resulted from them, were the key to OMS' success in Mexico.

With the location established and a growing prayer team developed, Max formulated a plan for the ministry in Mexico. He concentrated on the three main goals of OMS: evangelism, church planting, and leadership training.

They would begin with evangelism and church planting. The first OMS missionaries to Mexico arrived in 1990—one in July and two more in September. Right away in September, a missionary and their first national coworker began knocking on doors, looking for someone willing to open their home to a Bible study. Most of the people they encountered were not interested. However, after 18 rejections, in the nineteenth home they visited, they found a woman who was willing to host. She invited a few neighbors, and their first Bible study began. Over the following months, more Bible studies were started, gradually expanding the OMS work. It was a small beginning, but it was something.

~ * ~

August 1990

Dixie climbed into the car, struggling to hold back the tears. They had just dropped off Joe, their youngest son, at Valparaiso University to begin his freshman year of college. They were now officially "empty

---

23 March 1990.

nesters"—and what's more, their "nest" was moving! On this very same day, they were leaving for Edinburg, Texas, to begin their semester of language school. They were scheduled for four months of school to convert their Portuguese to Spanish before moving to Mexico in January.

Max and Dixie drove back to Winchester to pick up the remainder of their packed items; then they headed out for the several-days' drive to Edinburg, which was near the Mexican border. They would make this drive countless times over the next several years. Dixie cried most of the way across the country; she couldn't help it. Her baby was in college, all alone with no parents nearby; the country house that had finally become home was disappearing behind them; and before them, they faced the challenge of a new language, a new culture, and yet another new living situation. As they neared the end of their trip, driving across Texas, Dixie saw a car in front of them exit the highway to follow a little country road. *Oh,* she thought, *they're going home.* The tears began afresh as she grieved her loss of home.

Language school was hard, just as it had been when they studied Portuguese 20 years before. Knowing Portuguese both helped and hindered their study. Because the languages were so similar, they had an advantage in understanding, but mastering the differences to speak Spanish instead of Portuguese was difficult. It made Dixie feel like someone was playing tricks on her. With every Spanish word, it seemed like they had just taken the Portuguese word and changed it just a little, either adding a syllable or a vowel or taking one away. Furthermore, as she set her mind to really learning Spanish, she felt like her Portuguese was slipping away ... and she had to let it go. There was no other way to make it work for her; but boy, did it hurt. As usual, Max had trouble remembering any of the new information; he joked that he had a "Teflon" brain! Back in Indiana, Joe gradually adjusted to college life. Though it was difficult to be far away from his parents, he was thankful to have Sharon in his life. Eventually, he connected with other Christians at school as well as other kids who had grown up overseas like he had.

The Edwardses welcomed two more family members in 1990: Kendra Joy, born in April to Jeff and Laura in Brazil, and Jenna Pauline, born in October to Jan and Rod in Canada. Max and Dixie enjoyed grandparenting whenever they had the opportunity.

~ * ~

Thought for thinking: Change is the mother of challenge.
—Edwards prayer letter, January 1994

After Christmas back in Indiana, Max and Dixie officially moved to Mexico in January 1991, to join the other missionaries and national Christians in expanding the work. By this time, five Bible study groups existed, and in March, these groups combined to form their first congregation. Through the OMS organization "Every Creature Crusade"[24] or ECC, they were able to fund a team of Mexican Christians to do evangelism and plant churches. By July 1991, the OMS ministry had yielded 81 new Christians. In 1992, a second OMS church was planted. As more new missionaries arrived on the field, the OMS Mexico field was able to further expand their work. They held their first baptism in November, 1991.

The missionaries were struck by the problems in Mexican family life and the high divorce rate. Because of this, they decided to call their new church group *Familias Unidas en Cristo,* or "Families United in Christ." They tried to put emphasis in the churches on families and counseling, in addition to discipleship. Max was eager to start the seminary, in order to train Mexican pastors who could go out and plant more churches. However, he needed trained professors in order to make this dream a reality. At first, he thought these professors would be a missionary couple whom they knew from Brazil. They arrived in Mexico in September 1991, eager to start the new seminary. In March and April 1992, they held two classes in the Edwards' dining room with five enthusiastic students. However, soon after these classes were completed, they were told that they would have to return home due to a lack of finances.

Max was disappointed; they'd had such a promising start! What would they do now? Determined to make the seminary a success, he began to explore other options. After much planning, prayer, and several phone calls, he found a solution, at least for the time being. The seminary would run on a modular system: 12 Spanish-speaking professors from other

---

24   Now "Every Community for Christ."

OMS fields agreed to take turns coming to Mexico to teach intensive courses. In this format, the seminary officially opened in August 1992. By the following spring, the student body had expanded from 5 to 14.

Though Max and other leaders were pleased that classes were up and running, Max knew that there was another thing they needed for the seminary to function: property. The locals told him that they would have to buy property in order to succeed long term; otherwise, Mexicans wouldn't trust that they were there to stay. Max couldn't agree more. But finding the right property was a challenge, and raising the money for it would be more challenging still.

Max looked at several pieces of land, but none of them seemed quite right. Then one day in January 1992, he visited a property in an area called *Lomas de La Hacienda*. The property was an abandoned school, which had been standing vacant for more than three years. It was run-down with few facilities, but the basic structures of the buildings seemed solid.

As Max stood on the property, his imagination took over—just as it had when he had first seen the Panorama and the Shalom properties in Brazil. He could see buildings renovated and expanded to form a thriving seminary with room for classes, offices, a church, and housing for missionaries or professors. He saw a place where Mexican Christian leaders could be trained and prepared to reach their nation for Christ. Moved in his spirit, he claimed the property for God's work in Mexico, asking Him to provide the means for them to obtain it.

As soon as he could, Max went with some of his colleagues to find the landlord. They found that the landlord was willing to rent the property for $4,000 a month—much more than they could afford. Disappointed but not ready to give up, they sent out a call to friends, family, and supporters; they asked for prayer that the rent be reduced. In November 1992, they had another meeting with the landlord. This time, he agreed to reduce the rent to $2,000 a month with an option to buy after the agreed-upon rental period. The missionaries and their national partners thanked God for His provision.

Soon after, they signed a rental agreement with the landlord. That very same day, Max was told by his own landlord that he would need to vacate his home by the end of January. Plans were quickly made to begin renovation on the *Lomas* property so that Max and Dixie could move there. In January, an MFM group came for two weeks. During that time they ran electric wiring, installed plumbing, built kitchen cabinets, painted, and moved Max and Dixie into their new home! Other groups soon followed to develop the property so that it could house the seminary, a church, and the OMS offices.

Though it took several years of fundraising, eventually OMS was able to purchase the property, which served as an excellent location for the growing seminary. Max was pleased to see their plans beginning to take shape.

~ * ~

This new life in Mexico wasn't easy for Max and Dixie. It seemed like they were always on the move. They drove back and forth between Mexico and Indiana frequently to work on recruitment and fundraising in the U.S. and to bring supplies back to Mexico. Furthermore, for various reasons, they changed residences at least four times during their few years in Mexico. Max knew instinctively that God had not called him to stay in Mexico long term; his goal was to work himself out of a job.

"As soon as I can," he told Dixie, "I'll find somebody that will take my place and do much better than I." Because of this, they didn't take much time to put down roots and become accustomed to the culture, although they did as much ministry as they could whenever they saw opportunities.

Making the several-days' drive back and forth in their old van was certainly an adventure for Max and Dixie. On one occasion, they were headed to the U.S. from Mexico City. They were driving through the mountains and had been on the road for several hours. The day was dreary, and it was chilly up in the mountains. Dixie was starting to feel drowsy.

"I'm gonna take a little nap," she said.

"Okay," Max responded.

As she started to doze off, Dixie felt the van begin to go around another curve. Then all of a sudden, she felt a jerk, and Max's hand on her shoulder.

"Honey, we're goin' down!"

Her eyes popped open to see trees flying by the window. On her other side, Max was gripping the steering wheel. He had hit an invisible slippery spot in the road, and the van had slid off and down the side of the mountain.

The van bumped down the slope for a few minutes, then came to an abrupt halt. Looking out the front windshield, they could see that a small tree had temporarily stalled their descent.

"That won't hold for long," Max commented. Dixie's heart was pounding in shock and fright.

"I'm getting out of here!" she declared. And with that, she opened her door and jumped out.

"Don't, Dixie!" Max exclaimed. But it was too late. Dixie's exit loosened the van from the tree, and it took off down the hill again. Panicking, Dixie ran after it.

The van barreled down the mountainside until it reached a level spot at the bottom. Its momentum took it forward a little farther until it rolled to a stop next to a corral of sheep. Dixie paused at the bottom of the hill to catch her breath, putting her hands on her knees. It almost looked like it had been on purpose—like Max had just driven down the mountainside and parked next to the corral! The sheep watched disinterestedly as he climbed out of the van and walked over to Dixie.

"Why did you do that?" Max exclaimed.

"I wasn't thinking," Dixie responded. "I'm sorry. Are you okay?"

Max nodded, looking back at the parked van. "If we had to go over the side of the mountain, I guess this was an ideal place to do it," he said.

Dixie glanced back up toward the road and saw a man standing there. She tapped Max's arm and pointed. It looked like the driver of the semi-truck that had been ahead of them had seen them go over and had stopped.

"Are you all right?" the man called down in Spanish.

"Yes, we're fine. Thank you!" Max called back. He smiled and waved at the man. The driver waved back and left. Max looked around and tried to assess their situation. They saw a little dirt road ahead that looked like it led back up the mountain to the highway. Max went over and looked at it. Returning, he said, "You know, I think the van can make that incline. We're gonna try it!" So they both climbed back into the vehicle, and Max started the engine. The van chugged along the road back up the mountainside, and soon they were on their way again.

Sometimes in their travels, the van was the source of their troubles. On one trip heading into Mexico City, the van struggled as they went up a steep hill. They were on a busy highway, and it was already dark. As they crawled up the hill, the engine started choking. Max pressed the accelerator, but to no avail.

"Honey, I don't know if we can make it to the top of the hill," Max said.

Dixie was alarmed. What would they do if they couldn't make it? There was no place to stop along the side of the hill, although they could see lights in the distance at the top. "Let's pray," she responded. So Dixie began praying aloud. She kept praying as Max pulled over to the right lane of the highway and tried to coax the van to keep moving. The other traffic whizzed by them, but Dixie kept praying.

After what seemed like an eternity, they crested the hill and turned into the filling station at the top. Immediately the van sputtered to a stop. Max and Dixie could never explain how they made it except that God heard their prayers and brought them to safety. The establishment where they stopped had both mechanics and a small hotel, so they left the van with the mechanics and spent the night at the hotel. In the morning, it was ready to go again.

Besides the difficulties of frequent traveling, Mexican culture was a big adjustment for the Edwardses. This was perhaps harder for Dixie than for Max; Max loved interacting with people and could usually get along with anyone, though his Spanish was even worse than his Portuguese. For Dixie, on the other hand, it was much more difficult to build relationships. It was hard not to compare Mexico to Brazil, which was a much different culture.

On one occasion, when Dixie felt that she had gotten to know some of the women in her neighborhood, she decided to invite them to a little get-together in her home. She hoped they could get better acquainted, and hoped also to read a bit of Scripture and talk together. However, when the day came, not one person showed up. She went outside to look around and saw that there was no one in sight—even though it was a time of day when children were usually out playing. She concluded that the people were afraid of her because she was an evangelical. *Lord, what am I doing wrong?* she prayed. Dixie was disappointed and confused about how to reach the people. And even though they spent several years in Mexico, she felt that she never quite learned how to reach the local people.

Nevertheless, she was eventually able to start a Bible study with a few ladies, and she learned to appreciate the Mexican Christians whom she got to know. She developed some good relationships with people in the church as well, and she enjoyed being involved there and assisting with the Sunday school. Even though Mexico was hard, she could see how God was using her and Max to advance His kingdom. And she knew that was what really mattered.

~ * ~

By 1993, Max had finally found the couple he felt could replace them as field directors: John-Mark and Susan Brabon, who had been serving in Ecuador. It was arranged that they would begin as field leaders on July 1, 1993. Once he had found someone to replace him on the Mexico field, Max felt it was time to request to be transferred back to the U.S. He believed he could best serve the OMS Mexico field by dedicating himself to full-time recruiting and fundraising. OMS granted his request, and Max and Dixie became "Mexico missionaries assigned to the U.S." They moved back to Indiana in the middle of 1993. By that time, there were 22 missionaries recruited for Mexico, who were already there or raising funds to get there. Their first church in Mexico City had a regular attendance of 80, the second church had 40, and the seminary was growing.

One piece was still missing from the Mexico field: a full-time seminary director. They needed someone qualified with a Ph.D. who could earn the respect of the local Mexicans and lead the seminary effectively. Max had been praying and searching for the right person for a long time, but so far, he'd had no luck. Then in November 1993, when Max was in New Jersey on a recruiting trip, he met a man named Leroy Lindsey. Leroy was in the process of completing his doctorate degree in theology. He and his wife, Kay, had previously worked as missionaries in Mexico through their denomination. Leroy had experience as a seminary professor and was fluent in Spanish. Max took him to lunch on the spot and talked to him about the opportunities in Mexico. A few days later he returned home, ecstatic.

"Dixie!" he exclaimed. "I think I found the man God wants down there!" Soon after, he received a letter from Leroy about beginning the application process with OMS. The Lindseys moved to Mexico after Leroy finished his doctorate a couple of years later. Leroy took over the position of seminary director, and Kay worked as the registrar.

Max thanked God for the way that He was working in Mexico. It hadn't been his easiest assignment, but it was always an honor to be in the center of God's will, doing God's work.

> *None of the above has been easy or without a struggle.*
> *Satan has fought us all the way. Thanks to the interces-*
> *sor crusaders who came before we began and caught*
> *a vision to intercede in prayer. God is the victor.*
> —Max and Dixie, "OMS Mexico history," January 1993

Chapter 20

When the Roll Is Called Up Yonder

Your love, LORD, reaches to the heavens, your faithfulness
to the skies. Your righteousness is like the highest mountains, your justice like the great deep. You, LORD, preserve
both people and animals. How priceless is your unfail-
ing love, O God! People take refuge in the shadow of your
wings. They feast on the abundance of your house; you
give them drink from your river of delights. For with you
is the fountain of life; in your light we see light.
Psalm 36:5–9 (NIV)

Spring 1995

*M*ax paused next to his tractor and took a deep breath. He could
smell the soil of the bare, brown earth that stretched around
him, canopied by a bright-blue sky. A breeze swept by his face—chilly
but not cold. What a perfect day for planting. Max smiled. Even after
all of his travels and experiences, nothing could beat the feeling of an
Indiana spring day. "Thank you, God," he breathed.

Over the last couple of years, Max and Dixie had readjusted to Indiana
life. They had remained "OMS Mexico missionaries" for about a year
after returning to the U.S., focusing most of their efforts on recruitment
and fundraising for Mexico. Max had also gradually resumed some of
his MFM activities. Now, Max and Dixie were officially back with MFM,

this time with fewer responsibilities. Max covered seven U.S. states. He enjoyed it as much as ever, and Dixie came with him on more of his trips. As always, they especially looked forward to their trips to Brazil, where Jay and Jeff still resided with their families.

Speaking of his children … Max was pleased that they were all married now. Joe and Sharon had married in June 1993, and they stayed in northwestern Indiana. Jan and her family had moved to Indonesia as missionaries in February 1995. Though Max and Dixie missed their children, they were so happy that they were each serving the Lord.

Max climbed onto his tractor and started it. This was another new development for him—he was back to farming! He only had a little land, so this was more of a hobby than anything else, but it sure was nice to be back! Though he hadn't farmed for himself since 1968, the old saying proved true: "You can take the boy off of the farm, but you can't take the farm out of the boy." No matter what other titles he held or jobs he performed, Max would always be a farmer. And though he didn't expect to make big money from it, he planned to add to his land and his equipment in the future, so the farming would contribute a good supplementary income.

Max had also found another way to fill some of his spare time. One day he had felt led by the Holy Spirit to volunteer his services at one of the larger churches in downtown Winchester, the Winchester Congregational Christian Church (WCCC). He met with the pastor and explained his background and current situation.

"I'm not here all of the time," he concluded, "but when I am here, I'd be happy to help with visitation, if that is something you might need." The pastor nodded vigorously.

"Yes!" he exclaimed. "We could definitely use your help."

So, Max was brought on as a care pastor, and he helped with visitation of members who were home-bound, in nursing homes, and in the hospital, whenever he was in town. He and Dixie began to regularly attend WCCC. Switching to a new church was an adjustment, but over time Max and Dixie got to know other attendees and felt at home there. By visiting people in their homes, Max became close to many of the church members. He was widely loved and respected in the church.

Over the next few years, Max enjoyed being as busy as ever with these various activities to fill his time.

Meanwhile, OMS was working toward opening another field—this time in Mozambique, one of the poorest countries in the world. Max joined some of the survey trips there, and in November 1996, he and Dixie took their first intercessor crusade there. It was an enlightening trip for the crusaders as well as for Max and Dixie. They were struck by both the poverty and the potential of the nation. They enjoyed that the people spoke Portuguese there! It was different from Brazilian Portuguese, but it was Portuguese nonetheless.

During their trip to Mozambique, Max got a nasty bite of some kind on his leg. A few days after their return home, Dixie noticed that the bite didn't seem to be healing. Looking closer, she saw a red line extending out of the bite up his leg.

"Max," she said, "have you been watching this?"

"It's just a little bite," he responded.

"Maybe, but isn't it strange that it hasn't gotten better? And now there's a red line coming out of it."

Max shrugged. "I feel fine," he said.

Dixie shook her head. "You know, honey, I really think we oughta go to the doctor for this."

"It's Thanksgiving week," Max protested.

"It's Wednesday. His office will still be open," Dixie responded.

In the end, Max agreed to see the doctor. The doctor took one look at Max's leg, and concern spread over his face. "I don't know what this is, but we've got to get you someplace and put you in isolation until we find out."

"Isolation? Is it that serious?" asked Max.

The doctor shook his head. "Like I said, I don't know," he responded. "But considering your travels, it's better to be safe than sorry."

The doctor made a few calls, and soon Max and Dixie were on their way to a large hospital in Indianapolis. Max drove. In spite of the doctor's concerns, he didn't see any reason why a bite on his leg should hinder his driving.

When they arrived at the hospital, the staff quickly ushered Max into a separate area.

"You can't come in here," they told Dixie. "We're going to run some tests, and we'll keep you informed."

As she watched them go back to work, Dixie felt strangely empty inside. Her husband was hospitalized with some unknown African disease, and there was nothing she could do but go home and wait by the telephone. Discouraged and frightened, she walked back to the car.

Dixie had never driven back from Indianapolis alone before, and now it was dark outside. As she exited the hospital's parking garage, she reminded herself that she could do more than wait by the telephone—she could pray. And pray she did, through the whole hour-long drive home.

As she reached familiar countryside, Dixie recognized landmarks, even in the dark. She turned off the highway onto Bloomingsport Road. Soon she would pass New Liberty Church, where they had attended for so many years. Even though they currently attended WCCC, they still knew most of the people at New Liberty; they were like extended family. From a distance, she could see lights on at the church. It was Wednesday night prayer-meeting time.

I have to stop and tell them, she thought suddenly.

So Dixie turned into the little parking lot, parked her car, and went in. When the church members saw her, they stopped what they were doing and allowed her to share about the day's events. They prayed with her, and she knew that she had made the right decision to stop by. These people cared about her and Max; it didn't matter if she interrupted their meeting. She left feeling warm and full inside. God was in charge, and He was taking care of them.

The awaited call came the next morning. The doctors had a diagnosis: South African tick bite fever. Apparently Max had been bitten by an infected tick in Mozambique. He would have to stay in the hospital a little longer, but he was being treated with antibiotics and was doing fine. She could visit him now; they knew what he had, so they had taken him out of isolation. Overjoyed, Dixie made the trip back to Indianapolis—this time in the morning sunshine.

So Max and Dixie spent Thanksgiving 1996 in the hospital. Later in the day, Jeff joined them, and they watched football in Max's hospital room. They knew they had much to be thankful for, including health and good medical care. Max was released from the hospital the next day. Just another adventure in missionary life!

In spite of his run-in with an exotic disease, Max visited Mozambique a couple more times and was privileged to witness the beginnings of OMS' ministry there. He also visited other countries, including Brazil, Haiti, and Indonesia. Sometimes he took MFM teams for intercession, work, or evangelism. Other times he went with smaller groups to do surveys or promotional videos.

Max never lost his enthusiasm for taking groups to the mission field. In a prayer letter, he wrote:

> *Hopefully, when you read this I will be in Brazil with a group of 12 ... Of the twelve, eleven are first-timers. Some are young and some older. It is my vision that all will return with an excitement and love for lost souls that they could never experience any other way. I pray there will be a burning in their hearts that will never stop. I pray that while there, some Brazilians will meet Christ. If any or all of this happens, my excitement for going "one more time" with "one more group" is heavenly justified.*[25]

~ * ~

Though Max still enjoyed working with MFM, more and more of his time was going to his work at WCCC. When the church's pastor resigned in 1999, Max felt moved to apply for the position. He sensed that God had been preparing him to fill this role; the church needed the kind of leadership that he could provide. Max and Dixie both knew that this was what God wanted. The church invited him to be the head pastor, and he began in September 1999.

As Max was taking on this full-time job, he realized that it was time to retire from OMS. After 30 years working for the mission organization, it was a bittersweet decision; but he and Dixie both knew that it was time. Jay, Jan, and Jeff were all missionaries now. Jay and Jeff continued their work in Brazil. And just that year, Jan and her family had also moved

---

25   August 1997.

to Brazil, and had decided to become career missionaries with OMS. Max and Dixie Edwards had passed on their passion for God's work to the next generation. They wrote a letter to their supporters, stating their decision and asking them to prayerfully consider transferring their support to their children. Many of Max and Dixie's supporters did transfer their support, which was one of the key reasons that Jan and her family received the funding they needed to stay in Brazil. The whole family thanked God for His perfect timing.

Max and Dixie were in their element again—pastoring WCCC where they would remain for the next seven years. Because of Max's biblically based, straightforward messages and unique object lessons, those in the congregation would remember his sermons for years. On one memorable occasion, he brought an ox yoke to the church. Since he didn't have an ox yoke at home, Max had made this one himself from scrap wood on the farm. Calling one of the youth up to help him, he used the yoke to illustrate Matthew 11:28–30 about being yoked to God. Yes, church with Max was often quite interesting! He always challenged his congregation to grow deeper in their faith and to follow God further, just as he had learned to do. His sermons were filled with personal stories, making them memorable and authentic. He often urged church members to go on mission trips, which impacted their lives and their perspectives on the world.

Dixie made her mark at WCCC mostly through involvement with the children's ministries. She taught Sunday school, led a children's choir, and much more. Max and Dixie sought to reach out to the congregation on a personal level, both by visiting church members when they had needs and by hosting various church groups at their home for events. The haymow in their barn was converted into a useable space for church gatherings, and Max enjoyed giving kids (and their parents) hayrides in the fall and inviting them to pick sweet corn in the summer.

Though they knew they were getting older and would not be able to do this forever, Max and Dixie enjoyed this season in their lives, ministering to God's people and enjoying their home and their family. They now had 10 grandchildren, ranging from small children to college-age young adults. There had been four additions in recent years: Anna, born to Joe and Sharon in 1996; Cristiana, born to Jay and Kirsten in 1997;

Nathan, born to Joe and Sharon in 1999; and Sophia, also born to Joe and Sharon in 2002. Later in 2008, Joe and Sharon would have their last child, Joelle, bringing the number of grandchildren to 11. Max and Dixie enjoyed seeing them whenever they could and hearing how God was working through their family in ministry.

~ * ~

After several years of pastoring at WCCC, Max began to sense that his time there was drawing to a close. After all, he was over 70 years old now and was beginning to feel a need to slow down. In the fall of 2005, he presented his resignation letter to the church leaders.

"I believe that I have done all that God called me to do in this position," he explained to the elder board. "I'll stay until you find a new pastor, but this will give you plenty of time to start looking. Whenever you find a pastor, I'll step down and serve as care pastor—or whatever you would like me to do."

In January 2006, the church found a new pastor. As planned, Max stepped down in March. He thought his days of serving as a head pastor were finished ... but maybe God had other ideas. With the new pastor in place, Max and Dixie felt that perhaps it was best for Max to be away from WCCC for a while. But where would they go?

On June 5, 2006, their anniversary, they drove to a small country church called Jericho Friends Church for a funeral. The woman who had passed away had attended Jericho Friends, but the current pastor hadn't known her. Max had visited her as part of his care-pastor ministry, so the church invited him to perform the funeral. What a way to spend their fiftieth wedding anniversary!

When Dixie walked into the church that day, memories flooded her mind. She had been here before; Jericho Friends was only a mile from the home where her family had lived when she was very small. It was the first church Dixie had ever attended. Though they hadn't been a Christian family at the time, occasionally they would visit Sunday services there. As she looked around at the small sanctuary, the wooden pews, and the red carpet, she felt peaceful in a way that she hadn't expected. As Max stood behind the pulpit and gave the message, somehow he looked like he belonged there. After the service they walked to the cemetery for the burial.

A few clouds scurried across the sky as a breeze swept along the ground, rippling the grass and rustling the women's dark skirts. The tombstones sat quietly and unmovingly, as if they were impervious to wind. After the burial, Dixie stood apart from the groups of attendees, since she didn't know anyone there. The pastor of the church approached her and asked about their current situation. Then he said to her, "I won't be here much longer. This church could use a man like your husband."

Surprised, Dixie smiled in response but could not think of any words to say. On the car ride home, she told Max about it. He nodded.

"One of the church members approached me too," he said. "I think this could be God's answer to our question of where He wants us right now."

Dixie agreed; she had felt as much in her heart. Soon after, a couple from the church asked to meet them for lunch and talk to them about possibilities. Max and Dixie saw confirmations everywhere they turned. This was where God wanted them.

So Max became pastor of the Jericho Friends Church, and he and Dixie left WCCC for the time being. The transition was somewhat difficult for them, just as all transitions are. Nevertheless, they loved the people, and the congregation welcomed Max as their pastor.

Another venture Max took on at this time was the position of county councilman. He was elected in November 2006 and continued in the position until 2010.

A couple of years into their time at Jericho, Dixie noticed that Max was having some cognitive difficulties. Sometimes when he was preaching, he would lose his place and seem to draw a blank when he tried to remember what he had planned to say. Dixie wasn't sure if anyone else noticed it, but she did, and she wondered how much longer Max could remain a pastor.

In 2009, Max felt that it was time for him to move away from some of his major responsibilities. That fall he turned in his resignation to Jericho Church.

"I'm ready to leave," he said. "I think God wants me to. You can start lookin' for a new pastor." By the following January, the church had found a replacement.

Max also decided that 2009 would be his last year of farming. Eyes twinkling, he said to Dixie, "When the machinery is smarter than the farmer, it's time to quit."

From then on, he rented his land to neighbors who could keep up with the physical and mental demands of farm work. Max was 77 years old and was ready for some form of "retirement."

~ * ~

During the last year of farming God began to give me what I now call my last assignment. God clearly spoke to me and instructed me that I was to spend the rest of my days visiting nursing homes and hospitals … At this time in my life I am experiencing the blessing and presence of the Holy Spirit in a unique way. There is no doubt in my mind that I (am) where He wants me doing what He wants me to.
—Max, 2010

November 2010

Dixie held Max's latest medical records, her hands shaking slightly as she read, "Alzheimer's." There it was in black and white, a formal diagnosis of what they had suspected for some time.

At this point, Max was still functioning well. He had some memory gaps, but he could carry out his usual activities. However, they had other friends and family who had suffered from this disease, so they knew what to expect. The prospect of watching her husband gradually slip away terrified Dixie. Max didn't say much, but she knew that he was frightened too. As always, they turned together to God in prayer and sought to prepare for the future as much as they could.

In spite of his limitations, Max knew that God still had some work for him to do. Throughout his time of pastoring, visitation had remained a large part of his ministry. Now Max felt God calling him to make that his main focus. He and Dixie returned to WCCC, where he was placed back on staff as care pastor. He continued to visit the people he knew from both churches who were in nursing homes or hospitals, as well as adding any others whom God brought across his path. He talked to the people, prayed with them, and shared the Gospel message if they were open to it. Through this ministry, Max saw many people come to the Lord.

Max formed a schedule for himself, visiting different nursing homes and facilities on different days of the week. Interestingly, even as he began to have more difficulty managing other aspects of everyday life, for a long time he always remembered his visitation schedule and the people he needed to see. He saw God enabling him to complete his "last assignment," as he called it, even as his mind was failing him.

Over time, however, Max did have to limit more and more the ministry that he did.

In May 2012, he broke his right hip. Recovery was slow, and this further hindered his ministry. In 2014, as Max's mental ability continued to decline, he and Dixie agreed that he should be removed from the church staff as care pastor. Dixie wrote a letter to the pastors and elders explaining this decision and thanking them for their continual love and support. Max would still visit nursing homes on his own but not in an official church-related capacity. The elders brought Max and Dixie into their meeting one evening to lay hands on Max and have special prayer for him. Max and Dixie were touched and thankful to have such a loving church family.

The year passed, and soon January 2015 was upon them. As Dixie stood in the kitchen one day, she had a flashback to January 1970, 45 years before. At that time, she had stood in this same kitchen, surrounded by boxes, barrels, and piles of their belongings, as they packed to leave for Brazil. She remembered feeling perplexed, scared, and excited, knowing very little of what lay ahead of her. Perhaps it was a good thing that she had known so little! She doubted now that knowing would have eased her anxiety. At the same time, she was so thankful for the blessings that had followed her and her family, as she and Max had followed God's leading.

As she glanced out the window, Dixie saw Max walking out to the barn in the snow. He wore his overalls, his big brown jacket, and his green John Deere cap—the same kind of outfit any Indiana farmer might wear. He moved slowly now, in both body and mind, but Dixie remembered when he had energetically followed God away from this place, 45 years ago. He had never looked back, though he had left everything he knew. Later that evening, Dixie wrote some of her thoughts to her children:

> *His life is such an example to me. My emotions have highs and lows … I rejoice and I cry. I want God to spare him further embarrassment with the decline and take him to heaven, but yet, I want to always have him beside me. Tonight, after we had devotions, I sat on his lap and asked him to pray. Words weren't always correct, but God looks and listens to the heart anyway. He was warm … I relished both the physical and spiritual warmth of the minutes.*

Less than two weeks later, Max slipped on some ice and broke his left hip. As Dixie reflected later, this injury and the necessary surgery that followed was, in a way, a blessing from God. It facilitated Max's moving away from activities for which he no longer had the mental capacity. He no longer drove the car, even though driving had been one of his favorite activities. When he had healed enough physically to drive again, Dixie simply told him that she wanted to drive, and he gave her little trouble over it. Later Dixie explained, "Looking back, I think it was his graciousness and kindness that motivated him to just give in, not wanting to hurt me by insisting. Always the gentleman."[26] Max remained sweet and loving, especially toward Dixie, throughout his mental decline. Those who knew him attributed this to his many years of allowing the Holy Spirit to shape his character, so that character remained even as his mind slipped away.

Max wanted to return to his visitation ministry after his hip recovery. One day Jeff accompanied Max to one of "his" nursing homes. Jeff, who now lived in the Indianapolis area, helped to steady Max as he walked. The visit did not go well for Max. He could not function, mentally or

---

26   Dixie, in an email, March 2018.

physically. Jeff saw this clearly, but Max was able to sense it, too, and did not try to continue visitation after that.

~ * ~

> A person's steps are directed by the LORD. How then can anyone understand their own way?
> Proverbs 20:24 (NIV)

In the following years Max and Dixie mostly spent their time at home on their farm, caring for the house and yard, feeding the cats that "adopted" them, and relaxing in front of the TV. Dixie taught Sunday school at church, and Max accompanied her.

It was hard for all the Edwardses to understand what God's plan might be in these difficult circumstances. Max had always said, "If you have warm blood in your veins, it's because God isn't finished with you." Max was ready for heaven and wanted to go as soon as he could no longer do the ministry the Lord had given him; so why was he still here? As Max tried to remember people, do household tasks for Dixie, and function on a day-to-day basis, he sometimes felt like he had lost his usefulness and his purpose. It broke Dixie's heart to watch him struggle, but she tried to help him bring all of the hurts and the thoughts—scattered though they may be—to the Lord in prayer. They spent many hours crying and praying together, seeking what God wanted to show them through this trial.

Dixie and other family members reminded Max that he had done everything God had asked of him. He had worked hard, and this was his time to rest. The family learned more during this time about praise and thanksgiving. They thanked God for Max and Dixie's full lives, their family, their home, and His goodness and grace through any and every hard moment. It was an uphill battle, but the spiritual lessons they had grasped over the years came back to them, even in a seemingly senseless situation.

Friends and family eagerly helped the Edwardses when they could. Church friends would come sit with Max or take him for a ride in a pickup truck. Dixie took him to an adult day-care facility a couple days a week, which gave her an opportunity to take care of errands outside of home. And of course, their children visited and helped whenever possible.

In spite of all of the loving help, the day-to-day responsibility of caring for Max still fell on Dixie, and it became increasingly difficult for her to maintain. Max rarely slept through the night. Sometimes he would fall, and she would not be able to get him up without help. With the encouragement of family and friends, Dixie finally decided to explore the option of moving him to a nursing home.

The closest facility was Randolph Nursing Home, which was one of the places Max had visited regularly as a care pastor. Many of the staff there remembered Max and Dixie, and they were warm and welcoming. In September 2017, Dixie took Max there for a visit to see how he would do. She hoped that God would show her what was best for her husband. The night before the visit, she sat in bed and prayed over him as he slept: *Lord, this man is Your faithful servant. Please give us Your direction and guidance as we visit Randolph Nursing Home tomorrow. If this is Your plan, please let me see a positive response from Max during the visit.*

As they approached the nursing home building the next day, Max began to make positive comments, in his own way. It almost seemed as though he recognized the place from his many years of visiting. The home's director, Marilyn, met them at the entrance and walked them to the memory-care unit. Dixie observed Max as he moved slowly down the hall and interacted with Marilyn. Max seemed calm and peaceful, even happy. He made humorous comments as they walked.

When they reached the common area, Marilyn called to a woman who was leading a group activity. She introduced Max to the staff member, who smiled warmly.

"We're playing a game!" she said. "Would you like to join us?"

"Well, sure!" Max responded. The worker led him to the group where residents were hitting a balloon back and forth. Dixie watched as he participated in the activity, hitting the balloon and "besting" all of them. He looked at her and smiled. She smiled back, tears pricking her eyes. She had her answer. Later she described the visit in an email to family:

I can't deny that God answered my prayer. I wanted to see him positive there … and I did. There is one bed available now. Marilyn asked me if I wanted to reserve it and I said "yes." I must be faithful to respond obediently to God's answer for me. Some heaviness has lifted from my spirit. I know you all have prayed for God to help me make the right decision and at the right time … The "pieces" seem to be falling in place as orchestrated from heaven. I'm not saying this will be easy, but I will be obedient. We are headed into a new ministry now … the Alzheimer's ministry!

Max moved into the Randolph Nursing Home in September 2017. It was a difficult transition. Dixie mourned the loss of her husband, and she wondered if she had done the right thing. She visited him every day and did her best to make sure all of his needs were met. Family and friends visited him too, when they were in the neighborhood. Dixie began to see the nursing home ministry as hers now. When she visited, she sought to minister to the other residents as well as Max; she also began to reach out to the nurses and other staff. It was never easy, but she continued to believe that God had a plan for Max's life and for her own. All she could do was what her husband had always done: Respond in obedience and trust the Lord to take care of the details.

Dixie continued with other ministries that God had brought her way in this season. She taught a children's Sunday school class at church, hosted a small group in her home, and mentored younger women.

In 2020, the advent of the COVID-19 pandemic restricted Dixie's access to the nursing home to visit Max. However, she continued going as often as she could to stand at the dining room window and talk to Max through the glass. Occasionally other family members were able to visit and go with her. By this time, Max did not recognize any of them, but they hoped that his spirit heard them as they talked and sang. In December, Max contracted COVID-19. Dixie was allowed to visit him three times, wearing full protective gear. She talked, sang, and prayed with him. On her third visit, Dixie sensed that it would be her last time with Max as he struggled for every breath. Lovingly, she said goodbye to her earthly partner. She knew she would see him again in heaven.

On her way out of the nursing home, Dixie stopped to witness to the young man at the front desk. Though much of her ministry had been restricted due to COVID, she had continued encouraging and praying for the nursing-home staff.

In the early-morning hours of December 15, 2020, Max Eldon Edwards went to be with Jesus. Family members who were able to travel gathered for a small, quiet funeral, which was livestreamed for the many people, both in the U.S. and in Brazil, who knew and loved Max. As the family shared stories of Max's life, they were challenged yet again by his tireless devotion to God. They were inspired to carry on his legacy as they sang together one of his favorite hymns:

> Let us labor for the Master from the dawn till setting sun,
>> Let us talk of all His wondrous love and care;
> Then when all of life is over, and our work on earth is done,
>> And the roll is called up yonder, I'll be there.
>> … When the roll is called up yonder, I'll be there.[27]

---

27   James M. Black, "When the Roll Is Called Up Yonder," 1893.

Postlude: Boldly Obey

$\mathcal{A}$s I read this story, I can hardly believe it is my own! I had no idea when I was writing weekly letters to our parents, Joe and Pauline Brumfield and Russel and Maud Edwards, that they were saving every letter, preserving our ministry and family history.

I wrote on both sides of parchment-thin airmail paper to minimize weight and expense. The ink leaked through, and I am amazed that the letters were legible enough after all these years for my granddaughter Danna Jo to transcribe them. Her great patience and perseverance over the past few years have paid off, as you now hold the resulting story in your hands. Thank you, Danna Jo!

Max and I were just farm kids—farm kids who married and expected to live and die on the farm. But God had other plans. I had the privilege of living with a servant of the Lord. I miss him so much. My consolation is this: "Be still, and know that I am God" (Psalm 46:10 NIV).

However, I WAS and AM blessed because of his obedience to our God. Our children, Jay, Jan, Jeff, and Joe, are blessed because of their daddy's obedience. Our grandchildren are blessed because of Grandpa Max's obedience. Our great-grandchildren are blessed because of Great-Grandpa Max's obedience.

After years of battling Alzheimer's, Max finally received his reward in heaven. I smile when I think of the welcome he must have received there, hearing the words of his Lord: "Well done, good and faithful servant!" (Matthew 25:23 NIV). And I also wait in great anticipation to hear those words. But until then, I remain "Rejoicing in hope; patient in tribulation; continuing instant in prayer" (Romans 12:12 KJV).

And with grateful hearts, my family and friends say together:

"Now to the King eternal, immortal, invisible, the only God, be honor and glory for ever and ever. Amen" (1 Timothy 1:17 NIV).

Dixie Anna Brumfield Edwards

Where Are the Four Js Now?

*A*s Max always told his children, "God calls the whole family," he believed that God called all of them to minister to Brazil and he was an example to his kids of how to continue to follow God's call throughout life. Max and Dixie's legacy continues in their children, who seek to boldly obey the Lord, just as their parents did. Here's a glimpse of their stories.

Jay

Jay found the Lord in family devotions before Max and Dixie left the Indiana farm. He served the Lord to the best of his ability from that point forward. He graduated in 1976 from PACA in São Paulo, Brazil, where he finished his last two years of high school. Jay attended Asbury College where he met Kirsten Webster, who had accepted Christ personally in eighth grade at a lay-witness mission in the United Methodist church her family attended in Kansas. Jay and Kirsten were married in 1979 and began farming near Winchester, Indiana.

They returned to Brazil as short-term missionaries in 1987 to serve in administration at *Acampamento Shalom,* the second camp Max and Dixie built. Two years turned into five, plus one year of furlough, as they stayed on to help with the treasurer's office and a church plant. Then, instead of returning to farming in the U.S., Jay and Kirsten partnered with an investor group and bought farmland in the pioneering region of eastern Mato Grosso, Brazil. They moved there in 1994 with their two oldest children: Jason, 10, and Aaron, 7. Despite precarious conditions, Cristiana Kay was born there in the frontier town of Querência in 1997.

In addition to developing farmland and running the farming

operation, Jay taught Bible classes in the public school for six years. The family held Sunday school for neighborhood children, led weekly home Bible studies, and founded a Christian bookstore and day-care center. Kirsten taught English in different venues, homeschooled the children, and led women's prayer groups and Bible studies.

After an extended furlough in Enid, Oklahoma, Jay, Kirsten, and Cristiana moved to Boa Vista, Roraima, northern Brazil, in 2005. There they started another farm project, built a recording studio, and served as laypeople in two local churches.

Aaron works in agribusiness, based in Florida. He and Lorena have three children. Jason has a doctorate in education and is principal of Leman Charter School. He and his wife, Andrea, also have three children. Cristiana married Joseph Verissimo, and is pursuing a career in nutrition.

Jay wrote the book *Daniel: Absolutes in a Gray World, and Power, Business, and Politics,* a work of Christian fiction inspired by his identification with the Daniel of the Bible as he navigated the challenges of agricultural business in Brazil.

> Jay reflects: *When I left the farm as a boy, I was devastated, thinking that God had ruined my life. When I left the farm as an adult, I knew better, but the same feelings still crept in. But you know what? As I look back over life so far from age 60, I see God really did know best. Without the love of farming, I never could have lived with, worked with, and ministered to the Brazilian pioneer farmers. I could have never identified with the farmers in the first location, and now in the second, if I were not like them in this significant way. As we look forward, God really does know best.*

Jan

Jan married Rod Dormer, a Canadian, in 1986. The first eight years of their married life were spent pastoring a church in Ontario, Canada. Then the Dormers became missionaries with OMS. Their first overseas ministry took them and their two young daughters, Danna Jo and Jenna, to work in a school in Indonesia.

After three and a half years there, they returned to the U.S. briefly and then went to Brazil. After five years of ministry with Camp Shalom and the seminary in Londrina, Brazil, the Dormers unfortunately did not receive their permanent visas and could not remain in Brazil. Thus, after a furlough in Canada, they returned to Indonesia for another term.

Danna Jo and Jenna both graduated from Wesley International School in Indonesia, while Rod and Jan worked with the OMS seminary there. They then spent two years back in the U.S. to be near their girls while they started college, and as Rod began doctoral studies. Then, Rod and Jan spent a year in Kenya, leading a Bible school there. Rod has a doctorate in organizational leadership and continues to serve with OMS, primarily working in theological education in Africa. Jan has specialized in teaching English to speakers of other languages (TESOL), which has been her area of ministry everywhere they have served. She holds a doctorate in TESOL education and is professor of TESOL in the graduate program in education at Messiah University in Pennsylvania. She has written six books, including *Teaching English in Missions* and *Language Learning in Ministry.* This latest book, to help missionaries prepare for learning a new language, was inspired by Max and Dixie's story.

Though the Dormers now make their home in the U.S., they are often found somewhere else in the world, teaching classes or speaking at conferences. When they are in the U.S., their travels often take them to see their daughters and grandsons: Danna Jo and Shogo Matsuki, with Kaito and Yoshiki in Michigan, and Jenna and Brendan Strahm, with Owen in Virginia.

> Jan reflects: *I feel incredibly blessed to have had the upbringing I had. I experienced every kind of education possible, and that is probably what led me into the field of education. Amidst every change, there was the anchor of faith in God and family time reading, learning, playing, praying, and of course, singing together. It was because of the positive impact of my growing-up years in Brazil that*

> *I wanted to raise my own daughters as MKs. It's still a*
> *very, very important part of my identity, 40 years later.*

Jeff

All of Jeff's formative years (ages 6 to 18) were spent in Brazil, except for the two and a half years the family furloughed in the U.S. He loved growing up at Panorama Camp and then graduating from PACA in São Paulo, where he was active in all the sports the school offered.

In January 1980, Max, Dixie, Jeff, and Joe returned to Brazil after a furlough. At this time, Jeff met Laura at Panorama Camp where they were both counselors for a children's camp. Laura, a Brazilian, had accepted Christ in a Japanese Holiness Church in São Paulo at the age of eight. She went to Panorama with the church youth group because of the church's OMS connection. When Jeff and Laura met that January, it was *like* at first sight! They became good friends, which morphed into dating, engagement, and eventually marriage in August 1983.

In 1987, they started their career service with OMS by becoming missionaries to Londrina, Brazil, where they served until 2008. During that time, they served the Shalom Community Church in various pastoral roles; Jeff was lead pastor for their final eight years in Brazil. Laura taught at the Londrina Bible Seminary for many years and served the broader church of Londrina through church-based counseling. During furlough years, they were both able to complete master's degrees from Wheaton College Graduate School: Laura in clinical psychology and Jeff in theological studies. Afterwards, Jeff completed a doctorate in pastoral care and counseling from Trinity Evangelical Divinity School, and Laura completed a doctorate in educational psychology from Regent University.

Jeff and Laura live in Noblesville, Indiana (the Greater-Indianapolis area). Jeff continues to serve with OMS. For several years, he served as the regional director for Latin America and the Caribbean, overseeing the broad scope of ministry in the region and working alongside field directors. He now serves as the executive director of OMS Global Ministries, which broadens his role to managing all regions of OMS' global ministry. Laura teaches psychology at Taylor University. They have two daughters. Katie is married to Thiago Cesar, and they have three sons: Lucas, Sam, and Caleb. Katie has a regular podcast to strengthen Brazilian Christian families, called *"Projeto do Coração."* Kendra is married to Mark Thomas, and their children are Cecilia and Leo. Kendra holds a doctorate in psychology, and is a professor at the University of Indianapolis.

> Jeff reflects: *I consider myself to have had the easiest time with our parents' missionary venture due to my age. I was six when we left the farm (too young to have roots) and remained connected to Brazil until I was 18 and off to college. So all my formative years were in one place (except furloughs, of course). This made life easier for me than for my siblings. I've always considered it a privilege to grow up bicultural and to have acquired Portuguese and not have to learn it. Okay, it was "hillbilly" Portuguese, and Laura had to refine it into respectable and cultured, but it was a huge benefit. I've told countless people that I was blessed to grow up in a truly Christian home. My parents practiced what they preached. What a head start for me and my siblings.*

Joe

Joe was born in Brazil and preferred it to the U.S. by the time Max, Dixie, and he moved to rural Indiana in 1983. A couple years later, a seminary student working as a youth pastor in Anderson, Indiana, became enamored with Jan and worked to make points with her by inviting her kid brother Joe to youth-group activities. That youth pastor is now Joe's brother-in-law Rod, and that youth group had a girl named Sharon in it, who is now Joe's wife.

Joe completed high school in Winchester, Indiana, where he translated his Brazilian soccer skills into kicking an American football. American football opened an opportunity that helped pay for Joe's college at Valparaiso University. Joe and Sharon married in 1993, and Sharon completed her master's degree in TESOL shortly thereafter in Chicago, Illinois.

They then moved to Phoenix, Arizona, where Joe completed his master's in international business at Thunderbird School of Global Management. He then spent 10 years with Citibank, mostly working with international banking across Latin America. At one point, Joe and Sharon moved with their children to Panama.

In 2005, the family moved to Dallas with Citibank. In 2008, Joe left the corporate world to be an entrepreneur, and today, along with three Argentinian partners, he runs a digital agency called W3 and a user-experience shop called Tonic3. Joe and Sharon have four children: Anna, who is married to Ethan Eismont, Nathan, Sophia, and Joelle. One was born in Arizona, two in Florida, and one in Texas. Sharon spends much of her time homeschooling and teaching in a classical education framework. Joe and Sharon have dedicated more than 20 years to youth ministry and enjoy investing in teens through discipleship, mentorship, and teaching apologetics and worldview.

> Joe reflects: *While I was in the university, a godly couple with an OMS connection, Jim and Lois (Greenlee) Stuck, sponsored a campus group for Third Culture Kids. Their friendship and teaching helped me and my future wife understand how this MK life had affected the person I am. Certainly, the life you've read about made growing-up hard sometimes, but it was incredibly rich with every kind of spiritual blessing I can imagine. I am grateful for the example of three older siblings who boldly follow God and especially grateful for godly parents who consistently set before me an authentic model of believing faith. Rich Mullins could have been describing them when he said, "They worked to give faith hands and feet and somehow gave it wings."*[28]

---

28   Rich Mullins, "First Family," 1989.

Sources and Acknowledgements

*I*n the early stages of my work on this book, I called it "The Family Project." This reflects not only that it tells the story of our family but also that putting it together was truly a family effort. The primary sources for this book were Grandma Dixie's letters from Brazil to their parents, prayer letters to supporters written by Max and Dixie throughout their ministry, a handwritten document that Grandpa wrote of his story, and interviews with various family members.

I was able to get a few interviews with Grandpa Max before his Alzheimer's became advanced; after he could no longer tell his stories, Grandma Dixie and the rest of the family continued for him. While I wish I could have heard more stories from Grandpa himself, I also treasured the opportunity to hear all the perspectives and memories from different family members. Even though there's now a book, I hope my family members will continue to tell each other these stories; there's something special about times together when you hear the tales that shaped your family's history. Other sources for the book were various family documents and pictures, and documents from OMS headquarters. Many times Grandma reached out to people with specific questions, and various individuals provided additional details and information. I'm sure I can't remember all the names of those who contributed, but we want them to know that we are deeply grateful for the help in putting together this story.

I want to thank Grandpa, Grandma, and the whole family for entrusting me with this incredible project. Everyone in the family was generous with their stories and input and gracious in allowing me to gather the information and put it together how I saw fit. A project like this, which records people's personal lives, could lead to arguing over how things are presented, but there has been none of that with compiling this book. Everyone wants only to see God glorified and this story preserved.

The two people most closely involved in the writing of the book have been Grandma Dixie and my mom, Jan Edwards Dormer. Every step of the way, they have read each chapter, fact-checked everything, and given inspiration and input. This book would not exist without them, and my gratitude for their support is inexpressible.

I want to thank my dear friend Jessica Fry (J.M. Butler) who read an earlier version of some of the chapters and gave me key writing advice. She helped me learn how to write this as a story rather than a history book. A few other friends also read portions of the book and provided encouragement. Thank you!

My husband, Shogo Matsuki, is my rock and encouragement in everything I do. Thanks for always believing in me, dear!

And, of course, at the end of the day, the Person who deserves all thanks, glory, and honor is God, Who transformed my grandparents' lives and, consequently, many more lives as they obeyed. I trust that He has been guiding the writing of this book, and that He will use it for His glory. Amen!

—Danna Jo Matsuki

The Four Js and Their Families

Jay Dee and Kirsten Rene (Webster) Edwards

- Jason David and Andrea Michelle (Mendel) Edwards
  - Elijah William
  - Ezra Jay
  - Elissa Grace
- Aaron Jonathan and Lorena (dos Santos) Edwards
  - Noah dos Santos
  - Benjamin dos Santos
  - Julia dos Santos
- Cristiana Kay (Edwards) and Joseph Verissimo

Jan (Edwards) and Rodney Glenn Dormer

- Danna Jo (Dormer) and Shogo Matsuki
  - Kaito Dormer
  - Yoshiki Edwards
- Jenna Pauline (Dormer) and Brendan Strahm
  - Owen Bruce

Jeffry Max and Laura (Mendonça) Edwards

- Katie Cristina (Edwards) and Thiago Cesar
  - Lucas Max
  - Samuel James
  - Caleb Jeffry
- Kendra Joy (Edwards) and Mark Thomas
  - Cecilia Joy
  - Leo Edwards

Joe Russel and Sharon Lynn (Hanson) Edwards

- Anna Lynn (Edwards) and Ethan Eismont

- Nathan Russel

- Sophia Marie

- Joelle Grace

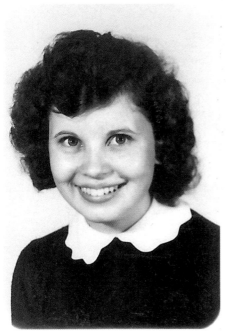

Dixie in high school, 1955

Max in military, 1954

Max and Dixie's wedding, 1956

Wedding with parents, Russel and Maud Edwards and Joe and Pauline Brumfield

Max with Jay and Jan, circa 1963

Max and Dixie and Family, circa 1963

Dixie's choir at New Liberty, the Sunbeams, circa 1965

MFM Action cover, 1967

Max and Dixie, 1967

Peaceful Valley Church, circa 1967

Brazil Crusade Team: Back row) Fred Zuhl, Max Edwards, Rowan Messerschmidt, Bob Taber, Katherine Messerschmidt, Maynard Meyers, and Burton Schoepf; *Front row)* Emma Zuhl, Dixie Edwards, Harry Burr, Lois Taber, Mary Polasky, and Betsy Schoepf; *Not pictured)* Sammy Poole.

Crusade trip to Brazil, 1967

PUBLIC SALE

Of Late Model Farm Tools

As we are preparing for the Mission Field, we will offer for sale at Public Auction the following described personal property located 3 miles west of Lynn, Indiana on Hwy 36 to the Bloomingport Road, then north 1¼ miles, on

Saturday, January 20, 1968

Sale to Begin at 12:00 o'Clock Noon

2 Tractors - 4 and 6 Row Equipment Picker-Sheller - New 1967 McCurdy Elevator - Combine - Farm Tools

1964 Ford 6000 Diesel tractor with Select-O-Speed, wide front end, dual wheels, new rear tires, wheel weights, very good condition; 1965 Ford 4000 Diesel tractor with Select-O-Speed, wide front end, wheel weights, in A-1" condition; 1964 Ford 5/16 inch semi-mounted plows with cover boards; 1965 Ford 3/16 inch mounted plows with cover boards; 1965 Ford loader with large bucket, hydraulic control; 1966 Ford 7 ft. rotary mower; Ford 7 ft. mounted mower; 1965 Ford 12 ft. wheel disc; Ford grader blade.

1966 JOHN DEERE NARROW ROW, 6 ROW PLANTER WITH HERBICIDE AND INSECTICIDE, MINIMUM TILLAGE, DISC FERTILIZER ATTACHMENT, DISC OPENERS, PLANTED 2 CROPS, A-1 CONDITION; 1966 JOHN DEERE NARROW ROW, 6 ROW REAR MOUNT CULTIVATORS.

1964 Burch 4 row rotary hoe; 1966 New Idea narrow row Picker-Sheller; 1963 John Deere 42 combine, 9 ft. cut; 1967 McCurdy 40 ft. elevator with Briggs & Stratton engine, power lift; John Deere R tractor spreader; 1966 John Deere wagon running gears with new 6 ply truck tires and KilBros gravity bed; flat bed rubber tired wagon with side boards; Case four bar rake on steel; 14 ft. all steel harrow; Ford 10 ft. lime spreader; 3 two-way cylinders, one with 21 ft. hose; end gate seeder; overhead gas tank and stand.

TRUCK: 1957 International 1½ ton truck with hoist.

PULL TOGETHER HOG HOUSE—HOG EQUIPMENT
MISCELLANEOUS

Six pen pull together hog house; 2 Pax 45 bushel feeders with cast iron bottoms, like new; 2 Pax Creep feeders, like new; 12 bunk sheep feeders; 60 hole bolt bin; very few items to be sold from the wagon.

HOUSEHOLD GOODS

2 Ashley wood burning heating stoves with thermostat on draft; Magnavox console TV; round pedestal dining room table; youth bed; 2 three-quarter size beds; crib; chest of drawers; large two-drawer closet; 2 rockers. (Household goods will be sold first.)

TERMS OF SALE—CASH

(Nothing to be removed until settled for.)
Not responsible in case of accidents.

MR. and MRS. MAX EDWARDS

FISHER & FLESHER, Auctioneers   GERALD SHARP, Clerk

Missionary Internship, the Central Singables choir at Freewill Baptist Church, 1969

On the ship headed to Brazil, January 1970

Opening barrels after arrival in Campinas, 1970

After putting together the motorcycle brought across the ocean in pieces!

Panorama Camp entrance, 1971

The 3 Js singing in a tent church, 1971

The family after arrival
in Panorama, 1971

The family, 1971

First record cover, 1972

LP M 483

The 3 J's

sing from

BRAZIL

Jan * Jay * Jeff

Panorama house, circa 1972

Max and others holding snake skin, circa 1972

Max holding a snake, circa 1972

Dixie teaching Sunday school at the local brick factory, circa 1972

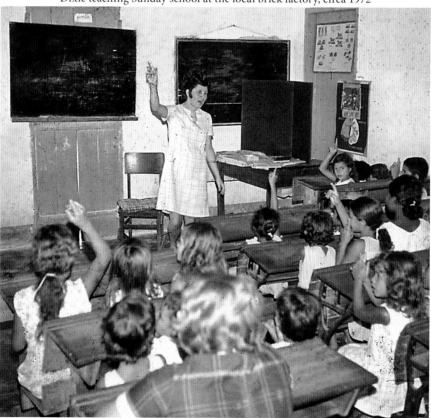

Walking to Sunday school, circa 1972

On the Parana River, circa 1972

Playing in the River, circa 1972

Playing in the River, circa 1972

Campers having fun at Panorama Camp, circa 1972

The 4 Js, 1973

Work crew at Panorama, circa 1973

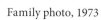

Family photo, 1973

4 J's photo, on OMS
magazine, 1975

Second record cover, 1976

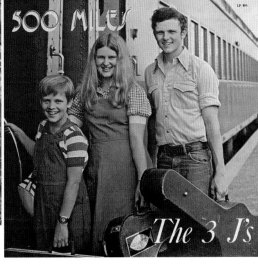

In front of the red Panorama Camp truck, circa 1975

Campers at Camp Shalom, 1978

Max supervising construction
at Camp Shalom, circa 1981

Max and Dixie's 25th anniversary, Camp Shalom, 1981

Camp Shalom Chapel, 2000

São Saverio church front, circa 1982

São Saverio baptism,
circa 1982

1990/3

MEN FOR MISSIONS INTERNATIONAL
The Laymen's Voice of OMS International

MFM
GIVES
ITS
OWN

MEXICO

Going to Mexico;
MFM Action cover, 1990

Mexico, circa 1991

Work in Mozambique,
MFM Action cover, 1997

Max in MFM, with Dale Larrance and Dave Fisher, 2008

Danna Jo Dormer Matsuki, the author of this book, with her Grandparents, 2007

50th anniversary, 2006

Max, Dixie, Jay, Jan, Jeff and Joe, 2015

Edwards family photo, 2015